THE TRIALS OF
PATRICK CARRAHER

EDITED BY

GEORGE BLAKE

LONDON   EDINBURGH   GLASGOW

WILLIAM HODGE AND COMPANY, LIMITED

MADE AND PRINTED IN GREAT BRITAIN BY
BUTLER AND TANNER LTD., FROME AND
LONDON, 1951

TO
THE RIGHT HONOURABLE
LORD COOPER, O.B.E., LL.D.,
LORD JUSTICE-GENERAL AND LORD PRESIDENT
OF THE COURT OF SESSION
THIS VOLUME
IS
BY KIND PERMISSION
RESPECTFULLY DEDICATED

PREFACE

ANY report of a lengthy trial for murder—in this case two trials—is necessarily a work of collaboration, and I have many obligations to acknowledge, thus:

To the Clerk of Justiciary for making available the shorthand transcription of the Notes of Evidence taken at the two trials; and to the Senior Depute for courteous assistance and wise advice;

To the Honourable Lord Russell for revising, not only his Charge to the Jury in the second case, but also that of the late Lord Pitman in the first;

To Chief Superintendent William Ewing, M.B.E., and his officers of the City of Glasgow Police, Criminal Investigation Department, for their valued advice and for the use of photographs and charts used as illustrations hereafter; also the Photographic Department of the City of Edinburgh Police for taking, by special permission, the photograph of the interior of the High Court of Justiciary, Edinburgh.

The leading medical witnesses in the second case—Professors Allison and Blyth, and Drs. McNiven, Scott and Black—have all been good enough to go over their testimonies; while the leading advocates concerned in the fate of Patrick Carraher—the Solicitor-General, Mr. Douglas Johnston, K.C., M.P.; the Dean of Faculty, Mr. John Cameron, D.S.C., K.C.; and Mr. J. R. Philip, K.C.—have been courteous in sparing time to revise the reports of their speeches.

It will be understood that these distinguished gentlemen, whether Officers of the Crown or not, are in no way responsible for my comments on the facts and conduct of the cases.

It is an honour that the Lord Justice-General and Lord President of the Court of Session, the Right Honourable Lord Cooper, has graciously agreed to accept the dedication of this addition to a notable series of studies in crime.

October, 1950.   GEORGE BLAKE.

CONTENTS

CONTENTS

SECOND TRIAL

First Day—Thursday, 28th February, 1946

Evidence for the Prosecution

CONTENTS

ILLUSTRATIONS

INTRODUCTION

I

EVEN if the City of Glasgow had no other claim to fame, it would be dear to all students of crime, and of the legal processes consequent on crime, as the scene of four murder cases quite exceptionally rich in social and detective interest—the cases in which Madeleine Smith, Dr. Pritchard, Jessie M'Lachlan and Oscar Slater figured, rightly or wrongly, as the accused.[1]

These cases were remarkable, in the first place, that three of them are still of grimly mysterious interest. If the guilt of Dr. Pritchard was never in any doubt, the beauteous Madeleine's escape under the notorious not proven verdict can still provoke either grave shakings of sober heads or the cynical smiles of the more flippant. It has been quite openly suggested that the convictions of Jessie M'Lachlan and Oscar Slater were as near miscarriages of justice as makes no matter.

In all these cases persons of considerable means were involved. In all, the shame associated with a charge of murder fell on middle-class families in the Victorian pattern. Jessie M'Lachlan's employers were substantial members of an accounting firm, of which that most elusive protagonist of the drama in the basement, old John Fleming, had been a member. Miss Smith's father was an architect in a very profitable line of practice. Miss Gilchrist, the aged victim in the Oscar Slater case, was possessed of substantial means: otherwise, indeed, she might well have been spared to die quietly in her bed.

A quite remarkable circumstance, as Mr. William Roughead once pointed out, is that the four famous murders (even if Dr. Pritchard's was a mass-production effort) were all committed within short distances of Charing Cross, which, towards the western end of the legendary Sauchiehall Street, is to Glasgow much as the West End is to Edinburgh's Princes Street or, say, the Marble Arch to West London. The lethal deeds were all committed in dwellings of substance. Miss Smith's father occupied a solid mansion in Blythswood Square, with a basement all too convenient for philandery and the passing of cups of cocoa through the window of what is now, one understands, a ladies' lavatory in an agricultural college. Even Miss Gilchrist's flat in West Princes

[1] Each of these cases appears in the *Notable British Trials Series*.

Patrick Carraher.

Street was a roomy and comfortable abode in a long street of good tenement buildings, peopled by solid citizens. Except in so far as a few of the involuntary participants in these affairs were of the working order of society, most of the principal players were well-to-do if not positively prosperous in their periods.

Now, in the case of Patrick Carraher and the two murder trials in which he was involved, we turn from the respectability of Glasgow to its degradation. We shift—in geographical measurement—about a mile East from the artificial Charing Cross to the region about the real, historical Glasgow Cross. We pass from gentility, however cold and grim in its undercurrents, to the frank, free, crude, drunken brutalities of the Have-Nots of a great industrial city. We turn from even respectable tenement flats to a region in which quite decent people may regard four sleepers to a small room as luxury; in which the inhabitants of several households may have to share a common, and inefficient, privy on the landing; in which the privileges of dividend and cheque book are wholly superseded, or anticipated, by begging, pilfering, peculation, assault, battery—a region in which, in fact, it is at once hard to bring up a family in decency and still harder for the family to resist the degrading social pressures about it.

The more murderous activities of this man Carraher were conducted in regions on or near the main axis running North–South through the most ancient part of the City of Glasgow. As the map shows, this runs from the neighbourhood of the venerable Cathedral steeply downhill past the site of the original College of Glasgow, then past the Tolbooth Steeple and the Cross; again down the Saltmarket and across the bridge over the Clyde into the district known as the Gorbals.

This section of a populous and crowded industrial city has in recent times acquired an adventitious notoriety. That somewhat ramshackle but authentic play, *The Gorbals Story*, as performed by the Unity Theatre of Glasgow, has carried the name and a legend of beery shiftlessness into the consciousness of intelligent Britain as a whole. Even the ballet, taking a somewhat romantic view of the scene, has popularized "Miracle in the Gorbals". On the whole, one fears, a vast number of people have been given an impression of a region of high, tottering, reeking tenements, peopled exclusively by characters in the *apache* class.

The real Gorbals is a much less picturesque district than the modern stage would suggest. Regarded as a bit of town-planning, most of it would be rather admired by contemporary architects.

GORBALS CROSS, GLASGOW

Introduction.

The streets run wide and straight, on the whole with plenty of light and air; the tenement buildings do not give that impression of utterly overwhelming narrow streets as they do elsewhere. An orderly colony of Jews of the poorer sort is respectably established in the area. It is, in fact, one of those old, solidly-built, central districts of Glasgow in which the westward movement of the more prosperous created a vacuum, and into which, in turn, there flocked the poor and a good many of the shiftless.

Gross overcrowding was an inevitable result of this process. Good old houses were divided and then sub-divided, and the greed or ignorance of distant landlords did not fairly meet the needs of a rapidly expanding population. Patches of insanitary slum were created. And thus, inevitably, there appeared in the body of the historical Gorbals the canker of crime. The bad boys and girls of a clotted city, racked by racial and religious differences, tended to gravitate to those transpontine fields; and they gave the place a bad name. It is merely necessary here to lay it down that the Gorbals is much less of a stew than many a corresponding area in other seaports; that the incidence of crime is indeed rather less seriously marked than in other districts of Glasgow alone; and that the vast majority of the local population strives at once to maintain decency in difficult conditions and aspires to escape into more agreeable homes in wider fields.

It was hereabouts, however, that a male child christened Patrick Carraher was born in 1906; and it is of importance that his father was a decent, respectable working man. We shall see later on how this Patrick Carraher developed as a hopeless breaker of the law. Our immediate concern is with the fact that, in the early hours of the morning of 14th August, 1938, he first used an edged weapon and killed a fellow-creature.

II

Gorbals Cross is the natural focus of the life of the district. This is quite a spacious circus, with a traffic island at its centre, and a crossing of importance in the city's transport scheme. North–South traffic by the Victoria Bridge across the Clyde is heavy throughout the working day, and it remains considerable until late at night, with trams, buses, taxicabs and private cars carrying the considerable population of the suburbs on the South Side home from work or recreation on the more sophisticated North Side. Altogether a lively nexus of transpontine life, it is inevitably

3   B

Patrick Carraher.

the favourite meeting place, and lounging place, of many of the inhabitants of a grossly overcrowded area.

At 11.15 p.m. on the evening of Saturday, 13th August, 1938, an 18-year-old working girl, Margaret McKay McNicol, arrived at Gorbals Cross to meet by arrangement a 19-year-old window cleaner called James Durie. The hour may seem late for such an assignation, but it would still be quite light in those northern latitudes and, as we shall see, the nocturnal habits of the Gorbals folk are apt to be eccentric. Margaret's first encounter at the rendezvous was with a man she knew as Paddy Carraher. He was alone, and she perceived that he had drink taken. Carraher's desire was that this young girl should go and act as intermediary with a woman called Katie Morgan, a former lady-love from whom, it appears, he had been parted by misunderstanding.

Margaret McNicol declined this delicate embassy. As she put it in court subsequently: "Well, the two of them fell out, and I didn't want anything to do with it." In the light of the evidence printed hereafter we may imagine that this young girl, undoubtedly knowing Carraher's criminal record and alarmed by the truculence which had come upon him with drink, was chiefly concerned to get out of his company as quickly as possible. She even came to know that he had a knife about his person; and this would seem to suggest that Carraher, in his sour mood, boasted of his lethal possession and his intention to use it if necessary. Even at this early stage the reader should note the overtone of theatricality in all the more desperate utterances of Patrick Carraher.

Alarmed by her encounter with this sinister personality—a girl of 18 against an habitual criminal of 32—Margaret McNicol looked about for succour and saw her boy friend, James Durie, not far away. She ran towards him. But Patrick Carraher followed her and grasped at her arm, tugging her away from Durie. This young Durie caught her by the other arm and tugged in his turn: the young woman helpless between them. In the issue of this formless brawl, the girl escaped from between Carraher and James Durie, and the two men came to grips.

This was a climax of some importance as the High Court of Justiciary came to consider it later on. The burden of the evidence is that Carraher seized young Durie by the lapels of his jacket with his left hand and, with an open knife in his right, threatened him direly: the point of the knife menacingly aimed at the youth's midriff. This, if the evidence for the Crown is to be accepted, was assault in an advanced degree.

4

Introduction.

The intelligent reader will, however, study with care the relevant passages in the various testimonies. It was maintained by witnesses for the Crown that Carraher and Durie remained in this statuesque pose "for five or ten minutes", and one wonders if even a couple of film stars could have so brilliantly "held" such a powerful scene over such a great length of time. The presiding judge at the consequent trial in the High Court, the late Lord Pitman, almost contemptuously dismissed this single issue in his charge to the jury. Considering the reported case after a lapse of twelve years, the layman may reasonably feel that the Crown—in the sense of mere tactics at least—put an excessive emphasis on this episode of technical assault and thus in fact, by dividing the interest, weakened the case of murder against Patrick Carraher.

However that may be, the two young people extricated themselves from the grip of Paddy Carraher at Gorbals Cross and made towards Peggy McNicol's home in Eglinton Street, about a quarter-of-a-mile away to the West. They would have done well to leave it at that, but it appears that, after a colloquy in the close leading up to the girl's home, they decided to return to the Gorbals and continue the dispute. In fact, they made for 163, Hospital Street, where young Durie's older brother lived under the roof of his mother-in-law, Mrs. Morgan. This John Dickson Durie, aged 24, was then an unemployed labourer. Hearing his brother's tale of threatened assault with a naked knife, he rose, dressed and went down with the others to Gorbals Cross. He conceived it his business to see that his junior "got a fair fight"—that is, against Carraher—but we may reasonably imagine that the Duries went out in force to maintain the family honour against a notorious troublemaker. This was a clan feud.

These Duries were not gangsters. The family record with the police was clean enough. They were rather of the class known in the *argot* of Glasgow as "Neds"—that is, the rather shiftless lads who hang about street-corners and watch and wait: without much purpose, without definitely criminal intent, but with a wary eye for the main chance: the loungers on the edge of active society.

When these two Duries got down to Gorbals Cross at a late hour of the night Paddy Carraher was not immediately in sight. They had, however, reinforced themselves. Peggy McNicol had gone home by this time and may now be forgotten; but with the Durie brothers at Gorbals Cross there were now Charles Morgan, aged 16, John Durie's brother-in-law, and Peter Howard, aged 23, and a shunter in good employment. By midnight or thereabouts the Durie clan thus felt itself no doubt ready for anything. In due course they spotted their man and went across to have it out with him.

According to the evidence of the Duries and their henchmen, their proposition to Carraher was that he should there and then agree to a fair fight with bare fists with one or other of the Durie brothers. To this Carraher would not agree, and we may share the presiding judge's view that this was only a prudent decision. He had a good deal of drink taken, and he rightly feared that, according to the code he knew so well, he might ultimately be beaten up by the Durie faction. The argument became heated; Carraher was heard to declare that if he had only two other men like himself he would "redd the corner"—that is, clear the place of the Duries and their friends. It is one of the small curiosities of this case that Carraher is more than once reported as speaking in good braid Scots instead of the debased *patois* of his native city.

There then appeared upon the scene a strangely ill-fated young man. This was a young Regular soldier, James Sydney Emden Shaw—a name of some interest to the student of naval history. Now, it is important that Shaw was little known, or not known at all, to the Carraher-Durie group. As they say, he butted into a private quarrel, perhaps with some drink in him. He appears to have overheard Carraher's brave boast of redding the corner, and he remarked to this dangerous citizen that he "spoke like an Englishman", or words to that effect. This observation, which might gratify a certain type of Scotsman, could not be construed by a man of Carraher's stamp as anything but an insult. The ball of controversy passed from the Duries to Shaw; and they were all making such a noise that the policeman on the beat intervened, telling them to "take a walk"—the Glasgow equivalent of the London Bobby's "Move on, now".

The party, Shaw still of the company, started to move eastwards from Gorbals Cross along Ballater Street, and Carraher and the soldier continued their highly personal argument. They were "throwing cracks" at each other; that is, they were insulting each other, and there is no doubt at all that Carraher was nagged and provoked by this intruder. Reaching the corner at Thistle Street, the older Durie wisely decided that he and his relatives should go home, and they started to move away. Peter Howard, however, lingered awhile on the edge of the pavement, Carraher and Shaw still wrangling in the roadway a few yards away. It appears that Shaw insisted on continuing his argument. The evidence here-

Introduction.

abouts is somewhat obscure, but it is fairly clear that, as Howard was turning to follow the Duries, a scuffle on the roadway caused him to look back; whereupon he saw Shaw "haudin' his neck"—that is, holding his neck with his hands—and pointing towards Gorbals Cross as if he looked for succour in that direction or hoped that Howard would seek it there. Carraher had meanwhile disappeared in the darkness. It was now after one o'clock of a Sabbath morning; and Paddy Carraher had the gift of swift disappearance from scenes of violence.

Peter Howard thus became, willingly or not, the leading actor in a tragedy. He was alone with a man bleeding to death from the jugular vein. A minor complication, of which the Defence ultimately made the best it could, was the appearance on the scene of a man in a light suit. From this passer-by Howard borrowed a handkerchief to stanch the flow of blood from Shaw's neck, and then he, also, disappeared into the shadows of the Gorbals. The episode seems to make a sinister convolution in the pattern of that night's dark doings, but we may agree with the view of Lord Pitman that it was not a material point, and that any one of us, encountering such a situation late at night in a notoriously dangerous area, would readily produce a handkerchief and even more readily escape the scene of an affair so obviously involving police proceedings. The stranger in the light suit was in fact never traced.

In the meantime, Shaw had staggered to the pavement at the corner of Thistle and Ballater Streets, and there he collapsed. It was afterwards discovered that the pool of blood at this point was even larger than that at the point on the roadway where he had been struck. Then he rose again and, according to Howard, "ran" westwards along Ballater Street towards Gorbals Cross: the trail of his blood clear to the detectives when they came to examine the scene. He passed under the viaduct that carries the railway lines across the Clyde into St. Enoch Station and then, having covered some 150 yards, finally collapsed in front of a picture house. A policeman watching a shop nearby attended to him, and an ambulance duly arrived to carry the unfortunate soldier across the bridge and up the hill to the Royal Infirmary. He died as they were taking him to a ward. The detectives on the spot in the Gorbals arrested Peter Howard.

The bush telegraph of the slums works fast. Even at that small hour of a Sunday morning people were abroad, including one female witness who "decided to go for a walk along with my

7

Patrick Carraher.

daughter about 12.45 on the Sunday morning". It very rapidly got about the Gorbals that a man had been killed, and that Howard had been arrested. A woman called Mary McCafferty, an unemployed domestic servant, aged 22, went out with her friend Kate Docherty to see what was afoot, saw Shaw being put into the ambulance in Ballater Street about 1.40 a.m., and gathered that Peter Howard had been arrested. This Kate Docherty was friendly with Howard's older brother, Robert, and the two women went to inform him of what had happened. Their subsequent movements are of rather curious interest.

On their way towards the house in Portugal Street where Robert Howard was staying—that is, westwards and beyond Gorbals Cross—the girls encountered Carraher. He was in Norfolk Street, near its junction with Buchan Street. He spoke to them, no doubt anxious to have the latest news of what was happening, and he went with them to the close giving entry to No. 12 Portugal Street. There, while Kate Docherty ran upstairs, he waited with Mary McCafferty but said nothing. Shortly they were joined by Robert Howard and Kate Docherty, and the strange foursome then proceeded across the Albert Bridge towards the Central Police Station not very far away. Short of this establishment, in the narrow and picturesque thoroughfare known as the Bridgegate, Carraher and the girl McCafferty lingered behind while Robert Howard and Kate Docherty went on to discover at the Police Office how matters stood with the former's young brother. An astonishing conversation ensued.

One is strongly tempted to believe that Carraher had in him that streak of vainglory which is apt to go with the temperament of the third-rate killer. With a good deal of drink in him, possibly with memories of American gangster films, he seems to have posed as the big man, the strong-armed hero who has disposed of the enemy. At all events, he told this girl whom he hardly knew that it was he who had stabbed Shaw.

"I said, 'What for?' and he says, 'I was arguing with a fellow. He was very cheeky.' I said, 'How did you do it?' and he says, 'With a knife,' and he took a knife out of his pocket and showed me it. . . . It was like a pocket knife, a dark knife."

When the girl protested that it would now go hard with Peter Howard she had from Carraher the prompt and rather too romantic

8

Introduction.

assurance: "Oh, yes, they will let Peter Howard out because I will give myself up; I won't let him swing for it."

One might think that he could then have walked into the Central and told the police what he had just told Mary McCafferty, but the heroics of Paddy Carraher were hardly so perdurable as all that. They were rejoined by Robert Howard and Kate Docherty, and back across the bridges to the Gorbals the foursome started again. The careful reader of the evidence will note that Carraher walked next to the parapet, and that on the way home Mary told the others what Paddy had revealed to her as they waited in the Bridgegate. "Show him your knife," she urged, and Robert Howard asked: "Have you got a knife?" To which Carraher blandly replied, "No, I have not got a knife, but I possess a razor blade. It is still in the packet."

When the detectives arrested Patrick Carraher later on that morning they found this razor blade on his person, apparently still in its original packet. They did not find a knife, for Carraher had in fact, unseen by his companions, slipped it over the parapet of the bridge.

The subsequent trial of Patrick Carraher for murder is of only limited interest as an exercise in detection. That his was the hand which raised the knife to stab young James Sydney Emden Shaw to death there is no doubt at all. He was in a drunken condition, and we may think that he believed his blow to be aimed at an older enemy than the young and foolish soldier who had crossed his path by accident. The proceedings in the High Court of Justiciary were remarkable only for the brief, not to say brusque, nature of Lord Pitman's charge to the jury. Some of the odd considerations we have reviewed—the matter of the knife over the parapet of the bridge, for instance—were not so much as mentioned by his lordship. If ever a jury was directed to reduce the capital charge to one of culpable homicide (*anglice* manslaughter) it was never more marked than in this case. It is only fair to observe that Lord Pitman had much in mind the factor of drink.

In the issue, the fifteen good men and women and true who constitute a Scots jury in criminal causes returned the unanimous opinion that Patrick Carraher should be found not guilty of assault but, by the majority verdict allowable in Scottish procedure, that he was guilty of culpable homicide. Lord Pitman thereupon sentenced Paddy Carraher to penal servitude for three years, and we may well think that the prisoner in the dock was a very lucky man.

9

Patrick Carraher.

One point must be made here—a point that has baffled many serious students of crime in Scotland alone. From 1928 onwards until the end of the Second German War there were no hangings in Scotland. During trial after trial over a period of at least fifteen years, it was seen that the Crown was only too ready to reduce a charge of murder to one of culpable homicide, mixed juries only too ready to accept the lessened responsibility with relief. In one notorious case of a shooting near Perth the jury found the accused guilty of rape but the charge of murder not proven; whereas it was obvious that the man in the dock could not have outraged the young woman in the case if he had not first killed her sweetheart. We can only assume that the authorities chose for a period to use the criminal courts of Scotland as laboratories in which the abolition issue might be tested over a long period. Lord Pitman's charge to the jury in the first Carraher case seems to show the influence of instruction.

The circumstances and the official temper had completely changed when, in March, 1946, Paddy Carraher appeared before the High Court of Justiciary for the second and last time on a charge of murder committed on a November night of 1945. It is worth recording at this point, without prejudice one way or another, the unofficial view of the City of Glasgow Police that two or three hangings during the 1945–6 period notably reduced the post-war exuberance of the local gangsters.

III

After his release from prison Carraher appears to have deserted his native Gorbals and transferred his operational headquarters to the Townhead area of Glasgow, on the other side of the river. The attraction here was a woman, Sarah Bonnar; and her brother, Daniel Bonnar, a rather notoriously aggressive citizen, became Carraher's henchman in many an escapade. Given Bonnar's adventurous temperament and Carraher's prestige as one who had done time for killing his man, this couple were at once able to exert considerable influence in their district and class and to be almost certainly destined for more serious trouble with the police.

The Townhead of Glasgow is utterly unlike the Gorbals in lay-out and general character. It is an older settlement by far, and it scrambles over and along the slopes of those clay drumlins, or ridges, which are so marked a feature of the city. Historic and important buildings stand in or about it. The Cathedral, the ancient

Introduction.

house known as Provand's Lordship, and the mass of the Royal Infirmary are at hand. Allan Glen's School, the Maternity Hospital, the Royal Technical College, and even the City Chambers lie within the grouping, which also includes more than one printing establishment of international repute. Many of the older domestic buildings are of great architectural interest and even charm, but too many of them have been overwhelmed by the internal pressures that are the curse of a great industrial city with narrow boundaries and are now only festering slums. As distinct from the Gorbals of the broad level streets, the Townhead is rather a clotted congeries of twisting lanes and dark, steep streets lined with the tall, grey tenements of the industrial West. Public-houses abound.

In this favourable environment, then, in February, 1943, Carraher and Bonnar enjoyed an orgy of violent misbehaviour. The Indictment at the subsequent trial charged Bonnar with breach of the peace, assault with a bottle and kicking a woman; the items against Carraher included vicious assault on a man in a public-house in George Street—punching, kicking and slashing with a razor to his severe injury—and then a turning on three women with a razor, putting them in a state of bodily fear and alarm. For about a week between the 9th and 17th February that year these two men seem to have been in an extreme state of offensive madness or drunkenness. The trial, however, which took place on 11th May, is of no criminological interest. The case was a plain one of lurid hooliganism. Carraher was sent back to gaol for three years.

We may notice here how Carraher's development as a criminal was now not to be halted; it was proceeding only too rapidly. He had started in early youth with theft and assault and some clumsy burglaries; but once he had wielded a weapon and got away with it, as they say, and doubtless as he relied more and more on the stimulus of drink, arrogant brutality grew upon him. The circumstances of the period, moreover, favoured the lone wolf, the reckless enemy of society. Carraher was unfit for military service, having a weak chest and a bad stomach, and he luxuriated in an atmosphere in which easy money, deserters on the run from the Services, the black-out and psychological strain sombrely coloured low life in all British cities. Honest liquor was scarce, but the lack of it could be made up with cheap and potent wines, sometimes fortified with methylated spirit to form a cocktail of lethal strength. Shortages, controls and the black market, along with the strain on

Patrick Carraher.

depleted police forces, completed the picture of a gangster's paradise.

We should understand, however, that Carraher was in fact not a gangster in the literal sense. He neither commanded nor belonged to a large and organized clan of law-breakers. He seemed to be content to operate with the able and enthusiastic assistance of his "good-brother", that is, brother-in-law—though it was not actually in law in this case—Daniel Bonnar. Indeed, the sensitive student of the proceedings in both trials may get from the evidence an uncomfortable sense of Carraher's essential loneliness and will certainly note the fact that in neither of his two fatal assaults was he the original provoker of the conflict. In the Gorbals case he was threatened by the Duries and nagged by the intruding Shaw; in the second and final case we are now about to study the pot of trouble was undoubtedly stirred mainly by Daniel Bonnar on one side and Duncan Revie on the other. Carraher's austere function was that of Lord High Executioner: the man with the knife or chisel, prepared at the critical moment to redd the corner. We may fairly see that he was doomed by his temperament and circumstances sooner or later to overstep the limit a fairly tolerant society imposes on its bad boys.

At the time of his last trial Carraher was nearly 40 years of age, and his person was showing the signs of wear and tear. His height was rather below the average, being 5 feet, $6\frac{1}{2}$ inches; his sandy fair hair was thinning above the temples. His eyes were the most remarkable features of his appearance. Seen in profile they were heavily lidded, hooded, so that from the front they appeared to be mere slits. It was a sinister and apparently merciless visage, so far as these outward stigmata matter at all.

It was on the night of Friday, 23rd November, 1945, that Carraher committed his last crime. That his was the hand which struck another fatal blow at a fellow-creature, another slash with a weapon at a man's neck, there can be little room for doubt. At the same time, the evidence is highly confused, like the topographical nature of the scene; and counsel on both sides were dealing mainly with people of indifferent education and low mentality: some of them quite obviously concerned to make a show of their own innocence. It is perhaps legitimate here, however, greatly to simplify the story and take a short cut through the tangle of testimony, described by the Advocate-Depute as "a mosaic of evidence which is rather like the disconnected pieces of a jigsaw puzzle".

Introduction.

IV

On the afternoon of this Friday in November, 1945, then, three brothers of a family called Gordon left their father's house about 4.30 p.m. These were John, Joseph and Edward Gordon: the first-named the oldest, with 18 years' service as a Regular soldier in the Seaforths and not long released from imprisonment in a German camp since Dunkirk.

These Gordons—there were eight brothers in the family—were not unknown to the police, but they had the reputation of being sufficiently clean fighters in the petty warfare of the poorer quarters, and they were not of the workshy type. It is of pathetic interest that John, the old soldier, was notoriously the quietest of the family, and it is of at least a little importance that until the evening of his last day on earth he had remained indoors and had not touched drink. Apparently the Gordons had fallen foul of the Carraher-Bonnar faction, but whether for racial, denominational or merely family reasons we do not know, and there is no evidence to show that they went looking for trouble in the first place.

Their first port of call was a house at 139, McAslin Street, in the Townhead, where there lived a sister married to one, Duncan Revie—another of those somewhat unfortunate "good-brothers" with a too highly developed sense of family loyalty. This Revie was a deserter from the Army and on the run, able to visit his wife with safety only on occasion. At the statutory hour of 5 p.m. the four men went into the "Coronation Bar" next door to 139, McAslin Street, and there remained, drinking steadily, until about 7 p.m. They then decided to go down to the Rottenrow to Cameron's public-house (now vanished in a slum-clearance scheme) where John Gordon was well known, and there again they drank until near closing time, 9.30.

There is no indication that there was any sensible pause for a bite of food. Indeed, the two younger Gordons passed out under the influence of alcohol and may now, for our present purposes, be forgotten. In Cameron's pub the Gordons had meanwhile encountered a young man called John Keatings, another deserter, but from the Navy in this case. In evidence he admitted that when he, John Gordon and Duncan Revie emerged from Cameron's pub they were all half-seas over.

In the meantime, probably unknown to the Gordons, Carraher and Bonnar had been drinking more or less steadily throughout the day and had passed the evening in Thomson's public-house,

Patrick Carraher.

not far from Cameron's in the Rottenrow. Apparently they left this place about 8.45 p.m. and went down to Daniel Bonnar's house in the same street; with them a little man called Thomas Connelly Watt, "Wee Watt", who was to prove the absolutely fatal witness against Carraher in the subsequent trial. The Carraher-Bonnar party in the house in the Rottenrow, womenfolk among them, then decided that they should have a sing-song, and Bonnar went out to secure supplies of drink and bring in such kindred spirits as he might encounter on the way. He thus made his way up the Rottenrow and opposite Cameron's pub encountered the Gordon clan and its adherents either emerging or just emerged from the premises.

We cannot now safely surmise whether or not this meeting was foreseen or planned; we do not know exactly why the parties should have leapt so swiftly into violent action. We do know that the handsome, fair-haired boy called Keatings, of the Gordon faction, immediately roared his intention to clear the street of lesser men, and that Bonnar on his part doffed his jacket, laid it on the roadway, and prepared for battle against this obvious enemy. It is safe to surmise that both Keatings and Revie made for Bonnar, and it is certain that Bonnar ran away, pursued by Keatings at least. It is also fairly clear that there must have been an exchange of blows. After a brief chase, however, the affair fizzled out. Keatings, in a tolerably advanced state of drink, disappeared from the scene and close students of the case have little more interest in him. But he had done his bit to set the heather on fire.

Bonnar now retired to the house of a sister in College Street, his blood up, and there borrowed (a) a hatchet and (b) a woman's costume jacket to replace his own jacket that had been left on the roadway opposite Cameron's pub. Thus strangely attired and heavily armed he returned to the fray, and on the way he met Carraher and "Wee Watt" near Weaver Street. These alert citizens had been warned that the good-brother was in trouble with the Gordons, and they had come out to support their friend. A Mrs. Helen Josephine Colquhoun, wife of a soldier and a temporary postwoman in her own right, had been cleaning her windows, even at 9.30 p.m., and had seen Bonnar chased along Rottenrow by Keatings. She had thus conceived it her neighbourly duty to go down to Sarah Bonnar's house in Tarbet Street and tell her that her brother was in a fair way to be seriously assaulted.

The details of the next phase of the operations will probably remain forever shadowy. It is merely a safe short-cut through the

Introduction.

jungle of rather suspect testimony to say that, after the first encounter with Bonnar and the disappearance of Keatings, John Gordon and Duncan Revie went up from the Rottenrow into McAslin Street; and that, in the meantime, Carraher and Bonnar, with "Wee Watt" in attendance for a while at least, executed a flanking movement through the dark, dull streets and came upon their enemies again near the intersection of McAslin and Taylor Streets.

Whether "Wee Watt" was actually present or not does not matter now. It is certain that the factions then clashed. Revie went for Bonnar, and again Bonnar executed a rapid retreat downhill, pursued by John Gordon's pugnacious good-brother. It seems equally certain that John Gordon, no doubt swaying pretty hopelessly on the edge of the pavement, was pounced upon by Paddy Carraher. When next seen by a fellow-creature he had collapsed on the pavement and was bleeding copiously from a wound at the back of the neck.

Of this tragic scuffle late at night and at an ill-lit corner there were, however, four good witnesses, if from various distances. Two more than middle-aged tradesmen, both respectable painters, had been chatting at the corner nearby. They did not claim to have heard sounds of scuffling, but they did hear voices raised in sundry incitements to violence, and they saw certain things happening. From some 60 yards away two much younger men heard the commotion and had seen very much what the painters had seen.

None of these witnesses could identify any of the men taking part in the brawl, and they differed as to the number of men involved: an agreeable symptom of their honesty. They all agreed as to the shouting of the men fighting, and they all saw two, or three, men running away down McAslin Street, one (or two) apparently in pursuit of another. They all saw still another figure advancing and "punching" the man who stood on the pavement's edge. They all agreed that, when they went to the aid of the man who had been seemingly "punched", he was bleeding copiously from a wound at the back of the neck. This man was John Gordon.

The evidence becomes slightly confused again at this point, but it is perfectly clear that some of these four witnesses started to help John Gordon to the Royal Infirmary, not far away. An unidentified sailor came to their assistance. The two ageing painters prudently disappeared from the scene. One of the two remaining

15

Patrick Carraher.

witnesses—a young private in the Royal Marines called Neil Campbell—hastened to call a taxi to take the wounded man to hospital. The latter collapsed at the junction of Stanhope Street with McAslin Street as they were helping him along, but he appears to have been persuaded to his feet again. And then, an extremely odd incident, Duncan Revie reappeared, took the wounded person of his brother-in-law on his shoulder, and carried him up to the second-floor landing of the close at 139, McAslin Street, even if he might have seen that Gordon was rapidly bleeding to death.

We may surmise that Revie was in a state of high excitement and even apprehension; no doubt he had in his confused mind the notion of getting his good-brother into the care and protection of his own clan. Marine Campbell, however, had meanwhile found a taxi-cab, and Gordon was rushed to the Royal Infirmary. There he died exactly a minute after the doctor on duty at the gatehouse had made a superficial examination of his injuries.

Approximate silence then fell on the Townhead of Glasgow. From the evidence it is clear, however, that the affair had made a stir, and that sundry parties concerned continued to hang about, awaiting developments, their sombre curiosities not unnaturally aroused. One of the most important of these as a fatal witness against Carraher was a tall, 27-year-old part-owner and driver of a taxi-cab, John Douglas Stewart by name.

It was he who had been with Marine Campbell at the corner not far from the scene of the assault. He had helped to get John Gordon along McAslin Street towards the Royal Infirmary. Whatever he had done with himself thereafter, at about 11.30 p.m. that night, in either Cathedral Street or its brief extension into Stirling Road, he encountered an acquaintance, George Ross Elliott, nicknamed "Gasser" Elliott, apparently on account of his conversational proclivities. These two discussed what had happened, and they set off together, near midnight, to look for Daniel Bonnar, whose name was being freely mentioned as the author of the crime. It is merely fair to say that Stewart knew little of the parties concerned and proved to be an intelligent and useful witness.

Elliott and Stewart thus went first to Bonnar's house in the Rottenrow. There was nobody there, and they proceeded to Sarah Bonnar's home at 14, Tarbet Street. Into this dwelling they were admitted by Bonnar after some hesitation. Men and women were assembled in the kitchen, Carraher among them, and we get from the evidence a strong impression of excitement, now height-

16

Introduction.

ened by Stewart's intimation that Gordon was dead. It is of importance that Stewart had never seen Carraher before. Ultimately, after a great deal of talk backwards and forwards, the latter invited the former into a room apart. The report then reads:—

"Do you remember one of the people in the house coming up to you and asking you to speak apart?—Yes, the accused asked me who I was, and I told him it did not matter. He said 'Where do you come from?' and I said, 'Over the road.'

"Where did this conversation between you and the accused take place?—In the kitchen. That was when he asked me, and he said, 'Well, come here a minute,' and he took me through a door into another room. . . .

"What happened when you and the accused were in this other room?—He told me that he was having a cup of tea in the house when someone came and told him Bonnar was in trouble in the Rottenrow, and he went out and met Bonnar, and the two of them went to a close in McAslin Street, but they didn't see anyone there and they went to the corner of Taylor Street and met the two fellows and the fight started. . . .

"Try and recollect the actual words the accused used?—He just said, 'I gave one of them a jag and ran away when the fight started.'"

Bonnar was later to testify in the same sense, but this was an astonishing statement to make to a stranger. Carraher seems to have had a purpose, however, for when they returned to the kitchen and Stewart showed a clear desire to escape from this alarming situation, Carraher slipped something into his hand, saying, "Chip that away," so that when Stewart found himself in the open air again with "Gasser" Elliott he was in possession of the short, sharp blade and the wooden handle of a woodcarver's chisel.

We may wonder that Stewart did not march straight to the Central Police Station with this incriminating object, but we can make allowance for the excitement and alarm of the situation and for the presence of Elliott. In the issue, they dropped the blade down a stank in the High Street—that is, through the grating over a gutter drain—and the handle down another some yards away, having to use force to get the bulbous wooden part between the bars. These objects were recovered by the police within a few days.

17

Patrick Carraher.

This was not such absolute proof of Carraher's guilt as a judge and jury would accept out of hand, but the odds were narrowing.

Elliott followed Stewart in the witness-box and added some useful detail. He had seen Carraher draw the weapon from his hip pocket and break it into its two parts before handing it to Stewart. He had seen the accused wipe it with a dishcloth, but had not noticed any stain resulting. He had seen Bonnar take off a blood-stained shirt but understood that this was the result of one of his scraps with the Gordon faction; and Bonnar testified that he had been struck on the side of the head. Elliott had observed that Bonnar was excited, Carraher calm.

With regard to the nature of the wound of which John Gordon died there was some interesting testimony from the medical witnesses. It ran *upwards* from near the back of the neck to penetrate the cerebral canal; and at the post-mortem examination it measured four inches by the probe, whereas the effective length of the carver's tool was only about $2\frac{1}{2}$ inches. The Defence naturally sought to make the best of this disparity, but expert evidence for the Crown was able to show that (*a*) in the case of a blow delivered with force the surface tissues would "give" considerably under the impact, and (*b*) that there would ensue a considerable swelling or infiltration of the soft tissues by subsequent bleeding. Professor Allison's citation of the swelling seen in a case of mumps provided a convincing illustration. So far as the upward track of the wound is concerned, it is not difficult to see that Gordon probably crouched head downwards to receive it, and that the assailant would be pulling a clenched fist towards himself at the nadir of his stroke. The discovery of a cut on the ring finger of Gordon's right hand would surely indicate the involuntary raising of a hand to protect the vulnerable neck.

We may now return for a moment to the scene of the scuffle at the corner of McAslin and Taylor Streets, if only in order to clear away some of the confusions surrounding the figure of Carraher in that setting. Was it certainly he who was seen to "punch" Gordon in the view of the four detached witnesses?

Whatever the motives of those pugnacious "good-brothers" Revie and Bonnar, they exculpated each other in their separate testimonies. Revie was quite certain that he chased Bonnar down the street, Bonnar that he retreated before Revie, both leaving Gordon alone of his faction on the pavement; and Revie swore that he had seen Carraher menacing John Gordon. Was "Wee Watt" among those present? Bonnar insisted that he was, but the

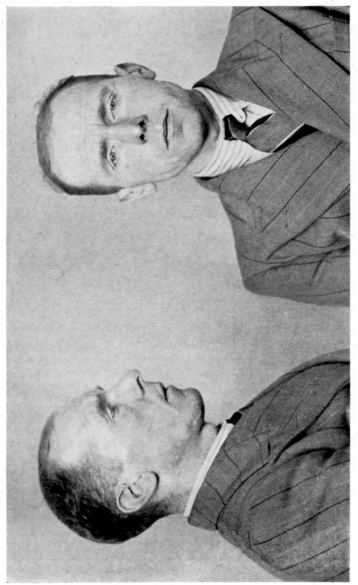

PATRICK CARRAHER IN 1941

Introduction.

Defence, though naturally concerned to imply the possibility, made no overt suggestion that he struck the fatal blow nor suggested that he had ever been in possession of a weapon.

If Carraher was not thus indicated as the assailant beyond any reasonable doubt it was left to "Wee Watt" to tell a story of damning and lurid circumstantiality.

Poor Paddy Carraher! one is almost tempted to exclaim; he was so scurvily served in the witness-box by those who had been his cronies and sycophants. As will be seen from his evidence, Thomas Connelly Watt, aged 47, was at some pains to tell the whole truth as he knew it of the happenings during that fatal November night, and it should be observed that the keenest cross-examination could not break his story. Briefly, it went thus:

Watt was with Carraher and Bonnar in the latter's house when, after the session in Thomson's pub, it was proposed they should have a sing-song and Bonnar went out to bring in a friend. Then the news had come in that Bonnar was being chased by the young sailor, Keatings, and Carraher and Watt had emerged to see what was happening. Then, according to Watt, the carver's tool was in Carraher's breast pocket, the sharp edge showing. "He showed the blade from the top pocket," said Watt. He ran his thumb across the cutting edge, and he said to Watt, "This is the very tool for them."

If that was not enough, Carraher was to make in Watt's presence another candid confession of his guilt. This was when, the fighting over but before the arrival of Stewart and Elliott with the news of Gordon's death, the Carraher-Bonnar faction had reassembled in Daniel Bonnar's house in the first place. In this instance Carraher demonstrated how he had dealt with his enemy, dancing on tip-toe like a boxer, the right hand swinging backward and forward, and then the upraised arm and the vicious stroke downwards. "He said he did not know whether he had got him down the side of the face or shoulder," Watt testified.

The presiding judge, Lord Russell, invited Watt to demonstrate these sinister movements, and those who were present in court declare that "Wee Watt's" vivid pantomime of a vicious assault was far and away the most telling evidence the Crown produced during the three days' hearing of the case. They also report that, throughout the proceedings, Carraher bore himself coldly and glumly, like one who knows his doom is sealed, his narrow eyes hooded and never a glance towards one of his enemies or his former friends in the witness-box.

Patrick Carraher.

In the early morning of 24th November, 1945, the Glasgow C.I.D. acted swiftly and arrested several of the principal participants in the brawl. Most of these were ultimately convicted for breach of the peace, while Carraher alone faced the charge of murder. The trial took place on Thursday, Friday and Saturday, 28th February and 1st and 2nd March, 1946. After the judge's careful charge it took the jury only twenty minutes to return a unanimous verdict of guilty. On 6th April, 1946, after an unsuccessful Appeal, Patrick Carraher was hanged in Barlinnie Prison, Glasgow; and most of us would agree that society was thus well rid of a vicious pest.

V

The case for the Defence rested entirely on medical evidence, provided by two experts who presented the view that Carraher's was a psychopathic personality and suggested that the then rather newfangled doctrine of diminished responsibility should apply to his violent actions.

In his able speech for the defence Mr. G. R. Philip, K.C., covered a great deal of ground, perhaps attempting, one may think, to cover too much. He made his plea for Carraher under three distinct heads.

In the first place, quite legitimately, learned counsel set out to discredit certain leading witnesses for the Crown, notably Revie, Bonnar and Watt, and so to handle the confusing evidence as to suggest that another hand than Carraher's, perhaps Bonnar's, had struck the fatal blow; and in this passage naturally, he emphasized the apparent disparity between the length of the carver's chisel and the length of the wound in post-mortem conditions. With the evidence on paper before us we may feel that these attempts were hopeless in the light of Stewart's detached testimony, and the evidence of the doctors for the Crown.

Mr. Philip, then, momentarily accepting the hypothesis that his client had been the killer, not altogether unreasonably argued that, considering the confusion of events and the amount of provocation supplied by Revie at least, this was no case of deliberate intention to kill. All the lurid events of the evening had been working up to a clash in which hard blows would inevitably be exchanged. This, argued learned counsel, justified the view that Carraher's crime, if any, was rather in the nature of technical homicide than in that of murder.

Finally, and most onerously, he rested his plea on the issue of

Introduction.

diminished responsibility spoken to by his three expert witnesses as against the evidence and the firm opinions of Dr. Scott, the prison doctor.

The careful reader will no doubt give close attention to these separate testimonies, for here is an issue which, in view of the latterday campaign for the abolition of the death penalty, involves the whole structure of our penal system and the public attitude towards crime. Judge and jury were invited in this case to consider a measurement or assessment of human responsibility that must at any time be infinitely more difficult to make with certainty than the sufficiently onerous assessment of a degree of lunacy. It will be noted that none of these experts for the defence would have certified Patrick Carraher insane. His was a psychopathic condition, he had alcoholic tendencies in a marked degree, and therefore his general sense of social responsibility was so far impaired that he could not properly appreciate the consequences of his acts. He knew the difference between right and wrong—but the distinction somehow did not apply to himself.

Another age would have called this sheer egoism, and the layman may wonder if the generalization could not be applied to the vast majority of criminals. However that may be, the student should address himself to Dr. McNiven's able exposition of the theory, particularly to the passages at the end of his testimony when, in re-examination by Mr. Philip, he uttered some easily understandable definitions. Also to be noted is his view that, so far from being willing to define a general line of demarcation in such cases, he thought each case should be taken on its own merits. There was again Dr. Blyth's somewhat alarming estimate that psychopathic conditions, just below the ceiling of certifiable insanity, affect two per cent of the population. Finally, there came Lord Russell's admirably complete and fair presentation of these issues to the jury, unanimously approved by the Appeal Court.

Carraher was not insane. At school he was a normal pupil. The Defence invoked a legend of the traditional stepmother who put him from the house at an early age, but this romantic interpolation must be qualified in the light of information that was not produced in court. Paddy's dismissal from his father's house was the deliberate act of both parents, sickened and saddened by his incorrigibility. The list of his convictions from first to last is a lengthy chronicle of misdemeanour and imprisonment over some twenty years, so that he spent much more of the second half of his life in prison than out of it, with a spell of Borstal intervening.

21

Patrick Carraher.

The man's father was an anxious listener in court at the first trial for murder in 1938, but he made no appearance at the second and last.

There were also introduced into the proceedings certain vague suggestions of a persecution mania. The medical witnesses for the Defence found Carraher harbouring a general grievance against the Law and the police, surely a familiar attitude among inveterate criminals. There was the account of his occasional trick of looking into cupboards for men who were not there, but if that was not a symptom of the irritability of the chronic alcoholic, one may think it not unnatural in one who lived with a lady who was not his legal wife. As for the man's grievance against people "piping" him in public-houses, who that has lingered in any East End pub does not know the sodden wreck with a chip on his shoulder, to whom even an accidental look is an insult to be wiped out only by abuse or assault?

On the whole, even the layman may think that if the defence had rested wholly on the plea of chronic alcoholism in Carraher's case it might have availed him more than the somewhat experimental plea of diminished responsibility, advanced by two doctors who had not seen a great deal of him, and then only when the strict regimen of Barlinnie had allowed the drink to work out of his system.

The fatal brawl was undoubtedly provoked and inflamed by drink. A telling fragment of Sarah Bonnar's evidence was to the effect that the man would rarely face a proper meal. A close student of this case, highly qualified to judge these matters, has privately declared that such as Carraher probably drank rather less in the average day than many a wealthier and better-fed man of invulnerable respectability, but that the absence of substantial food to absorb and offset the effects of alcohol would tend to enclose such as Carraher within, as it were, a glasshouse of morose illusion, into which a stranger might break only at the risk of violent assault by the lone wolf on guard.

The social problem symbolized by the public-house in such clotted cities as Glasgow is a heart-breaking one indeed. In Glasgow in particular it is complicated by the fact that strong pressure by the extreme elements of the temperance movement, working over a long period of years and with influence on the licensing Bench, has tended to turn the average public-house in the poorer districts of the city into a species of penal establishment. Even the most harmless games, such as dominoes and darts, are not per-

22

Introduction.

mitted, and the police are forced by superior instruction to exercise the strictest sort of supervision of licensed premises, while any effort by a progressive licensee to improve his premises to the standards prevailing in, say, England does not have the encouragement of the magistrates at least.

Even so, the public-house in those overcrowded districts of central Glasgow is an important part of the social structure. Given grossly overcrowded conditions of housing, the menfolk at least are simply driven out of their mean, stinking, insanitary and often bug-ridden homes. If it is not to be wholly a matter of hanging about the street corner with the other "Neds", it must be the pub, especially in a notoriously wet climate. It would be a vicious irony to suggest that the Glasgow working man's pub is his club. It is occasionally so, let us admit, but on the whole it is simply a refuge from the degradation of so many homes, from the meanness of the environment.

A terrible case has developed against those who have governed Glasgow during the past century. Throughout the long period of industrial expansion so little foresight went to the problems bound to arise when peoples of half-a-dozen races scrambled for work in an expanding city, when landowners and property-owners allowed dwellings and their sites to be divided and sub-divided, to be built over again and again, producing warrens in which the impoverished detritus of the old industrial order multiplied and festered. The maintenance of decency in such conditions is much more than a simple social duty; it is a feat.

Much has been made of gang warfare in Glasgow, and of those bands of pugnacious youths who, under fancy names, banded to fight each other on such pretexts as the old Billy and Danny rivalry, Protestants against Catholics. The pretexts are meaningless. The emergence of a Scoto-Irish breed, mainly huddled in the most degraded areas, did indeed complicate the pattern, but its basis was the essentially Scottish one of the clan system. Strong and violent youth unconsciously organized itself in groups in order, one had almost said, to fight its way out of sombre monotony. Theirs was only a special and unpleasant expression of the motive that bids millions rather more fortunately placed to sublimate their sense of frustration in blind loyalty to this or that football team. It is of touching interest that a sympathetic police official of one of the eastern divisions of Glasgow could, by 1942, show from his careful records that most of his notoriously bad boys were by then serving, if they had not already fallen, in North Africa or in the

23

Patrick Carraher.

various Commando raids on the European coasts. So badly did they need a way of escape from the home environment and from the doldrums of unemployment that so terribly afflicted the industrial regions of Scotland during most years of the third decade of the 20th Century!

It has been suggested here that Paddy Carraher was not cut out to be a good gangster. His morose and individualistic temperament fated him to operate within small groups and usually as the Big Man with a somewhat theatrical fondness for the part of the decisive killer: the vicious egoist *in excelsis*. It has not been suggested, despite modern psychological science, that he was aught but a rat, acute and resourceful within his limitations. It has not been claimed that he was ever involved in a case of subtle interest to students of crime. One would like to think, however, that this account of his killings, trials and subsequent punishment may assist in moving the public conscience and the authorities towards a more urgent sense of the appalling problems of housing and reconstruction, and of the gravity of the human problems arising out of bad environment, that still face many another British community besides Glasgow.

Leading Dates

1906

19th October   Carraher born in Glasgow.

1923

11th January   Sentenced to 14 days' imprisonment for theft and assault.

2nd February   £2 caution for six months or 14 days, for theft.

19th March   Sent to Borstal for 3 years for theft (four charges.)

1926

2nd June   Sentenced to 3 months' imprisonment for theft, and previous convictions.

1927

23rd July   Sentenced to 4 months' imprisonment for house-breaking with intent to steal and p.c.

7th December   Sentenced to 6 months' hard labour for theft, and p.c.

1929

8th August   Sentenced to 6 months' hard labour for theft, and p.c.

1930

3rd April   Sentenced to 12 months' hard labour for attempted house-breaking.

1931

15th June   Sentenced to 18 months' hard labour for theft by house-breaking.

1933

16th February   Sentenced to 18 months' hard labour for theft by house-breaking, breach of the peace, and p.c.

1934

10th September   Sentenced to 2 years' hard labour for house-breaking with intent to steal, possessing explosives, and p.c.

1938

Night of
13/14th August   Carraher alleged to have assaulted James Durie at Gorbals Cross.
Carraher, the Duries and Shaw quarrel.
Shaw stabbed with knife, and dies on way to hospital at 1.40 a.m.
Peter Howard detained by police.
Carraher arrested at 3.30 a.m.

Patrick Carraher.

12th September	First Trial of Carraher for murder opens in Glasgow before Lord Pitman.
13th September	Carraher found guilty of culpable homicide and sentenced to 3 years' penal servitude.
1943	
11th May	Carraher sentenced to 3 years' penal servitude for assault and razor-slashing.
1945	
23rd November	Clash between Revie, Keatings and Bonnar outside Cameron's public-house at 9.30 p.m. Carraher and Bonnar encounter John Gordon and Revie on corner of McAslin Street and Taylor Street at 10 p.m. John Gordon stabbed, and dies on admission to Royal Infirmary at 10.15 p.m.
24th November	Carraher arrested and charged with murder.
1946	
28th February	Second Trial of Carraher for murder opens in Glasgow before Lord Russell.
2nd March	Carraher found guilty of murder and sentenced to death.
20th March	Appeal dismissed.
6th April	Carraher hanged at Barlinnie Prison, Glasgow.

THE TRIAL

WITHIN THE

HIGH COURT OF JUSTICIARY, GLASGOW

ON

MONDAY, 12TH SEPTEMBER, 1938

Judge Presiding—
LORD PITMAN

Counsel for the Crown—

MR. JAMES WALKER, Advocate-Depute

MR. G. A. MONTGOMERY, Advocate

Counsel for the Defence—

MR. J. CAMERON, K.C.

MR. J. WHEATLEY, Advocate

27

First Day—Monday, 12th September, 1938.

THE CLERK OF COURT—Call the Diet of His Majesty's Advocate against Patrick Carraher.

MR. CAMERON—I appear for the accused along with Mr. Wheatley, and the accused adheres to his plea of Not Guilty.

A jury of 15 was then empanelled and sworn.

Indictment.

THE CLERK OF COURT—Patrick Carraher, prisoner in the Prison of Barlinnie, Glasgow, you are Indicted at the instance of the Right Honourable Thomas Mackay Cooper, His Majesty's Advocate, and the charges against you are (1) that on 13th August, 1938, at Gorbals Cross, Glasgow, you did assault James Durie, 1, Dunvegan Street, Glasgow, and did seize hold of him, take up a threatening attitude towards him and brandish a knife at him; and (2) that on 14th August, 1938, at the junction of Ballater Street and Thistle Street, both in Glasgow, you did assault James Sydney Emden Shaw, 3, Ballater Street, aforesaid, and did cut or stab him in the neck with a knife or other sharp instrument, and did murder him; and you have been previously convicted of assault.

JAMES WALKER, A.D.

Evidence for the Prosecution.

PETER HOWARD (23),[1] sworn.

Examined by MR. WALKER—I reside at 58, Norfolk Street, Glasgow, and am employed as a shunter with William Dixon Limited, in Crown Street. I have known the accused, Patrick Carraher, for some years and I identify him in the dock. I am friendly with John Durie and James Durie.

On Saturday, 13th August, 1938, did you go to 163, Hospital Street, where James Durie lives, to see if they were there?—Yes. None of them were in.

[1] Figures in brackets indicate age of witness.

Patrick Carraher.

P. Howard

When you found neither of them in I think you went down to the corner of Norfolk Street and Portugal Street?—Yes.

And there I think you met them along with the witness Charles Morgan?—Yes.

About what time would that be?—Before midnight.

You had set out before midnight and met these people before midnight?—Yes.

Along with them did you go to the Gorbals Cross and speak there with them for some time?—Yes.

As a result of the conversation with the Duries and Morgan were you on the lookout for someone?—No.

Did you ultimately see the accused at Gorbals Cross that night? —I seen him, yes.

Did you call the attention of anybody to the accused?—I called the Duries back because they wanted to see him.

And did they come back and speak to Carraher?—Yes.

I think you were a little distance away and did not hear anything that was said?—No, I never heard anything.

Did the Duries and the accused then go to the south-west corner of Gorbals Cross where, I think, you joined them?—Yes.

Did you hear something being said by the accused?—I never heard him saying anything.

Do you remember any young fellow joining the company?— Yes, Private Shaw.

That is now the deceased man?—Yes.

You had known him I think by sight at that time?—Yes.

Was there anything said by him to Carraher?—Yes, he asked Carraher did he come from England, and Carraher said: "No, what's it got to do with you?"

Was anything said about a blowhard?—No.

Was there any argument going on when you were present there?—Yes, the Duries were arguing with Carraher.

Was Shaw in the argument at all?—No, Shaw came walking in and just asked Carraher did he come from England. That was all.

He was not in the argument otherwise?—No.

I think after a little two policemen came and moved you people on?—Yes.

And after that did you walk along Ballater Street, that is going eastwards away from Gorbals Cross?—Yes.

Ballater Street leads east from Gorbals Cross, and some distance along Ballater Street you have Thistle Street on your left hand side as you are walking east?—Yes.

30

Evidence for the Prosecution.

P. Howard

Were you walking along Ballater Street in the direction of Thistle Street?—Yes.

Who were all there?—The two Duries, Morgan, Carraher, Shaw and myself.

That is six altogether?—Yes.

Were you all walking together in a bunch or were you with the Duries and Morgan?—Me and Morgan were at the back, and the Duries and Carraher and Shaw were walking in front.

When you came to the corner of Thistle Street did you stop there at all?—Yes, we stopped at the side of the pavement.

Was there any argument there?—No. James Durie says: "I am going home, it's kind of late." He took his brother and young Morgan with him.

So that left Shaw and the accused and yourself?—Yes.

Did you three remain any time at this corner?—A couple of seconds. I asked Private Shaw if he was going along the road and he said no.

Did you turn and go along the road?—I turned to go.

And did Shaw come with you?—No.

Did he remain with the accused?—Yes, he remained with Carraher.

Just as you were leaving them did you hear anything said between them?—Carraher told Shaw to go home and mind his own business.

Tell the jury from that point anything that you heard pass between Shaw and the accused while they were at the corner of Thistle Street and Ballater Street?—Carraher told Shaw to go home and mind his own business, and Shaw would not go away. He said: "No, I am going to stay here."

Anything else?—No, I just walked on the pavement to go home myself.

Did you look back at all?—I just got on the pavement and looked back and I saw Shaw haudin' his neck.

Did you see anything happen before that?—No.

Just tell the ladies and gentlemen of the jury how Shaw was holding his neck?—Shaw was haudin' his hand up to his neck and he was pointing along to Gorbals. He was trying to tell me to go along to the Gorbals.

Why did you say he was trying to tell you?—He was trying to make it out; he was pointing in that direction.

Was he able to say anything to you?—No, he couldn't speak.

31

Patrick Carraher.

P. Howard

He could not speak but he was pointing towards the Gorbals? —Yes.

And he was holding his neck?—Yes.

Did you see anything the matter with him?—I saw blood coming gasping out of his neck.

How far would you be away from him when you turned round and saw him holding his neck? Would you be a few yards or a few feet away?—I would be a couple of feet away from him.

By the COURT—Was there anybody else there at all?—No, there was no one there.

Examination continued—Did you know where the accused had gone?—I turned round and he was not there; he had disappeared.

Just before that you have told us that you had asked Shaw to come home with you. Was the accused still there when you asked Shaw to come home with you?—Yes.

You had just gone a few paces, had you, because you were only two feet away when you looked round and saw Shaw haudin' his neck?—Yes.

And the blood gasping out?—Yes.

Did you see Carraher when you turned round?—I just turned round and Carraher was away, disappeared.

You cannot say where he went?—No.

By the COURT—Was it dark?—There was a street lamp that was shining.

Examination continued—Did you see anyone else there who could have inflicted the injury on Shaw?—I never saw anyone else. The only one I saw was a man who passed by and gave him a loan of his handkerchief.

That was after you had seen the blood gushing?—Yes.

But up to that moment when you saw Shaw haudin' his neck there was no one else there who could have inflicted the injury?— I never saw anyone there.

But apart from the accused and yourself there was no one there, was there?—No.

Now after you saw Shaw holding his neck and the blood coming out, did Shaw move at all?—Shaw dropped at the corner of Thistle Street and Ballater Street.

Evidence for the Prosecution.

P. Howard

Did he do anything after that?—Then he got up and ran along Ballater Street towards the Gorbals Cross.

That is going westwards along Ballater Street?—Yes.

What was happening as he was running along?—He ran along to facing the Green's, and then he dropped there.

Facing Green's picture house. Was that on the south or the north pavement of Ballater Street? Going towards Gorbals Cross was it the left hand side of the street or the right hand side?—The right hand side coming from the Gorbals, the left hand side going to the Gorbals.

That is the side the picture house is on?—Yes.

And was that the side that Shaw was on?—No, Shaw was on the other side facing the Green's.

On the north side?—Yes.

Did he collapse at the Green's?—He collapsed just there.

Then did he get up again?—No.

Did someone come and assist him?—The police came.

Shaw was ultimately taken away in an ambulance, was he?—Yes.

Cross-examined by MR. CAMERON—You say you went to the police office. Were you taken there?—I was taken to the police office.

And were you detained there for some time?—About three hours.

And after you had given a statement were you allowed to go?—Yes.

Was there a street lamp quite near the place where Shaw was seen by you holding his neck?—Yes, a street lamp was just at the corner.

And was it quite a clear night?—No.

Was it raining?—It was not raining, but it was dull.

But you could see what was going on, could you, in the light of the street lamp?—Yes.

Did you know the name of the man who came along with the handkerchief?—No.

Did he come on the scene before the police arrived?—Yes.

Did you speak to him?—I only asked him for a hankie.

Did he give it to you?—Yes.

Where did he come from?—I couldn't tell you.

He must have been very close?—He was on the other side of the pavement.

Patrick Carraher.

P. Howard

The same pavement as you and Shaw were on?—No, the other side.

You say you don't know his name. Have you seen him since?—No.

Did you tell the police about him?—Yes.

Is he not one of the people you see quite often round about the Gorbals?—No.

So this was a mysterious stranger whom you had never seen before, and you have never seen him since?—No.

Do you know what became of his handkerchief?—No.

What was he dressed like?—I never took any interest in what he was dressed in.

Was he a tall man or a short man?—About the same size as me.

A young man?—Yes.

Was he quite sober?—Yes.

What time of night was this?—Between one and a quarter past.

There would not be many people about at that time of night?—No.

And what happened to the man after he gave you his handkerchief?—I just ran on and gave it to Shaw; I never saw the man.

Where did he go?—I couldn't tell you where the man went.

You say he took no interest in this?—Not that I saw.

Except to give you his handkerchief?—Yes, I asked him for it.

How did you know he had one?—I just asked him if he had a handkerchief to give to Shaw.

Did you tell him why you wanted the handkerchief?—Yes.

And you say that although you told him that you wanted the handkerchief to stanch the wound in this man's neck he just disappeared into the blue after giving you the handkerchief?—I never took any interest in the man; I just took the handkerchief and gave it to Shaw.

And he just went away?—Yes.

Took no more interest in this curious affair?—I couldn't tell you.

You do not know who he is?—No.

Have you made any enquiry since?—No.

By the COURT—Was that before Shaw went along Ballater Street?—Yes.

Cross-examination continued—And at that time the accused was not in sight, was he?—No.

34

Evidence for the Prosecution.

P. Howard

Did you not think it would be a wise thing to do to try and find out who this man was?—It was none of my business.

Did you not think you had better not make any enquiry? Was that it?—Why should I make enquiry?

May I take it you wanted to have as little to do with this as you possibly could?—Yes.

Well, now, I want to come back to your movements in the early part of the evening. You told us in examination-in-chief that you went to look for the Duries, James and John—went to their house, did you not?—Yes.

They are friends of yours?—I run about with them.

How many run about together?—About four of us: the Duries, Morgan and myself.

There isn't a fifth, is there?—No.

Are you sure?—Yes.

Whose house did you go to after you found they were not in their own house?—I went down to the corner.

And you saw them?—Yes.

Were they with Charles Morgan at the time?—Yes.

And was there a girl with them?—Yes, Peggy McNicol.

Whose girl is she?—James Durie's.

Whilst you were at the corner did James Durie go away to take Peggy McNicol home?—Yes.

Did you stay at the corner until James came back, or did you go away?—I stayed at the corner till he came back.

Did you not go down Norfolk Street whilst John Durie and Charles Morgan went down Gorbals Street until they got to the corner of Dunmore Street? Isn't that what happened?—No, the three of us stood there together.

Are you quite certain?—Yes, till young Durie came along and then we separated.

And you separated to go and find out where Carraher was?—No, I saw Carraher coming.

Did you not go to look for him?—No.

Did you not see him at a coffee stall at Gorbals Cross?—Yes.

And did you not sing out to the Duries that there he was?—Yes.

Where were they when you sang out to the Duries?—Going up home.

And you called them back?—Yes.

You knew that there had been some sort of an altercation between Carraher and the Duries?—Yes.

And you were looking for him?—It was none of my business.

D

Patrick Carraher.

P. Howard

Why did you want him? To fight him, was it not?—Yes.

So there were the two Duries, Charles Morgan, and yourself looking for Carraher?—Yes.

You were going to beat him up, were you not?—No.

Were you going to have a nice friendly chat with him?—It was the Duries that wanted to see him.

Did they want to see him to discuss the weather?—To discuss what they were arguing about.

They wanted to fight, didn't they?—I could not tell you.

And you were the scout who was sent out to look for him?—No.

Will you kindly explain why it was you sang out to the Duries, who were going home, that there was Carraher?—The Duries told me they were looking for Carraher. I saw Carraher coming to the coffee stall and I shouted to the Duries to come back.

By the Court—Did they not tell you what they wanted to see him about?—They wanted to see him about an arguing match about his young brother.

Cross-examination continued—Carraher was pretty drunk that night, was he not?—Yes.

He was staggering pretty badly, was he not?—Yes.

He was not able to look after himself very well, was he?—He could look after himself; he wasn't that bad.

You were quite sober though, were you not?—Yes.

And so were the Duries, and Morgan?—Yes.

A nice argument you were going to have with the drunk man, weren't you?—I had no argument with a drunk man.

You called the Duries back to the coffee stall. Was this about half-past twelve at night?—I cannot tell you the correct time.

Round about that time, was it not?—Yes.

Did they come back and go over to where Carraher was?—Yes.

And I think you and Charles Morgan stood watching from the corner of the street to see what was happening?—Yes.

Were you keeping under cover?—No.

Where were you standing? In a close mouth?—Standing at the corner of Freedman's shop.

And then did the two Duries bring Carraher over to you?—Yes.

They were arguing, were they not?—Yes.

Were they not trying to get him to fight? Was he not wanting to get home?—Durie wanted to have a square go with him.

Evidence for the Prosecution.

P. Howard

Did Carraher not make it quite clear that there was no chance of a square go if there were two Duries there to go into him?—Yes.

Carraher was not wanting to fight, because there were two Duries against him at least?—Yes.

And there were two of you as well, Charles Morgan and yourself?—Yes.

Did Carraher suggest that if he wished to have a fight he could have it on the Sunday when he was sober, but he was going to go home now?—No.

You did not hear that?—No.

In any event, you did not see Carraher fighting with the Duries?—No.

And they were apparently wanting to fight with him?—Yes.

By the COURT—Tell me this. You said they brought him up. What do you mean by that? When they brought him up had they their hands on him at all?—No, they were just at the side of him.

What do you mean by saying they brought him up?—They ran him along to the corner.

If it had not been for them he would not have come?—Yes.

Cross-examination continued—Where was Shaw at this time?—I had not seen Shaw. We were all standing together talking.

You were arguing, were you not?—The Duries were arguing.

And were you not making such a noise that the police moved you on?—The policeman told us to take a walk.

Were you moved on before Shaw came on the scene?—No.

Shaw had come on the scene before you were moved on?—Yes.

You were just making a nuisance of yourselves in the public street, and you were told to go home by the police?—No.

Were you not told to go home by the police?—No, to take a walk.

And was not the best place to walk, to walk home?—No.

What time in the morning was this?—It was about one o'clock.

Have you often been told by the police to take a walk at one o'clock in the morning?—Yes.

Are you in the habit of getting into trouble with the police?—No.

Did you take the policeman's advice and go home?—I went along Ballater Street.

Where do you live?—Norfolk Street.

Patrick Carraher.

P. Howard

Well, if you went along Ballater Street you were going away from home, were you not?—Yes.

Why were you going away from home when you were told to clear out?—The whole lot of us went together. I went along with the Duries.

Why didn't you go home: that is what I want to know?—Well, when the police told us to take a walk we were standing facing in that direction.

How far were you going to walk?—That depends.

How far were you intending to walk?—I couldn't tell you that.

Was the policeman following you?—No.

Where were you going to?—Well, I might walk along to Crown Street.

What was the attraction in Crown Street?—Going up to the Duries' house in Hospital Street.

You passed the entrance to Hospital Street, did you not?—Yes.

You went to the junction of Thistle Street and Ballater Street, and Thistle Street is beyond the street where the Duries live?—Yes.

So you were not going to the Duries house. Why did you pass Ballater Street and go on to Thistle Street junction?—I only took a walk along, that's all.

You cannot give us any better explanation than that?—No.

Was Shaw still with you at that time?—Yes.

Are you sure the Duries live in Hospital Street?—It is Thistle Street.

Oh, it is Thistle Street, now; it was Hospital Street two minutes ago. Is it Thistle Street now? Which is it?—Hospital Street.

Do they both live there?—No.

Who lives in Hospital Street?—The married one, the old one, John.

Where does the other one live?—I couldn't tell you.

You don't know although you are friendly with them and run around with them?—Yes.

Did Carraher tell Shaw to go away home several times?—Yes.

Was Shaw quite sober?—Yes.

And did Shaw refuse to go?—Yes.

Was he making various remarks to Carraher as you were going along?—I did not hear what they were talking about.

Did you tell him to go home?—I asked Shaw if he would come along and he said no.

Evidence for the Prosecution.

P. Howard

Why did you tell Shaw to go home?—Well, Shaw had no right to be in the company.

Was he being rather provocative?—Yes.

Was he provoking you a bit too?—No.

Who was he provoking?—Carraher.

And the Duries?—No.

How far away were the Duries would you say when you saw Shaw holding his neck?—The Duries were not there; they were away.

How far away?—I could not tell you.

Could you not see them?—No.

So you could not see either them or Carraher when you saw Shaw holding his neck?—No.

I think Ballater Street is a good straight street?—Yes.

And none of these three were in view when you saw Shaw holding his neck?—No.

And it was just after that that you noticed the man from whom you got the handkerchief?—Yes.

And who he is you do not know?—That is so.

Re-examined by Mr. WALKER—Do I understand you to say that Shaw had no right to be in the company that night?—Yes, it was none of his business.

He was a stranger to you, was he—at least you just knew him by sight?—Yes.

And whatever argument the Duries may have had with the accused, was Shaw, so far as you heard, taking any part in that argument?—No.

He had nothing to do with that, but he was a stranger butting into the company?—Yes.

And I think you told us that he had asked Carraher if he was an Englishman?—Yes.

Now, when the six of you who had gone along Ballater Street stopped at Thistle Street corner, you told me that the two Duries and Morgan had left?—Yes.

Did you see where they went?—Well, they said good-night and I saw them going away home.

Did they go away from the corner?—Yes, right up Thistle Street.

Out of sight?—Yes.

And so far as you know they went away?—Yes.

Were they away for any length of time before you asked Shaw to come along home?—About five minutes.

Patrick Carraher.

And during that five minutes am I right in thinking that Carraher had been telling Shaw to go home?—Yes.

And Shaw had been asserting his right to stay there?—Yes.

And, of course, you heard that and you were there?—Yes.

Was there anybody else in the company except the three of you?—I never saw anyone else there.

There was no one else there except Carraher, Shaw and yourself?—Yes.

Then you just asked Shaw to come home. At that time where was Shaw standing?—Shaw was standing with Carraher, the two of them in the street together.

Was he close beside him?—Yes.

Then you looked round and Shaw was holding his neck?—Yes.

What time would elapse, so far as you can remember, between you leaving Shaw and Carraher standing together and you looking round and seeing Shaw holding his neck?—I cannot tell you.

How far would you have gone along the street?—I was just on the pavement when I turned round.

How far were you away from Shaw when you turned round?—About ten yards.

So that you had just walked about ten yards after seeing Shaw and the accused standing together when you turned round and saw Shaw holding his neck?—Yes.

Now you were asked about whether you knew the man that offered you the handkerchief. Who got the handkerchief from this man; was it you or was it Shaw?—I got the handkerchief because I had no handkerchief myself, and I wanted one to stop the blood on Shaw's neck.

Had you seen the blood coming from Shaw's neck before you got the handkerchief?—Yes.

Did you ask this man for a handkerchief?—Yes.

By the COURT—Tell me, what day of the week was it?—A Saturday night. It was a Sunday morning when it happened.

Was it Sunday morning, 14th August?—Yes.

MARGARET MCKAY MCNICOL (18), sworn.

Examined by MR. WALKER—I live at 249, Eglinton Street, Glasgow, and am a machinist. I have known the accused, Patrick Carraher, for about two years. I also know James Durie, and I go about with him. On Saturday, 13th August, I had arranged to

Evidence for the Prosecution.

M. M. McNicol

meet James Durie at Gorbals Cross about 11.15 p.m. and I went down to the Cross about that time.

When you came to the Cross did you see the accused?—Yes, he spoke to me. He was by himself.

Did he ask you to do something for him?—Yes, he asked me to go a message for him.

Were you willing to do that or unwilling?—Unwilling.

Did you leave him; did you run away from him?—Yes, I went across to where James Durie was standing at the Gorbals Cross with Charles Morgan.

By the Court—Was the accused quite sober?—No, he had a drink in him.

Examination continued—Did you say something to James Durie about Carraher?—I just said he had a knife.

Did Durie ask Carraher to come over and speak to him?—No, the accused came to where I was standing with James Durie. He wanted to speak to me, and he got hold of me by the arm.

Did James Durie do anything?—He pulled me away towards him.

Tell the jury in your own words what happened then?—Paddy came forward and said he wanted to speak to me again, and James said he wanted to speak to me too, and the two of them got hold of me by the arm, and then Paddy got him by the lapel of his jacket. A crowd gathered, then, and I was put off the road.

You told us that Paddy, that is to say the accused, got hold of James Durie by the lapel of his coat. What kind of attitude was the accused taking up towards James Durie?—He had a knife in his right hand.

Who had?—The accused.

And how was he holding James, by the lapel of his coat?—He had him by his left hand.

His left hand on the lapel of James's coat, and the knife in his right hand?—Yes.

What was he doing with the knife? How was he holding it?—He was just showing the blade (demonstrating with clenched fist).

How long did the accused keep hold of James by the lapel and have the knife in his hand?—Between five and ten minutes.

Was anything said by either of them?—No, that I could not say. I got out of the road at the time.

Patrick Carraher.

M. M. McNicol

Did you hear anything being said by the one to the other?—No, James just told him to put the knife in his pocket.

As far as you were concerned did you form any impression at the time as to whether this was serious or not?—I did not know what he was going to do.

By the COURT—Did you say just now you did not think he was going to do anything?—I did not know what he was going to do.

Did you say before that you did not think he was going to do anything?—No.

Examination continued—Tell the ladies and gentlemen of the jury how the accused was holding this knife?—He had it in his right hand.

Whereabout was his right hand?—He had it just at the side of him—up like that (demonstrating)—and he had James by the lapel of the coat.

It was in his right hand?—Yes.

By the COURT—Was the blade open?—Yes.

Was he holding on to the handle?—Yes.

Did you think he was going to use it as a dagger, or what?—I don't know.

Was it an ordinary one-bladed knife?—Yes.

At all events you only saw one blade?—Yes, I only saw one blade.

Examination continued—Which way was the blade pointing when the accused was holding it?—Just like that (demonstrating).

Was it pointing towards James Durie or away from him?—Towards him.

You said some people gathered round?—Yes.

And the two ultimately separated?—Yes.

I think you went away with James Durie to where his brother lives at 163, Hospital Street?—Yes.

The brother John came down with you to the Gorbals Cross and there you met Peter Howard and Charles Morgan. Is that right?—Yes.

I think you stayed with that lot until after midnight?—Yes.

Then James Durie saw you home and you got in about half-past twelve?—Yes.

Evidence for the Prosecution.

M. M. McNicol

Cross-examined by MR. CAMERON—What was the message that you were to take for the accused?—He wanted me to go up to Katie Morgan.

And you were not willing to go. Why not?—Well, the two of them fell out, and I didn't want anything to do with it.

You mean Carraher and Katie Morgan had fallen out?—Yes.

What was the message he wanted you to take up to her?—He never said.

And you say he had a drink in him?—Yes.

Then, when you ran over to James Durie, he came and followed you and took hold of you—by the wrist, was it?—By the arm.

And then James Durie took hold of you by the other arm and they both began to pull?—Yes.

You have told us about James Durie being held by the lapel of his coat. Are you sure it was not both lapels he was holding by?—No.

What was he doing?—He just told him to put the knife in his pocket.

But what was he doing?—I can't mind.

Just think, and try and mind, because we want you to?—I don't think he had hold of Paddy.

Was he trying to get hold of him?—Yes.

So James Durie was trying to get hold of Paddy. Is James Durie your boy friend?—Yes.

Was he annoyed at Paddy Carraher speaking to you?—No, he wasn't annoyed at him, but he was annoyed at him pulling me.

Carraher went away after he had been told to go away, and then you and your boy friend, James, went to see his brother?—Yes.

This was between half-past eleven and midnight, was it not?—Yes.

Did you get the brother to come out to Carraher?—Yes.

When you got down to the street corner did you send Peter Howard to see if he could still see him at the Cross?—No.

Was Peter Howard still standing at the corner of the street when you went away?—Yes.

Did James say before he took you home that he was going back?—He just told me to stand in the close and he would be back again.

And he went to look for Carraher?—I don't know.

You had a pretty good idea?—Yes.

43

Patrick Carraher.

And your pretty good idea was that he went to look for Carraher?—Yes.

To beat him up?—I don't know.

But you had a fairly good idea that that is what they were after?—I don't think they were all going to get on him.

Not the lot of them?—No.

Only two or three?—No.

How many of them did you think were going to get after him? James and John?—No, just James.

Why did you go for John?—Just to tell him about the argument he had with him.

Why did you bring John out of the house?—To see that James would get a fair enough fight with him.

By the COURT—Why did James want to go for him?—Because he had hold of me. He was pulling me. And because he had hold of Jimmie.

It was not until after the accused got him by the coat that he wanted to go for him?—Yes.

Cross-examination continued—So John wanted to have a go at him because he had had hold of Jimmy?—No.

And Jimmie wanted to have a go at him because he had hold of you?—Yes.

What were Peter Howard and Charles Morgan going to do in the party?—I don't know.

Were they going to stand by and see fair play?—I don't know. They never said anything.

JAMES DURIE (19), sworn.

Examined by MR. WALKER—I live at 1, Dunvegan Street, Glasgow, and am employed as a window cleaner with the West Nile Window Cleaning Company of Glasgow. I have known Patrick Carraher for a number of years and I identify him as the accused. The last witness Margaret McNicol is my girl friend. On Saturday, 13th August, this year, I had been at the pictures with Charles Morgan, and was to meet my girl friend at Gorbals Cross after coming out. I went to the Cross shortly after 11, and saw Peggy McNicol coming over the Cross.

Did you see the accused that night?—Yes.

Did he speak to Peggy McNicol?—Yes.

44

Evidence for the Prosecution.

James Durie

Did you see anything happening?—No, he just pulled her arm and they were talking for a while.

Ultimately did she come across to where you were standing?—Yes.

Did Carraher come across after her?—Yes.

Just tell the ladies and gentlemen of the jury in your own words what happened when Carraher came across to you and Peggy McNicol?—Well, when I was standing talking to Peggy McNicol, Paddy Carraher came over and pulled her away, and when I saw Paddy Carraher pulling her away, I pulled her, and the two of us kept pulling her. Paddy Carraher started to shove me, and I shoved Paddy Carraher back again, and he grabbed me by the lapels and drew out a knife—he had a knife in his hand, and he was going to use it on me. After that the crowds gathered, and my girl friend took me home. I left my girl friend's home, but as I was going to leave I took her up to my brother's house, and I told my brother about Paddy Carraher.

Never mind what you told your brother at the moment. Just let us get this clear. When Carraher came over to you and Peggy, he pulled her and you were pulling her, and then you gave each other a push?—Yes.

Then the accused caught you by the lapel of the coat—and you said something about a knife. Which hand was the knife in?—In his right hand.

And his left hand was holding you by the lapel?—By the lapels of the jacket.

Did you see the blade of the knife?—Yes.

Where was it pointing?—He had it in his right hand, this way, and the left hand was that way (demonstrating). He had it low down, like that.

You mean at your waist line?—He just had it at my left hand side.

Where was the blade pointing? Was it forward from the thumb?—Yes, pointing towards me.

Were you being threatened at all?—Yes.

With what?—The knife.

Were you threatened with any words?—No.

How long was the knife kept pointed at you?—For about five or ten minutes.

What were you doing?—I just held him by the lapels of his jacket.

You were holding him and no words were passing?—No.

Patrick Carraher.

By the COURT—When he caught hold of you, did he let go Peggy?—Yes, he just let Peggy go, and Peggy walked away.

He let Peggy go and caught hold of you with his left hand?—Yes.

Examination continued—You say you had hold of him by the lapel. Was that with one hand or both hands?—One hand.

What were you doing with the other hand?—I had it down like this by my side (demonstrating).

With nothing in it?—No.

If the accused was pointing this knife in your direction for some minutes, can you tell the jury how it was that he did not do anything to you with it?—I cannot tell you that.

Did you think at the time that you were being threatened?—Yes.

After you and the accused separated, you told us, your girl friend took you away, and you went to your brother John's in Hospital Street. Did you ask him to come down to the Cross?—Yes.

What was he to do?—He was to see that I got a fair fight.

Were you wanting a fight with Carraher?—No, I feared maybe he would use the knife on me.

In any event, did John Durie come down to Gorbals Cross with you and Peggy McNicol?—Yes.

I think you there found Charles Morgan with Peter Howard?—Yes.

Was Charles Morgan present when Carraher was pointing the knife at you?—Yes.

Morgan was there but not Howard?—No.

When you came back with your brother John, Howard had joined Morgan. Was Carraher there or had he gone away?—He was away.

Ultimately I think Carraher did turn up at Gorbals Cross?—Yes.

Who was it that saw him first?—Peter Howard.

Did he call to you and your brother that Carraher was there?—Yes.

Did you and your brother go across and speak to Carraher?—Yes.

I don't want to know what was said, but what were you going to speak about?—I was going to ask Paddy Carraher if he would have a straight go with me, a straight fight.

46

Evidence for the Prosecution.

James Durie

Did you ask him that?—Yes.

Was there some further argument between you and your brother and Carraher?—Yes.

By the COURT—Argument about what?—It was just a confab; we just kept on arguing.

Arguing about what?—Fighting.

About a fight?—Yes.

Examination continued—What was Carraher's reply when you asked for a fight?—He said if he had to fight with me the two of us would give him it.

And it was about that kind of thing that you were arguing, whether there would be a straight fight or not?—Yes.

At that time you two brothers and the accused were all together. After a bit of an argument did you cross over to the south-west corner of Gorbals Cross and join Howard and Morgan?—Yes.

By the COURT—Does it come to this, that you wanted what you call a straight fight and you had got three friends and he had got none?—Yes.

Examination continued—What exactly do you mean by a straight fight?—I mean a fair fight.

Do you mean as regards numbers on each side, or do you mean as regards the weapons?—Well, fists.

Do you mean a straight fight with fists and not knives?—Yes, bare fists.

By the COURT—Did you say that?—Yes.

Did you say, "Fists and no knives"?—Yes.

You said that to the accused?—Yes.

Examination continued—We had got you to the south-west corner of Gorbals Cross, you and your brother and the accused and Howard and Morgan there together. Do you remember a young fellow joining you five?—Yes, there was a young fellow standing outside the pavement by himself.

Not one of your crowd?—No.

Did he take any part in the conversation of your group?—Yes.

Did you know him?—No, I did not know him at all.

Did he say anything to the accused?—He heard the accused

47

Patrick Carraher.

James Durie

saying that if he had a couple like himself he would come along and redd the corner.

Does that mean clear up the corner?—Yes.

What did this young fellow say?—He says to Paddy Carraher: "You talk like an Englishman."

And Paddy Carraher made some reply, did he?—Yes; he says: "No, I don't," or something like that.

And did the young fellow take some part in the conversation of your group of lads?—Him and Paddy Carraher started talking.

What about?—We didn't take any notice of that—just a confab.

That is how it started, by this young fellow asking Carraher if he was an Englishman?—Yes.

You were moved on by some constables, and the six of you walked along Ballater Street and got to the corner of Thistle Street?—Yes.

Just tell the jury what happened when you got to the corner of Thistle Street?—Paddy Carraher and this fellow Shaw kept on arguing until they came to Thistle Street, and they kept on arguing when they were standing at Thistle Street.

By the COURT—What about?—They were confabbing to themselves, throwing cracks at one another.

Did you hear what they said?—No.

How do you know they were arguing, if you could not hear what they said?—We couldn't hear the words.

Were they quarrelsome?—Throwing cracks at one another, shouting at one another, talking to one another.

Examination continued—Is that a form of repartee?—Yes.

Were they throwing jests at one another, or jokes, or were they quarrelsome words they were using?—Quarrelsome words.

But you don't know what it was about—is that what it comes to?—Yes.

You have got to the corner of Thistle Street. How long did you six people stay there?—For about five minutes.

And then did some of you go away?—My brother told me and Charlie Morgan—he said it was time to get home to bed.

And did you go?—Yes, up Thistle Street way.

The three of you?—Yes.

And did you go straight home?—Yes.

Which house did you stay in that night?—At Mrs. Morgan's, my brother's mother-in-law.

48

Evidence for the Prosecution.

James Durie

By the COURT—And you went home leaving the other three together?—Yes.

That is the accused——?—Yes, Patrick Carraher, the fellow Shaw and Peter Howard.

Examination continued—And you, your brother and Morgan all went to Hospital Street to Mrs. Morgan's house. When you left where were the three standing?—Paddy Carraher and the fellow Shaw were standing in the middle of Thistle Street, and Peter Howard was standing on the pavement next to the public-house.

That is "The Neuks" public-house at the corner of Thistle Street and Ballater Street?—I think that is the name of the pub.

Shaw and the accused were standing out in Thistle Street at the corner. Did you know if they were still talking to one another when you left?—Yes, they were still talking to one another.

When did you first hear that anything had happened to the young fellow Shaw?—My brother's good-sister, Katie Morgan, came up and told us. It was long after one o'clock—I just couldn't put the right time on it.

Just tell us as near as you can the time it would be when you left the three standing at the corner?—Between one o'clock and a quarter past.

What time would it be when you got word that Shaw had been injured?—I couldn't say for sure what time it was—after one o'clock.

Cross-examined by MR. CAMERON—Were you in bed when you were told about Shaw being injured?—No.

What were you doing?—Just sitting talking in the Morgans' house.

Why did you not go to your own house that night?—I usually stay there on a Saturday.

Why do you do that?—I don't like to go home on a Saturday. I just like to stay where my brother is staying.

Why don't you like to go home on a Saturday night?—I like to stay with my brother on a Saturday night.

Does your brother stay with the Morgans?—Yes.

I want to ask you about this argument you had with Carraher. You say that he had a knife in his right hand and he was holding it down by his side?—Yes.

Just show us with your own pocket knife?—I haven't got a pocket knife.

Patrick Carraher.

James Durie

Have you not?—No.

Whilst he was holding the knife like that, you had him by the lapels, had you?—Yes.

What were you doing with your right hand?—It was down like this (demonstrating).

By the COURT—Your right hand hanging by your side?—Yes.

Cross-examination continued—Why did you not use it?—I was afraid to use it, in case he would put the knife in me.

You were using your left hand?—Yes.

Did you not try to take hold of his right hand with your right hand?—No.

You made no attempt?—No.

What did you have your right hand there for?—To protect me.

But you never made any attempt to hold his right wrist?—No.

Or to touch him at all?—No.

Were you separated?—Yes.

Who separated you?—There were that many people separated us.

Their names?—I couldn't tell you that.

Did you try to strike him?—No.

What did your friends do with you after you were separated?—They just separated the two of us and I went for a walk with my girl friend.

And where did Carraher go?—I could not say.

He just went away?—Yes.

Are you quite sure you had nothing in your right hand?—Yes, nothing at all.

You have told us that you went for your brother, that is John, is it not?—Yes.

He had had a quarrel with Carraher, had he not?—That is so.

What had he quarrelled about?—He had a quarrel with Carraher.

Some time before this?—I could not tell you that.

Did you not know about that?—No.

I thought you told us he had a quarrel with Carraher?—He wanted a straight fight with him.

You could not have been very much afraid of his knife when you went after him that night?—I wanted to make sure he would get rid of the knife.

50

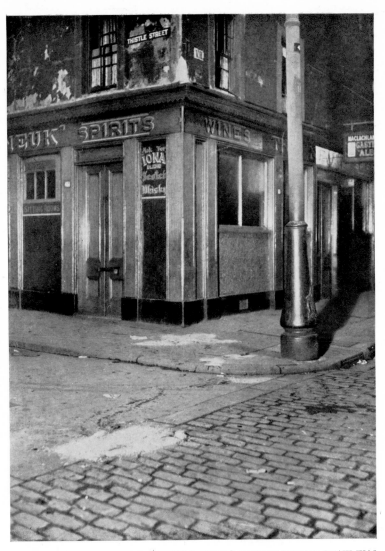

VIEW OF BALLATER STREET/THISTLE STREET CORNER WHERE SHAW WAS
STABBED. THE POOLS OF BLOOD ARE COVERED WITH SAND

Evidence for the Prosecution.

James Durie

In the course of the argument you had when you found Carraher did he not make it quite plain to you that he did not want to fight with you that night?—No.

Did he not say he was not going to fight that night with you?—No.

Did he not tell you it would not be a fair fight at all because your brother and his friends would join in?—My brother and I.

Well, have it your own way—he and you would go for him and he was not going to fight under these conditions?—Yes.

Did he not make it quite clear that he did not want to fight that night at all?—I would not say exactly that.

Put it your own way. Tell us what he did say?—That is all he did say. He said if he wanted to fight me, my brother and I would have fought him together.

That is exactly what would have happened?—No.

Why did you get your brother to help you?—I was afraid of the knife.

Did your brother not offer to fight?—It was the two of us. My brother asked him which one he would have a fair fight with.

And he said he would have neither?—He said if he fought with one of us the two of us would have fought with him.

Was he not quite right in that?—I don't think so.

Did he not tell you that if you wanted to have a fight with him he would fight you on the Sunday, the day afterwards?—Yes.

But he was not going to fight that night?—He didn't say.

But it was perfectly obvious to you that he wasn't going to fight?—I don't know about that.

But he did not fight with you, did he?—No.

By the COURT—Did he say anything about when he was sober?—Yes.

Cross-examination continued—Did he not make it quite clear that he was prepared to take one of you on when he was sober, but he was not going to risk the two of you when he was drunk?—No.

But he did tell you he was prepared to fight you when he was sober?—Yes.

But he was drunk that night?—Yes.

Very drunk?—I wouldn't say he was very drunk.

He could still walk, but that was about all?—Yes, he could walk.

Patrick Carraher.

James Durie

By the Court—Was he sober enough to know he was drunk?—Yes. He was quite sober.

Cross-examination continued—You said just now in reply to his lordship that he was quite sober. You told me he was drunk?—He looked quite sober to me.

Did you not know perfectly well he was drunk and had been drinking all evening?—Yes, he had been drinking.

And he was pretty bad when you saw him?—I didn't know whether he was pretty bad or not. I don't know how much these people drink.

Were you sober?—Yes.

Where were you when the police moved you on?—The corner of Freedman's.

What were you doing?—Standing arguing.

Making a noise?—Yes.

Making a disturbance on the street?—No, it was kind of quiet.

Except for the noise you were making?—No, there was no noise. Paddy Carraher was talking loudest.

And you were trying to get him to fight you?—Oh, no.

Just discussing the weather?—By that time the arguing was finished.

Why did the police move you on?—Because we were standing at the corner.

And making a noise?—Yes, I wouldn't say a loud noise.

A loud enough noise for the police to object?—They saw us standing at the corner and just moved us on.

What did the police tell you?—Just to move on.

Well, now, this man Shaw—was he sober?—Yes.

Did you know him before this?—No.

What had he got to do with this quarrelling?—He had nothing to do with it, he just butted in.

Was he noisy?—They were just talking—I wouldn't say he was noisy.

Talking loudly?—It wasn't loudly.

Was he trying to pick a quarrel with somebody?—I wouldn't say that. He just came over and asked Paddy Carraher was he an Englishman—Paddy says: "No, I am no Englishman."

There was a good deal more than that said?—Paddy Carraher said when we were first standing talking—when this young fellow was standing out on the pavement he heard Carraher saying if he had two like himself he would come along and redd the corner.

52

Evidence for the Prosecution.

James Durie

Did Carraher not try to get Shaw to go away home?—No.

Did Howard try to get Shaw to go away home?—I just can't mind that.

Have you got a bad memory?—No, sir, a good memory.

But you have not got any distinct recollection of the details of the quarrelling between Carraher and Shaw, is that so?—Yes.

But there was quarrelling?—Yes.

And you, I suppose, and your people were still quarrelling with Carraher?—No.

Why did you not leave the man alone?—My brother said it was time to go home to bed. We just walked along the street a bit to go up to the house.

Answer my question. Why did you not leave the man alone when you saw he was drunk and didn't want to fight?—Paddy Carraher was wandering along that way to Crown Street.

I still want an answer to my question. Why did you not leave the man alone?—He said he would take a walk along to Crown Street.

Why did you not leave him alone to take his walk?—We just wanted to go a walk with him.

And a few minutes before you had been looking for him to fight him?—Oh, no. The fight between me and Carraher was finished; it was all by by that time.

Because Carraher would not fight and wanted to go away?— No.

And you and your friends would not let him?—We were leaving it at that, me and my friends.

What were you looking for?—We were just walking. It was finished; we were leaving the argument finished at that.

Because you saw that you could not get him to fight?—No.

And was it not also the case that you saw the police had their eye on you?—No, I didn't know the police had an eye on me. I wasn't thinking of such a thing.

But you knew the police had their eye on you after you had been moved on?—I didn't know that.

Where did the policemen come from who moved you?—By Dunmore Street way.

Did they come on you quite suddenly?—Yes.

You weren't expecting the police to come to you at that time and that rather spoilt the evening's entertainment?—Oh, no, we were not thinking of fighting. It was finished, it was quietened down.

Patrick Carraher.

James Durie

Why was it finished?—The two of us were just quietened down.

Why was it quietened down?—I don't think any of the two of us wanted to fight.

You mean Carraher was not wanting to fight?—No, the two of us didn't want to fight.

You didn't want to fight him alone—was that right?—Oh, yes.

Where was Peter Howard when you last saw him that night?—We were just coming home and he came over and shouted at us and told us that Paddy Carraher was coming along.

Is that the last you saw of Peter Howard that night?—That is when we stood and started to talk for a minute.

Then what was the last thing you saw of him after that?—When we left him and Paddy Carraher and the fellow Shaw.

And what was Howard doing?—Standing at the pavement facing the public-house.

Do you know what he was waiting for?—I could not say that.

Had you any idea?—He would maybe be thinking of getting Paddy along the road or maybe a walk, or something like that.

Did you not ask Peter Howard to go home with you?—No.

Did he tell you what he was going to do?—No.

Was there a street lamp near where he was standing?—I cannot say for sure.

There was not, was there?—I could not say. There might be one there; I was not taking any particular notice.

How far away was Peter Howard from Shaw and Carraher when you last saw them?—From about here to that chair, there—about a yard or a few yards.

Was he taking any part in the discussion that was going on?—No.

Did you not hear his voice?—No.

And you do not know why he was there?—No.

Did you see anybody else in the street that night?—No.

Did you see Peter Howard the day after this happened?—No.

When did you next see Peter Howard?—I just cannot mind that.

Did he tell you about the man with the handkerchief?—No.

Did he not tell you he had borrowed a handkerchief to stanch Shaw's wound?—No.

I suppose Peter Howard has spoken to you about what he did on that night after you went home?—No.

Never at all?—No. Well, I don't know what he said. He just said he left them; at least he was standing at the corner.

Evidence for the Prosecution.

James Durie

Did he not also tell you he helped to stanch the flow of blood?
—No.

But you must have spoken to him quite a number of times about the events of that night?—No.

Why not?—I was not bothering about it.

A man was killed, you know?—Yes.

Do you suggest that you were not bothering about it?—We were not going talking to one another about it.

Why not?—We knew all about it, didn't we?

Did you?—Yes.

By the COURT—When did you first hear he was killed?—Shortly after one o'clock. It was when my brother's good-sister came up and told us. She did not tell us anybody was killed; she told us there was a fellow lying with his throat cut or something like that.

Cross-examination continued—Did she tell you who the fellow was?—No, she did not know the fellow.

When did you know it was Shaw?—It was the policeman that came up.

When the policeman came; was that early on Sunday morning?—Yes.

Were you taken to the police office?—No.

Do you seriously suggest that you were not very interested to know what happened from the lips of Peter Howard after you left him that night?—I did not see him after that.

When did you next see him?—I cannot tell you. I cannot mind all these things.

Have you not frequently discussed with Peter Howard what he knows about this?—Well, I have just asked him, did he see it.

Did he tell you about the mysterious handkerchief he borrowed?—No.

When did you hear about it?—To-day.

Was that the first time you had heard about a man with a handkerchief?—Yes.

Although you have talked about the thing quite often?—No, not quite often.

Did you not want to discuss the events of that night too closely with your friends?—What do you mean by that, sir?

Exactly what I say. Did you not want to discuss the events of that night too closely with your friends?—Well, we did not want other people to hear it.

55

Patrick Carraher.

CHARLES MORGAN (16), sworn.

Examined by MR. WALKER—I live with my mother at 163, Hospital Street, Glasgow. John Durie is married to my sister, and he lives at the same address. I am employed as a sheet iron worker with the Windsor Engineering Company in Glasgow. On 13th August, 1938, I was at a picture house with the witness James Durie, a brother of John. We went down to Gorbals Cross about 11.15 p.m. where Durie was going to meet his girl friend, Peggy McNicol.

You and James Durie were at the Cross when Peggy McNicol came on the scene?—Yes.

Did you hear her speak to the accused Carraher?—Yes.

And then she came over to where James and you were standing?—Yes.

Do you identify the accused man in the dock as Carraher?—Yes.

Did Carraher follow Peggy McNicol over to you and James Durie?—Yes. He came over and told Peggy McNicol he wanted to speak to her. James Durie shoved him, and they were struggling. The two of them grabbed each other's coats. Paddy brought out a knife, but he did not stab him; he just struggled with him. James Durie and Peggy McNicol then went down Norfolk Street. James Durie went up for his brother to come down and see what the fight was about.

I think you said that one caught hold of the other?—Yes. Paddy Carraher caught hold of James Durie.

Which hand did he catch him by the coat with?—His left hand.

Was he doing anything with his right hand?—I saw that he had a knife in his right hand.

Did you see the blade of it?—Yes.

Where was the blade pointing?—He had his hand hanging down, that was all.

Was the knife pointing forward or backward?—Forward towards James Durie.

Did you hear the accused say anything to James Durie while he was holding him in that manner?—I just heard him saying he had no right to push him.

And what was Durie doing?—Durie was just speaking back to him.

What was he doing with his hands?—I never saw him doing anything.

Evidence for the Prosecution.

C. Morgan

At the time did you form any impression as to whether the matter was serious or in jest?—I did not think it was very serious.

How did they come to part?—They let go each other themselves.

I think James Durie and Peggy McNicol went away, and you remained at the Cross?—Yes.

Peter Howard joined you at the Cross and then James Durie and his brother John came back with Peggy McNicol?—Yes.

And the lot of you were at the Cross after that, were you?—Yes.

By the COURT—Up to that time had the accused struck Durie?—No.

Did you ever see him strike or attempt to strike Durie at all?—No.

Examination continued—When James Durie came back with his brother John the accused had gone from the Cross, and ultimately I think someone discovered the accused at the coffee stall at the Cross?—Yes, Peter Howard.

And did he tell the Duries?—Yes.

I think at that time Peggy McNicol had gone home?—Yes.

Did the Duries come over and speak to Carraher?—Yes.

You did not hear what was said?—No.

After the Duries had spoken to Carraher did they come over and join you and Peter Howard?—Yes.

At that time did you see a young fellow joining in the conversation?—Yes, James Shaw.

Did you know him by sight at that time?—No.

Did he take some part in the conversation?—Yes; he came over and asked Patrick Carraher if he was an Englishman by the way he was speaking, and Patrick Carraher asked him why he was thinking that, and he said, "You speak funny," and the two of them started arguing. They argued for about half an hour and then a constable came along and chased them from the Cross and they walked along to the middle of Thistle Street, and then Paddy Carraher called James Shaw away and spoke to him at the middle of Thistle Street, and John Durie asked if they were going up home, and then James and I and John went up home and left the two of them standing there. Then a constable came up about four o'clock in the morning and told us about this thing.

That was how Shaw came into the conversation by asking Carraher if he was an Englishman?—Yes.

57

Patrick Carraher.

C. Morgan

So far as there was any quarrel between the Duries and Carraher, was Shaw, as far as you heard, taking any part in the quarrel?—No.

By the COURT—Can you give us any notion of which if any of the party, had drink?—Patrick Carraher had drink.
Nobody else?—No.
No sign of it in Shaw?—No.

Examination continued—Who was the accused walking with when you went along Ballater Street?—We were all walking in a row.
Was there anything in the nature of a quarrel or angry words passing while you were walking along Ballater Street?—Paddy Carraher and James Shaw were throwing jokes at each other going along the road.
I think you stood at the corner of Thistle Street for a little, and then you and the Duries went home?—Yes.
When you went home did you leave the other three men standing at the corner of Thistle Street?—Patrick Carraher and James Shaw were in the centre of Thistle Street and Peter Howard was standing on the pavement on the corner.
You and the two Duries went home. Did you go straight home?—Yes.
In which direction did you go?—Up Thistle Street.

By the COURT—By that time had all quarrels ceased?—Yes.

Examination continued—Shaw and the accused were standing together in Thistle Street, Howard being on the pavement at the corner?—Yes.
As you left and went up Thistle Street did you hear any sounds of quarrelling or anything of that kind?—No.
When did you first learn that Shaw had been injured?—Four constables came up at four o'clock that morning.
As near as you can tell us, about what time did you leave the accused and Shaw and Howard on the corner of Thistle Street?—Between one and half past one on the Sunday morning.

Cross-examined by MR. CAMERON—Who was in the house with you when the constables came in on Sunday morning?—My mother, my sisters, and the lodger, a girl, Margaret Davidson.

58

Evidence for the Prosecution.

C. Morgan

Did you know where the Duries were?—They were sleeping in my mother's house.

Do they stay there?—John Durie stays there.

But James does not, does he?—No.

What was he doing there that night?—He sleeps there every Saturday night.

Is there a Katie Morgan?—Yes, my sister.

Was she friendly with Carraher at one time?—Yes.

Did they quarrel?—I don't know, I can't say.

Were they friendly at this time?—Yes, I think so.

Were they going about together?—I don't know; they never told me anything about that.

Is John Durie married?—Yes, to my sister.

Is Peter Howard any relation of yours?—No.

Just a friend?—Yes.

I think you told us in examination-in-chief that when you first saw Carraher that night he and Peggy McNicol were talking?—Yes.

And then Peggy McNicol and Carraher came over to where James Durie was?—Peggy McNicol ran over to James Durie.

Carraher followed, and then James Durie shoved him?—Yes.

And then there was a struggle?—Yes.

Was Carraher complaining that James Durie had no right to shove him?—Yes.

That was the cause of the trouble, was it not?—Yes.

Carraher had obviously a good deal of drink in him that night, had he not?—Yes.

Was he pretty shaky on his feet?—He could keep his feet all right.

He could keep his feet but that was about all?—Yes.

Did you wait at the corner while James Durie went for his brother?—Yes.

Did you know John Durie had had a quarrel with Carraher some time before?—I was told they were arguing before.

But some time before this there had been a row between them when they were both drunk?—Yes.

And there had been some kind of fight in a house?—Yes.

Whose house was it?—My mother's house.

How long before this night had that fight taken place?—I cannot exactly say: about six months.

And since that time they had not been on friendly terms, had they?—I don't suppose they were.

59

Patrick Carraher.

C. Morgan

You knew they were not?—I never saw them speaking to each other.

They had been pretty friendly before that?—Yes.

On this night you say that John Durie was brought down by his brother for Carraher?—Yes.

Were John and James going to settle their differences with Carraher when they found him?—Yes.

And was it whilst the argument was going on as to whether there was to be a fight or not that night that you were chased away from the corner by the police?—Yes.

The Duries were wanting Carraher to fight and he was not wanting to?—I never heard them say that.

You knew that was what was happening?—Yes.

By the Court—They had stopped arguing about it, had they not, before you left?—Yes.

And, therefore, when you left there was to be no fight?—Yes, that is right.

That had been said?—Yes.

Cross-examination continued—Because Carraher was not wanting any fight that night?—No.

Why then were you walking along the road with Carraher and the Duries?—The constable chased us and we had to go somewhere, we had to walk. He told us to move from the corner.

The way you were going would take you to Glasgow Green, would it not?—Yes.

That is a pretty quiet place?—Yes.

Were you bound for Glasgow Green?—No.

Do you know whether the Duries were heading for Glasgow Green?—I know they were not going to Glasgow Green.

Where were they going?—Home.

They live in Hospital Street and you went beyond Hospital Street before you turned?—They were speaking and I didn't want to interrupt what they were saying.

What were they saying?—Carraher and Shaw were throwing jokes at each other.

What were the Duries doing in going past the end of the street where they lived?—They were just listening to what they were saying, and then went right back.

A nice quiet party?—Yes.

Did you know Peter Howard fairly well?—Yes.

Evidence for the Prosecution.

C. Morgan

When did you see him after leaving him at the corner of Thistle Street and Ballater Street?—Six o'clock that morning.

Where was he when you saw him?—In the house.

Had he been arrested in connection with this death and then let out?—Yes.

Did he tell you about a man whom he did not know from whom he got a handkerchief?—Yes, in our house.

What did he tell you?—He told us he held up James Shaw's head and a man gave him a hankie.

What room was he in at the time? Was it the sitting room?—Yes.

Was James Durie there?—No.

Was he not sitting there too?—No. He came in. He got up out of his bed and came in when Peter Howard came in.

Did he hear what Peter Howard had to say?—Yes.

And you say Peter Howard told you a story of how a man gave him a handkerchief on that occasion?—Yes.

Who was the man?—I don't know. He didn't tell me.

Did you not ask?—No.

Have you made any enquiries since?—No.

Were you frightened about what had happened?—I was not frightened. I had nothing to be frightened about.

When you left Peter Howard, Shaw and Carraher at the corner of Thistle Street was there anybody else about the street whom you saw?—No, I never saw anybody.

Of course, you were not looking for people, were you?—No.

Were there people going about the streets at that time in the morning?—I didn't see anybody.

Did you hurry home as quickly as you could?—I walked slow up the road.

Had anything been arranged about seeing Carraher the following day?—John had to see him the following day.

Who was it who told you that a man was lying with his throat cut in Thistle Street?—A boy standing over at the corner told my sister, and my sister told me when I went in.

Do you know who the boy was?—No, I didn't know, but he stands at the corner.

Do you know him?—No, my sister knows him.

Was Shaw quite sober that night?—Yes.

What was he doing with his hands when you last saw him?—He had them in his pocket.

61

Patrick Carraher.

Had he them in his pocket all along the road?—I was not taking any notice of that.

What business of Shaw's was it to interrupt your argument?—No business.

Did you hear anybody tell him to go home?—No.

You were not paying much attention to what was being said?—No.

Were you rather sleepy?—I was.

Re-examined by MR. WALKER—You suggested that Howard had been arrested on that Sunday morning. Who told you that?—Peter Howard himself.

What did he say exactly?—He said they arrested him and put him in gaol and they let him out again.

On this Sunday morning you say Peter Howard came to your house about five o'clock. Had the police been to your house before that?—Yes, about four o'clock.

Before that again did your sister or someone come and give you the information about a man being injured?—Yes.

What time would that be?—That would be about half past one.

When Howard came to your house that Sunday morning he told you a story about a handkerchief, I understand?—Yes.

Did he say who had got the hankie?—No.

He did not say whether it was he who had got it or where he had got it from?—No.

Did he tell you what he had done with the hankie?—He got it off a man, he said; he did not know who the man was, and he put it to James Shaw's neck.

Was that about all he told you?—Yes.

JOHN DICKSON DURIE (24), sworn.

Examined by MR. WALKER—I live at 163, Hospital Street, Glasgow, and am married to Mrs. Morgan's daughter. I live with my mother-in-law. At present I am unemployed. I have known Patrick Carraher for about six years. I identify him as the accused in the dock.

Now, do you remember on the Saturday night or Sunday morning of 13th or 14th August your brother James and his girl-friend, Peggy McNicol, came to the house to see you?—Yes, I do.

I think some statement was made to you—I don't want you to say what it was—but they told you something?—Yes.

Evidence for the Prosecution.

John D. Durie

Did you in consequence of that go down to the Gorbals Cross with your brother and his girl?—Yes.

And there you met the witnesses Charles Morgan and Peter Howard?—Yes.

Were you looking for anyone?—Yes, for Patrick Carraher.

I think he was not at the Cross when you went down?—No.

But after some time he turned up?—Yes, we were going home, and Peter Howard noticed him. We were at Dunmore Street when Peter Howard called on us.

And you and your brother went back to the Cross?—Yes, Carraher was over on the other side at the coffee stall. My brother and I went over to him.

What did you and your brother want the accused for that night?—To have a straight fight.

Who was to give him a straight fight?—My young brother or me; my brother asked him first.

Did you say to him that you wanted a straight fight?—Yes, we did. There was a policeman standing in the butcher's shop and he could tell. He heard us in the passing; he heard my young brother's remark.

That is what you and your young brother were looking for Carraher for, and you told him that?—Yes.

What was Carraher's attitude to you?—He thought the two of us would have assaulted him if he had had a fight with any of the two of us.

What did you mean by you wanted a straight fight?—No need to use anything. If you want a straight fight you take off your jackets and fight right with your bare hands, without using weapons.

By the COURT—Did you say which of you two was to have the straight fight?—Yes, the young brother first.

And were you going to take him on afterwards?—Not the two of us; there was only one going to fight.

Examination continued—Was the other going to be present at the fight?—No. The young brother asked him for a straight fight. There were other two there when we went over to the Cross again, Howard and Morgan, and they would have seen there was a straight fight.

Before you went to join Morgan and Howard, had you two

Patrick Carraher.

John D. Durie

brothers settled your argument or not?—We were still arguing when we got to the Gorbals Cross.

Had you settled whether there was going to be a fight or not? —It got kind of squashed up; it got kind of stopped.

And then you went over to where Morgan and Howard were? —Yes.

What did you do?—We stood there arguing. Carraher said if he had two men like him he would redd the corner.

Before you went over the Cross you and your brother and Carraher were arguing. What about?—To see who Carrahar was going to fight.

Does it come to this, that this argument about a straight fight fizzled out when you were going over the Cross towards Morgan and Howard?—Yes, it got kind of stopped when we got over there.

After that there was no argument?—Yes, he just said if he had two men like him he would redd the corner. That was all that he said when we were standing at Gorbals Cross.

Did you see a young fellow that night?—I never noticed him.

Do you know a chap Shaw whom you sometimes nodded to? —I saw him passing; I only knew him by passing.

You knew him by passing before this night?—Not this night —I knew him long before, I knew him by passing.

Just nodding to him?—Yes.

Did you see this young chap Shaw at the Gorbals Cross that night?—We never saw him until he came into our company.

When did he come into your company?—When Carraher mentioned if he had two men like him he would redd the corner, this chap Shaw came and said to Carraher: "Are you an Englishman?" and Carraher said: "I am no Englishman." Shaw said: "I thought you were by your talk." Shaw said: "If I had six or seven I would not try to come along and redd this corner." Carraher says to Shaw, "Who are you, anyhow? Do you come from Govanhill?" Shaw says: "No, I come from Barnhill."

That kind of back-chat was going on between Shaw and Carraher?—Yes, we had nothing to do with it. That was our argument finished.

Ultimately you were moved on by a policeman?—Two policemen came and just saw this chap Shaw was kidding Carraher on.

In words?—Yes, kidding him on like I said. He said, "You are a better man than Napoleon. Napoleon's dead."

Evidence for the Prosecution.

That kind of talk was going on between Shaw and the accused and you were moved on by two policemen?—Yes.

And the six of you went eastwards, along Ballater Street to Thistle Street?—Yes.

And the argument was going on still while you were going along Ballater Street?—Yes. We were not in the argument. They were still cutting one another up.

Then you came to the corner of Thistle Street and stopped?—Yes.

Did you and your brother and Morgan ultimately leave the other three?—Yes, we stood a couple of minutes and then went up Thistle Street. We went up Thistle Street and Howard was on the pavement we were going up Thistle Street on.

When you three, you and your brother and Morgan, left Shaw and the accused and Howard, what were they doing?—They were doing nothing. We left Shaw and Carraher in the middle of the street, and Howard was on the pavement. They must have been still talking to one another.

Did you hear any kind of angry words going on?—Not when we went up, no.

And you went up Thistle Street, did you?—Yes.

You went away straight home?—Yes.

Now what time, as near as you can, would it be when you left the accused and Shaw and Howard?—It must have been after one, I think.

By the COURT—You did not see the accused again after that? —No.

At that time had you seen the accused assault your brother? —No, I had never seen anything like that, never saw no knife or anything. I don't know anything about that assault.

You did not see him take up a threatening attitude towards him or brandish a knife at him?—No.

Examination continued—Then, Durie, what was the first you heard that Shaw had been injured?—I never heard it was Shaw that was injured. I was just in the house when my good-sister and her pal told me there was a chap with his throat cut out in Ballater Street and Thistle Street. We never bothered but went into our bed.

What time would that be?—I went home, and we were sitting in the house chatting for a while. I mind of getting wakened by the detectives at four o'clock.

65

Patrick Carraher.

John D. Durie

The detectives came at four?—Yes, and he said: "Were you with Carraher at ten o'clock?" and I said, "No."

You had not been with him at ten o'clock?—No.

Cross-examined by MR. CAMERON—When your brother came up for you that night were you in bed?—Yes.

Had you had a quarrel with Carraher some months before August?—No, I don't mind of it.

Did you not have a fight in your house one night?—I don't mind of it; I must have been drunk.

I think you probably were. Do you recollect that there was a fight in your house when you were drunk?—I cannot mind of it.

You may not mind the actual fight, but do you recollect that such a thing happened?—I heard about an argument but I never heard about a fight.

The argument ended in blows, did it not?—I cannot mind.

Were you so drunk as all that, that you cannot mind what happened?—Yes, I was drunk.

Were you sober this night?—The night this happened?

Yes?—No, I had a good drink that night too.

You were pretty drunk?—Yes, but I was home early and wakened later.

You went down to find Carraher to have a fight?—Yes.

Did he not refuse to fight with you?—He didn't refuse, he wanted to fight, but he thought the two of us would have assaulted him.

And wouldn't you?—You never know. It never came that way. It might have.

Just tell me this. Why did the police chase you away from the corner?—He always chases away a standing crowd.

You were making a noise, were you not?—If there was an argument there must have been a noise. Even if you do not make a noise he chases you away from the corner.

But you were making a noise that night?—He was arguing with the fellow Shaw at that time.

And you were taking part in it, were you not?—No, we were not.

Have you got a pretty hazy memory of what took place that night?—Yes, I have.

Because you were pretty tight, weren't you—pretty drunk?—I was not pretty drunk. I had a good drink but I got wakened up a couple of hours later.

POSITION IN BALLATER STREET WHERE SHAW COLLAPSED. SAND COVERS THE POOL OF BLOOD

Evidence for the Prosecution.

John D. Durie

You wakened a couple of hours later?—Yes, when my young brother came for me.

So you cannot help us very much about what happened that night?—I don't know what happened. I only saw Shaw was cheeky to him, taking him down.

He was very cheeky with him, and provoking him?—Yes, he was.

By the COURT—You said in answer to the suggestion that you both might have fought him—you said you never know?—I have never been in that position. If anybody is going to give your young brother a doing and he is losing, you never know what is going to happen.

Was the accused afraid of you both fighting him at once?—He must have been, two on to one.

There was a possibility of that, was there?—There is every possibility. If your young brother is going to get a doing what are you going to do? I am not going to say it was not going to happen.

DONALD CAMERON (37), sworn.

Examined by MR. WALKER—I live at 57, Surrey Street, Glasgow. I am a clerk by occupation but I am at present unemployed. On Saturday night, 13th August, I was walking along Norfolk Street in the direction of Gorbals Cross about eleven-thirty. On reaching Gorbals Cross I saw Peter Carraher holding a man whom I now know to be James Durie by the lapel of the coat, and threatening to assault him. He had a knife in his hand at this side (indicating the right hand side) but I do not think he intended to use it.

In which direction was the knife pointing?—I could not right say what way it was pointing.

You said he was threatening to assault Durie?—It looked to me like a threatened assault.

By the COURT—Was he brandishing the knife?—No, the knife was at the back.

Examination continued—Did you take a step forward and do something?—Yes, I took a step forward and went to speak to the prisoner, and I saw him put the knife in the right hand pocket of his jacket.

67   F

Patrick Carraher.

D. Cameron

Did you notice whether he had to close the knife?—No, I did not notice that.

Cross-examined by MR. CAMERON—Of course, when you came up to where this was going on the two of them were in grips, were they not?—Yes.

And you do not know how the affair began?—I do not.

And you do not know who began it?—No.

You have told us quite clearly what you saw. When you went up and spoke to the man you now know as Carraher, do you recollect what he said?—I said: "Give me the knife," but I don't think the prisoner heard me. His mind was a little distorted at that time; I think he was intoxicated a little.

And just as you spoke, immediately he put the knife away?—Yes.

Quite calmly and peaceably?—He put it in his right hand pocket.

And then did he let go of the other man?—Yes.

By the COURT—Had the other man got hold of him?—I could not right say, my lord.

Was there anybody else there?—There was a crowd congregated there at the corner.

Cross-examination continued—But nobody had interfered?—No.

Nobody separated the two?—No.

You saw what happened?—Yes.

And you saw them part?—Yes, they parted.

MRS. JANET MCLAUGHLAN (52), sworn.

Examined by MR. MONTGOMERY—I live at 428, Rutherglen Road, Glasgow. I remember 14th August, this year. On that evening I decided to go for a walk along with my daughter about twelve-forty-five on the Sunday morning. I arrived at Gorbals Cross at one-fifteen, and turned into Ballater Street and went eastwards. I stopped at Green's picture house in Ballater Street and looked at the advertisements.

Did you notice a policeman guarding a shop on the other side of Ballater Street where a window had been broken?—Yes.

Did you go along Ballater Street until you came to its junction with Thistle Street?—Yes.

When you came to that point did you hear something?—Yes, I

Evidence for the Prosecution.

Mrs. J. McLaughlan

heard peculiar groans, and looked towards the place from which I thought the noise was coming.

What did you see?—I saw a chap coming round the corner with his two hands at his neck. There was a chap with a light suit and another one with a dark suit, and the chap with the light suit gave the man with the dark suit a handkerchief.

What state was the man with the dark suit in?—Well, I didn't pay particular notice to that.

Were there any other people standing about?—There were not very many; the streets were quite bare.

By the COURT—Did you see two people standing together or three?—There were two at the corner. The chap with the light suit came forward, and I asked him what was the matter, and he told me they had got him through the jugular vein and he had given the chap a handkerchief. I told the man to run on, that there was a policeman waiting in a close further down. While I spoke to the chap in the light suit I looked after him and I saw he was swaying, and I ran after him, but by the time I got up to him the policeman had got him.

Examination continued—The injured man collapsed on the street and then a policeman came?—Yes; he blew his whistle, and he looked for the rest of the policemen to come and assist him.

Did you see the injured man when he was lying on the ground? —Yes.

Did you see anything about his neck?—Yes, I saw the wound, and it was bleeding.

Did you form any impression as to what kind of wound it was? —No, I did not but I knew it was a fatal wound anyway.

Then an ambulance came on the scene and the man was removed?—Yes.

Do you know a man called Peter Howard?—No.

Did you see a man speaking to a policeman?—Yes, there was a man speaking to the policeman when he fell to the ground.

Cross-examined by MR. CAMERON—You were coming along eastwards from Gorbals Cross along Ballater Street?—Yes.

Was it near the corner of Thistle Street that you heard the groans?—Just at the corner.

And was the man who was groaning on the ground?—No, he was on his feet.

Patrick Carraher.

Mrs. J. McLaughlan

Who were beside him?—There was nobody beside him.

Where were the two people whom you saw with the dark suit and the light suit?—The one with the light suit was in the middle of the street and was coming across the road in my direction, and we met in the middle of the road.

Where was the man with the dark suit?—I do not know where he was. He got the handkerchief from the man with the light suit.

And you did not see where he came from?—No.

Did you say there were four people whom you noticed standing at the corner of Thistle Street?—Yes. There were men talking at the corner of Thistle Street.

How far away would that be from the place where this injured man was when you first saw him? A few yards would it be? —About five or six yards.

I took you down as saying that one man told you that they had got him in the jugular vein?—Yes.

Who was the man who told you that?—The one with the light suit.

Did you say that you saw the injured man come round the corner from Thistle Street, into Ballater Street?—Yes.

So apparently his injuries had been sustained in Thistle Street? —Yes.

Were these four men whom you have described standing at the same corner of Thistle Street and Ballater Street as the injured man came round?—They were standing in the roadway between Thistle Street and Ballater Street.

And the injured man coming out of Thistle Street into Ballater Street would just pass where they were?—No, he came round the corner on the pavement and they were on the roadway.

Re-examined by MR. MONTGOMERY—Were you standing on the Green's picture house side of Ballater Street?—Yes.

When you heard, as you have told us, the sound of groaning and looked round, did you see these four men at the corner of Thistle Street and Ballater Street then, or did they come afterwards?—I could not exactly tell you, because it came so quick. It came on a sudden to me like that; I was not expecting anything of the kind. The injured man was by himself when I saw him first.

And did he come into Ballater Street round the corner from Thistle Street?—Yes.

70

Evidence for the Prosecution.

RICHARD McCALLUM (28), sworn.

Examined by MR. MONTGOMERY—I am a constable in the Central Division of the Glasgow Police Force. I remember on Saturday, 13th August of this year, being on night duty. On that night I was instructed to guard a shop at Ballater Street. That was a shop of which the window had been broken. I stayed in a close at 32, Ballater Street, while I was on guard.

Were you still there in the early morning of Sunday, 14th?—I was.

In the early morning did you hear sounds coming from somewhere in the direction of Thistle Street?—I did.

How far is Thistle Street from the shop where you were?—It will be about 130 to 140 yards.

Did you look in the direction of Thistle Street?—I did. I saw two men running towards me, on the south pavement of Ballater Street.

Did you know either of these men?—No, I did not.

Have you seen the witness Peter Howard since?—Yes.

Did one of these men speak to you, and if so what did he say? —Peter Howard came forward and told me that the second man had been stabbed in the neck with a knife. The second man approached me and I turned his head to see the wound that was in the left side of his neck. I saw it was serious so I took him eastwards in Ballater Street to nearer the street lamp. Blood was coming from a wound in the side of his neck. I asked the injured man what had happened and he was unable to speak.

Did you form any impression about the wound?—From the nature of wound I would say it was a knife that had caused the puncture.

What did you do after that?—I assisted him to the footway and endeavoured to stop the bleeding.

Did the witness Constable Turnbull come on the scene?—Not at that particular moment. When I first got to the injured man I attended to him as best I could and I asked someone to go and 'phone for an ambulance. As the ambulance was a good time in arriving I thought I had better go myself in case the person had difficulty in getting through on the telephone. So I went myself to the telephone and on the way I met Constable Turnbull. I told him to go to Ballater Street to the injured man and I telephoned to the Criminal Investigation Department. Shortly afterwards an ambulance arrived and the man was removed to the Royal Infirmary.

71

Patrick Carraher.

R. McCallum

Did you search Ballater Street to see if you could find any weapons?—I did.

Did you search right along Thistle Street?—Yes.

I think you did not find anything?—Nothing on the street at all.

Did you then search for bloodstains?—I saw bloodstains on the footway. There was a bloodstain on the centre of Thistle Street, or almost at the centre. There was a trail of blood towards the footway where there was another pool of blood.

Was that the point where the man collapsed?—No, that was at Thistle Street. There was a trail of blood then in a zigzag fashion to the close at 32, Ballater Street.

ALEXANDER MCKAY (40), sworn.

Examined by MR. MONTGOMERY—I am a sergeant in the Southern Division of the City of Glasgow Police, and I was on duty on the night of 13th August in the early morning of the Sunday.

Were you on duty in Oxford Street?—Yes.

Were you told there was something wrong at Gorbals Cross? —That is right. I went there and then went on to Ballater Street.

What did you find there?—I found the man Shaw lying on the south footway on Ballater Street.

What condition was he in?—Bleeding profusely from a wound in the neck. I took charge until the ambulance waggon arrived.

I think you asked the injured man who his assailant was but he was unable to make any reply?—No, he was not able to reply.

Did you accompany the injured man in the ambulance into the Royal Infirmary?—I did. I arrived there at one forty-three. He was attended to at the gatehouse by Dr. Cameron who had him removed to a ward. When he arrived in the ward he was found to be dead.

Did you immediately notify the Criminal Investigation Department that the man had died?—I did, and I then returned to the ward and assisted the nurse to remove the man's clothes.

MARY MCCAFFERTY (22), sworn.

Examined by MR. WALKER—I live at 92, Thistle Street, Glasgow, and am a domestic servant at present unemployed. On Sunday morning, 14th August, I went with Catherine Docherty to see what was the matter along Ballater Street, and I saw a man

Evidence for the Prosecution.

M. McCafferty

lying injured on the pavement. It would be twenty minutes to two. I waited there until an ambulance came. I know Peter Howard by sight and I saw him being taken away by the policemen. I thought at that time he had been arrested. My friend, Kate Docherty, is friendly with Peter Howard's brother, Robert, and she wanted to go along and tell Robert about his brother being taken away. I went along with her.

When you were on the way to Robert Howard did you see the accused, Patrick Carraher?—Yes. I see him in the dock.

When you saw him where was he?—Facing Buchanan Street in Norfolk Street.

That is the street that runs off Gorbals Cross away from Ballater Street?—Yes.

He spoke to you, did he not?—Yes.

Did you tell him where you and Kate Docherty were going? —Yes, and he said he would come with us.

Where does Robert Howard live?—12, Portugal Street.

When the three of you got to 12, Portugal Street, did Kate Docherty go up to see Robert Howard, leaving you and the accused in the street?—At the closemouth.

When Kate was away to speak to Robert Howard was anything said between you and Carraher?—No.

Did Robert Howard come down with Kate Docherty and did the four of you go along to the police station?—Yes.

To do that you had to cross Albert Bridge, the bridge over the Clyde that leads up to Jail Square?—Yes.

Were you and the accused Carraher left at the Bridgegate while Kate Docherty and Robert Howard went to the police station? —Yes.

By the COURT—Why did you go to the police station?—I went with Kate Docherty to see how Peter Howard got on.

Examination continued—You told us that you and Kate Docherty had seen Peter Howard being taken away from Ballater Street by the policemen and you thought he was being arrested, and that your girl-friend Kate was the girl-friend of Peter Howard's brother, Robert?—Yes.

She was naturally interested in Peter's fate and that is why the four of you went?—Yes.

By the COURT—The accused went with you?—Yes.

Patrick Carraher.

M. McCafferty

Examination continued—You and the accused were left at the Bridgegate while Robert Howard and Kate Docherty went to the police station to see about Peter Howard?—Yes.

When you and the accused were standing there did any conversation take place between you?—Yes.

Just turn to the jury, speak slowly and tell them what was said between you and Carraher at the Bridgegate?—I asked him was he there when it happened, meaning when the fellow was injured, and he said, "Yes" that he had done it. I said to him, "You done it?" and he said, "Yes." I said, "What for?" and he says, "I was arguing with a fellow. He was very cheeky." I said, "How did you do it?" and he says, "With a knife," and he took a knife out of his pocket and showed me it.

Do you remember which pocket he took the knife out of?—No, I can't remember.

But he showed you the knife?—Yes.

What kind of knife was it?—It was like a pocket-knife, a dark knife.

Do you mean the handle was dark?—Yes.

Did he say whether that was the knife he had done it with?—Yes, he told me that was the knife.

Did you say anything to the accused after that?—Yes; I said to him: "If it was done with a knife they won't let Peter Howard out," and he says: "Oh, yes, they will let Peter Howard out because I will give myself up; I won't let him swing for it."

Was anything further said between you and the accused?—No.

Did Robert Howard and Kate Docherty return then?—Yes.

In the presence of the accused did they say anything about Peter Howard?—Yes, they said he would be released in a few hours.

The accused was present so he heard it?—Yes.

Then did the four of you walk back over the bridge into Crown Street?—Yes.

Can you remember how you were walking?—Carraher was to the bridge and I was next, Kate Docherty was next to me and Robert Howard was to the outside.

Carraher was next to the parapet?—Yes.

Were you going down the road from the left hand side of the bridge?—Down the right hand side.

While you were walking southwards over the bridge did you say something to Robert Howard in the presence of the accused?—Yes, I said Carraher had a knife. I then said, "Show him your knife," and Robert Howard says: "Have you got a knife?" and he

74

Evidence for the Prosecution.

M. McCafferty

said: "No, I have not got a knife but I possess a razor blade; it is still in the packet."

Did he show you the razor blade?—No, he did not take it out of his pocket.

He said to Robert Howard that he had not got a knife and you had seen the knife just some minutes before that?—Yes.

But going over the bridge he said he had not got a knife but he had got a razor blade?—Yes.

When you got to Adelphi Street I think Carraher left the other three?—Yes. He said he was going home to his kip.

Did you learn later that the man who had been injured had died?—Yes.

So that up until the accused left you to go to his kip you had not heard that the man had died?—No.

Cross-examined by Mr. CAMERON—How long have you known Peter Howard?—I didn't know him very long.

Did you know Robert Howard better?—Yes.

How long have you known him?—About a year.

Are you very friendly with Kate Docherty?—Yes.

She is very friendly with Robert Howard?—Yes.

And also with Peter Howard?—Yes.

Were you worried when you found Peter Howard had been taken to the police office?—No, I was not worried; it was Kate Docherty who was worried.

Did you go along to the police office with the intention of finding out what you could about what had happened?—Yes.

And you met Carraher on the way?—Yes.

In what kind of condition was he?—He had a drink in him.

Quite obviously, had he?—Yes.

And a good deal of drink?—He hadn't an awful lot of drink.

He was speaking pretty wildly, was he not?—No, he was not speaking wildly.

Speaking pretty thickly too?—No.

He was not just his usual self, was he?—No.

You have told us a good deal of what he said to you about this thing. What else was he talking about that night?—He was not talking about anything else.

Nothing else at all?—No.

Had you ever seen him before?—Only once.

How long ago was that?—A week that night he spoke to me with Kate Docherty.

75

Patrick Carraher.

M. McCafferty

Did you know that he had been engaged in a scuffle with a man called Durie that night?—No.

Did you know at the time that in a scuffle with Durie Carraher had had a knife in his hand?—No.

When did you first learn that?—I didn't hear about that.

When did you first know there had been a scuffle with Durie? —I didn't know he had a scuffle with Durie.

And you did not know that in that scuffle a knife had been exhibited if not used?—No.

Is this the first you know about there being a scuffle with Durie?—Yes.

Do you know the Duries at all?—Yes.

Did you know Shaw?—No.

You did not know the name of the man whose injuries had led to Peter Howard being taken to the police office?—No.

So that when Carraher was talking to you in the way you have said you were speaking about somebody whose name neither of you apparently knew?—No.

You certainly did not. It was just a man?—Yes.

And you did not know that earlier that night Carraher when drunk had been engaged in a scuffle with James Durie and that a knife had been in his hand?—No.

Did you walk across Albert Bridge all together when you went to the police office?—Yes.

And when you came back again?—Yes.

Did Robert Howard ask Carraher if he had a knife, and he said he had not got a knife?—He said he hadn't a knife.

Then he said he had a razor blade?—He said he possessed a razor blade.

That was a funny thing to say?—Yes.

Did it strike you at the time as being a rather curious thing to say?—Yes.

As if he didn't know what he was talking about?—It seemed to me he did not want to tell them.

Why talk about razor blades?—I spoke about the knife.

And he said he hadn't got a knife but he had a razor blade? —Yes.

Did it not strike you as rather strange to bring into the conversation this razor blade?—No.

It did not strike you as being a stupid thing to do?—No.

Or just the kind of thing a drunken man in a half dazed way would come out with?—No, I never thought of it that way.

Evidence for the Prosecution.

M. McCafferty

What do you think of it now? Does it not strike you as being rather curious that he should mention a razor blade?—Yes.

And looking back on it now do you not think it was a kind of half-dazed remark as if he did not know what he was talking about?—I don't really know.

I understand that in the course of this conversation that you had there was nobody else present except yourself and Carraher, and you said that if it was done with a knife they would not let Peter Howard out?—Yes.

What did you mean by that?—I meant the fellow must have been pretty bad.

If it was done with a knife?—Yes.

"They won't let Peter Howard out"?—Yes.

Why did you say that?—I thought the fellow would be pretty bad if it was done with a knife.

How would that affect Peter Howard?—The police didn't know it was Carraher had done it. That is the way I took it.

And that it was Peter Howard?—Yes.

Were you rather worried that it might be Peter Howard?—No.

You did not know much about the thing?—No.

In fact, does it really come to this, that at that time of night when you met Carraher, a man whom you had only seen once before in your life, you knew nothing at all of the various happenings of that evening?—No.

And you did not know anything about scuffles or brawls he had been involved in that night?—No.

Or who he had been arguing with, or who had been cheeky to him?—No.

How was he walking?—He was walking quite straight.

What did his eyes look like?—I did not take much notice of that.

Were you not excited yourself?—No.

But it was rather an exciting event, was it not?—It was, after I realized he had done it.

Before that were you not rather excited to know that there had been somebody injured and that Peter Howard was in custody for it?—No.

You were not excited?—No.

You did not know very much about what had happened at all, is that not what it comes to?—Yes.

So does it come to this, that Carraher, according to your recollection then, was taking the blame of what had happened in place of anybody else?—He said to me he had done it.

77

Patrick Carraher.

M. McCafferty

You, whom he had never seen except once before?—Yes.

Quite openly?—Yes.

Did he appear proud of it?—No.

Just told you quite plainly and simply?—Yes.

Looking back on it now, if the case was that he was—as I am going to suggest—dazed with drink, do you not think he may very well have been mixing up the two things?—I don't think so.

But that is quite possible, if he had been involved in another scuffle?—It could be.

It might very well happen, might it not, that a man who had been drinking all the afternoon and night would not have a very clear recollection of what had taken place?—Yes.

That is quite a possible view, is it not?—Yes.

Re-examined by Mr. WALKER—When you and the accused were standing at the Bridgegate you asked him if he had seen the assault, and he told you what you have told the jury?—Yes.

What assault were you thinking of?—The fellow that was lying on the ground.

You had been along Ballater Street with your friend Miss Docherty and had seen the man lying on the pavement?—Yes.

And you had seen Peter Howard being taken away by the police?—Yes.

In your mind it was clearly associated that Peter Howard was being taken away in connection with the injury to the man that you saw lying on the pavement?—Yes.

Now, when you met the accused, Carraher, later, was any mention made between you and him of the injured man that you had seen lying on the pavement?—Yes, I told him how seriously injured he was, and he said: "Is he as bad as that?"

Of course, you told the accused where you and Kate Docherty were going, because of Peter Howard's arrest, as you understood it?—Yes.

Did you tell the accused what you thought he had been arrested in connection with?—I told him he was arrested beside this fellow.

That is the fellow who was lying on the pavement injured?—Yes.

By the COURT—Did you tell him what had happened to the man lying on the pavement?—Yes, we told him he was lying and losing a lot of blood.

Did you tell him what had happened to him?—No.

78

Evidence for the Prosecution.

You did not mention anything about bleeding?—Yes, we told him about bleeding.

Who told him about that?—We saw the fellow, and we told Carraher about the blood he was losing.

You told Carraher the man was bleeding?—Yes.

Did you tell him he was bleeding at the neck?—Yes.

Did Carraher seem to know anything about it?—He just said: "Is it as bad as that?"

Re-examination continued—After you had described the now deceased man's condition to the accused he said, "Is it as bad as that?"?—Yes.

Accordingly, when he came and spoke to you at the Bridgegate was it in relation to the condition of that man?—No, sir.

When you asked him about whether he had seen the assault was it in relation to the condition of the man who had been lying on the pavement?—Yes.

And at that time, I think you told me before, you had not heard that the man had died?—No.

CATHERINE DOCHERTY (23), sworn.

Examined by MR. WALKER—I live at 22, Portugal Street, Glasgow. The last witness, Mary McCafferty, and I were along Ballater Street on Sunday morning, 14th August, and saw the injured man. We also saw Peter Howard being taken away by the police and we went to tell Robert Howard about it. He came out along with us and we all went up to the police station over the Bridgegate.

You and Robert Howard went to the police station, leaving Mary McCafferty and the accused at the Bridgegate?—Yes.

After you got your information from the police station about Peter Howard did the four of you go back across the bridge? —Yes.

Now do you remember hearing any conversation or any statement made by Carraher about the assault that evening?—No.

ROBERT HOWARD (19), sworn.

Examined by MR. WALKER—I live at 58, Norfolk Street, Glasgow, and am a newsvendor, having a stance at the Gorbals Cross. I am the brother of the witness Peter Howard. I know the accused Patrick Carraher, whom I identify in the dock. On Sunday morn-

Patrick Carraher.

R. Howard

ing, 14th August of this year I was in my niece's house at 12, Portugal Street, when my girl-friend, Kate Docherty, came to the door about two o'clock in the morning. In consequence of what she told me I got up and dressed. When I came to the door I found the accused standing at the closemouth with Mary McCafferty, and the four of us went towards the Central Police Station.

On the way along the road how were you walking?—Kate Docherty and Mary McCafferty were at the front and me and Paddy were at the back.

Who had asked you to walk like that if anybody?—Paddy.

Did he say why?—No.

When you were walking along in that order, you and the accused together behind the two girls, did he tell you anything?—Yes, he told me that he had been fighting with a fellow and that he had used a knife on him.

Tell us what the accused said to you as you were walking along? —Going along Portugal Street, the accused, Patrick Carraher, told me that he had been fighting with a fellow.

Did he say who the fellow was?—No. He said that he had scratched his face with a knife.

Did he say how the fellow had been cheeky to him?—No.

Did he say where this had taken place?—No.

Did he say anything relating to Peter Howard, your brother? —Yes. He got told that Peter was in the Central Police Station, and Paddy said that if anything came out of it he would give himself up.

Did the accused know that you were going to the police station?—Yes.

About your brother being arrested, as you thought?—Yes.

By the COURT—Did he know that your brother had been arrested in connection with an assault upon the person whom he, the accused, had assaulted?—Yes.

It was the same person?—Yes.

He knew that?—Yes.

And what did he say?—Paddy said he would go over and give himself up and clear Peter's name.

Examination continued—At that time had anything been said between you and Carraher as to whether this scratch on the face with a knife was serious or not serious?—No. Paddy said he thought it was only a scratch on the face.

Evidence for the Prosecution.

R. Howard

We are told, I think, that you and Kate Docherty went up to the station leaving Mary McCafferty and Carraher in the Bridgegate. When you came back from the police station did the four of you walk back across the bridge?—Yes.

Now, just tell us how you were walking at the time. Were you behind each other, or in a line?—In a line.

Who was next the parapet of the bridge?—Patrick Carraher.

Do you remember anything said on the way back over the bridge?—Yes. Mary McCafferty brought up the subject about the knife.

Who did she speak to?—Paddy.

Did you hear that?—Yes.

What did Mary McCafferty say to the accused about the knife on that occasion?—She said: "Where is your knife, Paddy?"

You heard her say that?—Yes.

What did Paddy say?—He said he had no knife.

But he had told you earlier, I understand, that he had scratched a man in the face?—Yes.

With what?—A knife.

Now did he say what had happened to the knife that he once had had?—No.

He just said as you were going over the bridge that he had not got a knife at that time?—Yes.

Did he say anything about what other instrument he had?—He said the only thing was a razor blade, but it had never been opened.

I think when you got over the bridge the accused was leaving for his bed?—Yes.

Did you pull him aside and say something to him?—Yes, I told him to go back to my niece's house at 12 Portugal Street and I would come over and let him know how the fellow was keeping.

That was the man who had been scratched in the face with the knife, was it?—Yes.

And did Carraher make any remark again to what he would do?—He just said he would go right over there.

Did he say anything about Peter?—No.

And then he left you, did he?—Yes.

Cross-examined by Mr. Cameron—Did you know Carraher before this?—Yes.

Did you know him well?—Yes.

Did Peter know him well?—Yes.

Patrick Carraher.

R. Howard

Were you friendly with him and was he friendly with Peter?
—Yes.

Was he very friendly with Peter and did he sometimes do Peter good turns?—Yes.

I suppose Peter was a younger man than he was, was he?—Yes.

Did he ever help Peter out of scrapes or anything like that? —No, Peter was never in scrapes.

When you met Carraher that night I think he was intoxicated, was he not?—Yes.

He looked rather queer, and had a dazed kind of look on his face?—Yes.

And was he talking in a childish kind of way as if he did not know what he was talking about?—Yes.

That was obvious to you, was it not?—Yes.

Did you know when you were walking across to the Central Police Station that he had been mixed up in a brawl early that night with James Durie?—No.

Was it quite apparent from Carraher's attitude at that time that what he was talking about was a very, very minor thing?—Yes.

Just a mere scuffle in the street?—Yes.

Now, you said that he gave the explanation for scuffling with a man whom he had scratched that he had been cheeky to him, and I suppose that if one young fellow gives him a shove when he is drunk like that he might very well regard that as cheeky, might he?—Yes.

So that for all you know now it may have been, in his muddled condition, that what he was talking about was a scuffle with James Durie, which he thought your brother Peter was mixed up in? —Yes.

He apparently had no idea that what had happened later on was a very serious thing?—That is so.

That was quite clear, was it not?—Yes.

He obviously did not appreciate that what the police were worrying about was not a minor thing that had happened earlier that night but something very much more serious that had happened recently?—Yes.

And he was just gabbling on about some little scuffle that he had been engaged in?—Yes.

Let me put it this way. Was it quite obvious to you that Carraher had no appreciation that what you were worried about was a thing that might lead to a very grave charge indeed?—He did not want Peter to get into trouble.

82

HIGH COURT BUILDINGS, GLASGOW

VIEW OF CELLS IN HIGH COURT BUILDINGS, GLASGOW

Evidence for the Prosecution.

And what he thought his friend was in trouble about was a small scuffle about some cheeky boy?—Yes.

He apparently did not appreciate that what was really on foot was something very much more serious?—Yes.

When you came back over the Albert Bridge you were walking four abreast, were you not?—Yes.

And Carraher was nearest the parapet?—Yes.

Then who was next?—The lassie McCafferty.

Then you?—No, the lassie Docherty was next.

Then Docherty and then yourself?—Yes.

Were you walking arm-in-arm?—No.

Is that bridge lighted? Are there lamps along the parapet of the bridge?—Yes.

And they were lit that night?—Yes.

And was that the bridge you had come over on your way to the police station?—No.

Which bridge had you come over?—Stockwell Bridge.

And is that bridge quite well lighted?—Yes.

And was it lit that night?—Yes.

And you had walked across with Paddy Carraher?—Yes.

Re-examined by Mr. WALKER—When the accused spoke to you that night about an assault was it an occasion when a man had been scratched on the face with a knife?—It did not seem to be serious.

It was an assault that was not spoken of as a serious assault, but it was one in which a man had been scratched on the face with a knife?—Yes.

You have no doubt that that was what he was speaking about? —No.

And he said he did this?—Yes.

ALEXANDER JOHN SUTHERLAND (22), sworn.

Examined by Mr. WALKER—I live at 12, Portugal Street, Glasgow. I am unemployed and of no occupation. The witness Robert Howard is related to me by my having married his niece, and sometimes he stays with us. I remember that on Sunday morning, 14th August, Patrick Carraher came in. I know him well and see him in the dock. It was in the small hours, but I cannot tell the exact time.

Did he strike you as being drunk or sober?—Drunk. His eyes were very glazed.

Patrick Carraher.

A. J. Sutherland

I think you went out to the coffee stall to get something?—Yes.

Did Carraher go to the stall with you?—No, just down to the close.

And he waited there until you came back from the coffee stall? —Yes.

When you were out did you hear anything about a man who had been injured?—Yes, at the coffee stall I heard that some fellow had got murdered at the Cross.

When you came back to the close where Carraher was, did you tell him anything about a man who had died?—Yes, I asked him if that was what Peter was in for.

But did you tell him that a man had died?—Yes.

Did you ask him if that was what Peter was in for?—Yes. He said he didn't know. He said: "Is the fellow really dead?" and I answered: "So they say along at the coffee stall."

Did he make any reply to that?—He said: "That is bad." He said: "I think I'll go a walk over to the house," and then he left me.

Cross-examined by Mr. CAMERON—Had you seen Carraher earlier that night?—Yes. I came home from the dogs about half past nine that night, and the wife met me at Craigton Street coming off the car. We went into a tally shop and had ice-cream and then we came along the road, and I saw the accused on the other side of the street the worse for drink, standing on the street himself.

About what time would that be?—About a quarter to eleven or round about that.

What was the street you saw him in?—Norfolk Street.

That is not very far away from Gorbals Cross, is it?—No.

I think you go along Norfolk Street eastwards to Gorbals Cross, and then if you continue eastwards you are in to Ballater Street? —Yes.

Norfolk Street and Ballater Street are really one long street? —Yes.

Was he quite close to the Cross when you saw him?—Well, he was about a block away.

Was he trying to walk?—Yes.

Was he taking the whole width of the pavement?—Yes.

He was obviously very drunk indeed?—Yes.

And when you saw him again at two in the morning I think you told us that his eyes were glazed and he had obviously had a good deal of drink?—Yes.

84

Evidence for the Prosecution.

A. J. Sutherland

Did he appear to you just to be fuddled and dazed?—Yes, just like that.

So that when you came and told him the gossip you had heard at the coffee stall that a man had been killed and you asked him if that was what Peter was in for, he said he did not know?—Yes.

So that apparently he did not connect in his own mind what Peter was in for with the death of this man you had reported to him?—Yes.

And of course at that time you did not know the name of the man?—No.

From the way he took the news of the death of this man and from his behaviour, did you form the impression that he did not seem to appreciate that the death was anything to do with what he had been doing?—Yes.

Or indeed with anything that Peter Howard had been doing, or had been arrested for?—Yes.

Was it immediately after that that he said: "Oh, that's bad"?—Yes.

In a maudlin kind of way?—Yes.

And then did he just sit in a chair for a bit and then say: "Well, I think I will away home"?—Well, he didn't come up to the house the second time.

When was he in your house?—About two o'clock in the morning. That was the first I saw of him in the house. He came down to the close with me and stood there with two girls until I came back from the coffee stall. I took him aside from the two girls because I did not want them to hear, and asked him was this what Peter Howard was in for, and he said he did not know.

By the COURT—Does it come to this, that nothing had been said to you associating in your mind the accused with the death? —That is so. It never occurred to me at all.

MRS. CHRISTINA MAGUIRE (33), sworn.

Examined by MR. WALKER—I live at 75, Florence Street, Glasgow. I know the accused, Patrick Carraher, by sight. On Sunday, 14th August, the accused came to my house between three and four o'clock on the morning. He was wanting my husband. I let him in and asked him to sit down.

How was he looking? Was he looking well or ill?—I thought he did not look too well.

Patrick Carraher.

Did he say anything to you about himself?—I asked him what was wrong and he said he had had a quarrel and he did not know what had happened. I gave him a drink of water.

Did you ask him if it was serious?—Yes, I asked him, and he said he did not know.

Shortly after that did a motor car stop at your house?—Yes, about five minutes afterwards. Two detectives came in and took the accused away.

JOHN JOHNSTON (39), sworn.

Examined by MR. WALKER—I am a detective-sergeant of the Headquarters Division of the Glasgow Police, and I have fifteen years' service. I remember on 14th August of this year about two-thirty a.m. being summoned to the Central Police Office in connection with this case. Along with Dectective-Inspector Boyle, I went to the last witness's house at 75, Florence Street, and there I saw the accused Carraher. I formally asked him his name and I told him to come outside. When outside I cautioned him and told him we were making enquiry into the murder of James Shaw which was committed that morning in Ballater Street at the corner of Thistle Street, Shaw having been stabbed in the neck. He said: "Is he dead right enough?" and I said he was. He replied: "I was expecting you. I will gie ye the full strength of it," in broad Scots. I accepted that as an indication that he wanted to tell us the whole facts. I advised him it would be better if he told it to the officers in charge of this case. I then took him to the Central Police Office and he was formally charged and detained. I searched his clothing and found a safety blade in it. Label No. 18 is the razor blade that was in his possession.

Did you find any knife in his possession?—No.

Is that a safety razor blade in its paper wrapper?—Yes.

Does it appear to have been opened or used?—It appears not to have been used.

Did you examine Ballater Street about the corner of Thistle Street where the blood marks were?—I did. The first stain we examined was at the junction of Thistle Street and Ballater Street. It was a matter of nine feet from the footway, east of the footway. The second stain was actually on the footway at the corner of the building known as Neuk Bar, at the corner of Thistle Street and Ballater Street; that is the south-west corner of Ballater Street and Thistle Street. The second stain was on the footway immediately

Evidence for the Prosecution.

J. Johnston

at the corner. The first stain measured a matter of three feet square, and the second stain was about four feet square. The trail of blood extended the full distance of 136 yards west in Ballater Street to exactly No. 32. The trail of blood extended from Thistle Street to that point which is a distance of 136 yards.

By the COURT—That is before you come to Hospital Street? —No, you have already passed Hospital Street.

Under the railway?—Yes, under the railway arch.

And right along to half-way to Gorbals Cross?—Yes, half-way to Gorbals Cross from the railway arch. That is the point where the deceased dropped. The trail of blood had extended to that point. The first two stains I mentioned were, one at the corner of Thistle Street and Ballater Street and the other actually at the corner. Then there was a diagonal stain as if the deceased had staggered right across the footway.

Examination continued—Was the line of bloodstain along the south pavement of Ballater Street?—Yes, close to the wall, as if the deceased had been supporting himself with the wall. It was quite close to the wall, a matter of anything from 18 inches to two feet from the wall.

Then the man must have crossed Hospital Street without support?—Quite correct.

Patrick Carraher.

Second Day—Tuesday, 13th September, 1938.

MRS. JANE GALLACHER, sworn.

Examined by MR. MONTGOMERY—I reside at 3, Ballater Street, Glasgow. The deceased, James Shaw, was my brother. His full name was James Sydney Emden Shaw. He was a single man, 23 years of age, and lived with me. My house overlooks the street in Ballater Street.

Do you remember the early morning of 14th August this year hearing a police whistle sounded in the early hours?—Yes, it was about 1.30 I looked out, and saw something was wrong. Then a young man came to my house and said that my brother had been seriously injured. Later on I went to the Royal Infirmary, and on arrival there I was informed that James was dead.

On Monday, 15th August, did you go to the mortuary at the Royal Infirmary?—Yes. I identified my brother's body before a post-mortem examination was held.

Cross-examined by MR. WHEATLEY—When you looked out of the window did you see anyone in Ballater Street?—I seen somebody as if it was somebody lying, but I didn't know whether it was a man or a woman. There were a few people round at the time. I couldn't tell you how many policemen, four or half a dozen, and they were all running in the direction of the telephone.

Did the policemen come on the scene later?—Yes.

When you looked out of the window and saw the figure lying on the street, how many people were round about that figure?—There were not many people at that time.

Three or four?—More than that.

Six?—About a dozen, but I can't exactly tell you how many.

WILLIAM SHAW (58), sworn.

Examined by MR. MONTGOMERY—I reside at 69, Glenshee Street, Glasgow, and am a miner. The deceased James Sydney Emden Shaw was my son. On 14th August, 1938, about five o'clock in the morning, two reporters called at my house and told me that my son had been seriously injured and was being detained in the Royal Infirmary. I learned later that he was dead. On 15th

Evidence for the Prosecution.

W. Shaw

August I went to the mortuary at the Royal Infirmary, and there identified my son's body before a post-mortem examination was held. My son was buried in Janefield Cemetery.

DR. JOHN SPITTAL CAMERON (24), sworn.

Examined by MR. MONTGOMERY—I am an M.B. Ch.B. of Glasgow University and am a resident surgeon in the Royal Infirmary, Glasgow. In the early morning of 14th August this year I was on duty in the Royal Infirmary when James Sydney Emden Shaw was admitted. He was in a dying condition, and died when being transferred to Ward No. 22. I made a report subsequent to my examination of him.

Look at Production No. 4. Is that your report?—Yes. It is a true report.

Did you form any impression as a result of your examination as to how the injuries could have been caused?—I think they may have been caused by a sharp instrument.

Could a knife have caused the injuries?—Yes.

Was the cause of death the injuries to the neck?—Yes.

By the COURT—Could they have been self-inflicted?—I think they might have been.

Did you form any opinion about that at all?—No, I did not.

PROFESSOR JOHN GLAISTER, sworn.

Examined by MR. MONTGOMERY—I am a Doctor of Medicine, a Doctor of Science, and Regius Professor of Forensic Medicine in the University of Glasgow. Acting on the instruction of the Procurator Fiscal of Glasgow, I, along with Dr. Garrey, on 18th August, 1938, made a post-mortem examination of the body of James Sydney Emden Shaw in the Pathological Department of the Royal Infirmary. I produce our joint report.

Look at Production No. 5. Is that dated 18th August, 1938? —Yes, that is the joint report in question. (Reads report.) It is a true report.

You say at the end that death resulted from the effects of the incised wound on the left side of the neck which perforated the interior jugular vein and the pharynx together with the other tissues of the neck?—Yes.

Did you form any opinion as a result of your examination of

89

Patrick Carraher.

Professor Glaister

how that wound was or could have been caused?—In our view it was caused by a sharp cutting instrument.

Could it have been caused by the use of a knife?—Yes.

Did you form any opinion as to the degree of force which was necessary to cause a wound of that kind?—Yes, I considered that point.

What was the depth?—Measured on the probe, it was three inches including swelling, and making an approximate deduction for the swelling the penetration into the tissues would be in the region of two inches.

Did you form any impression as to the degree of force which must have been used to produce a wound of that kind?—Yes. Some force must have been employed, or alternatively the neck must have been thrust towards the weapon travelling towards it.

Can you express any opinion as to whether that wound could have been self-inflicted?—We were of the opinion that it was not self-inflicted.

Cross-examined by MR. CAMERON—I suppose it could have been self-inflicted, could it?—It is very unlikely, having regard to the two accompanying lesions.

The jugular vein was severed by this blow?—Partially severed.

That, of course, would cause considerable bleeding, would it not?—Yes.

But may I take it that you would not get the pulsation, the pulse motion, that you get if an artery is severed?—That is right.

So you would not get an instantaneous gushing of blood?—No spouting.

How long would it take from the time of infliction of that wound before there was any extensive bleeding?—I could not give an accurate answer to that question, but I should think probably some seconds.

When you say some seconds, would it be three or four seconds probably?—Probably exceeding the region of five.

Before any blood appeared at all?—That is speculative, of course, but that is the nearest I can get.

But you are speaking now from a pretty wide experience of these things?—That is true.

When you say that a knife could have caused that wound, I suppose you mean any sharp pointed or bladed instrument could have caused it?—Yes.

Evidence for the Prosecution.

Dr. G. Garrey

DR. GILBERT GARREY, sworn.

Examined by MR. MONTGOMERY—I am a Doctor of Medicine, hold the Diploma of Public Health, and am the Medical Officer of Duke Street Prison. I was associated with Professor Glaister in a post-mortem examination of the body of James Sydney Emden Shaw on 15th August, 1938. As a result of that examination Professor Glaister and I made a joint report, Production No. 5. It is a true report.

You say at the end of the report that as a result of the foregoing examination you and Professor Glaister were of the opinion that death resulted from the effect of the incised wound on the left side of the neck. Did you form any opinion as to how that wound had been caused?—We took it to be a stab with a knife blade.

Did you form any opinion as to whether a degree of force had been used to inflict that wound?—There must have been force.

Cross-examined by MR. CAMERON—It was not a mere scratch? —It was not.

I suppose that it was just, in a sense, bad luck that the knife or whatever it was happened to strike a certain vessel?—Well, that is quite possible.

There must have been other places in the region of that wound where a cut of a similar kind would have produced little or no serious result?—That is so.

MR. MONTGOMERY—I would ask leave, my lord, to put in a plan of the locus, two days' notice of which plan has been given to the Defence under Section 1 of the Criminal Procedure (Scotland) Act, 1921. I would ask leave to prove the plan.

SAMUEL PATON (37), sworn.

Examined by MR. MONTGOMERY—I am a detective-constable in the Eastern Division of the City of Glasgow Police. I have eleven years' service. Acting on the instructions of the Procurator Fiscal, on 18th August, I made a survey of Ballater Street, Gorbals Cross and the streets in the vicinity and I made a further plan on 19th August. Production No. 8 is the plan I made on 19th August. It is a true and accurate plan and is drawn to scale.

I want you to give me the distance between Gorbals Cross on

91

Patrick Carraher.

S. Paton

the one hand and the corner of Ballater Street and Thistle Street on the other?—590 feet.

What is the distance from the corner of Ballater Street and Thistle Street on the one hand, and a point in Ballater Street opposite to Green's picture house on the other?—420 feet.

Cross-examined by MR. CAMERON—If you go along Ballater Street eastwards, do you come to the river ultimately at Glasgow Green?—No.

Does the river not take a bend further east of Albert Bridge? —Yes—you would need to go to the extreme end of Ballater Street where the bridge crosses.

What is the name of the bridge?—King George V Bridge, I think.

No, I am talking of the east, not the west?—It is the new bridge crossing the Green.

And that would take you right on to Glasgow Green?—Yes, it takes you out on to James Street, Bridgeton.

How far is it from the corner of Thistle Street, that is to say the junction of Thistle Street and Ballater Street, to the place where you get to Glasgow Green, the river going along Ballater Street? Would it be about a quarter of a mile?—Fully.

Is that to over the new bridge?—Yes, it would be a quarter of a mile at least.

Glasgow Green at one o'clock in the morning is a pretty quiet spot, is it not?—Sometimes.

If there is nobody there causing trouble—is that what you mean?—Yes, and it is a district frequented by undesirables as a rule at that time in the morning.

Is there a great amount of undesirable conduct, riotous conduct?—Yes, as a rule.

Is it a place in which fights are not uncommon?—I could not speak to that because it is outwith my district.

But, after all, you are a Glasgow policeman and you must have a pretty good idea of what goes on in Glasgow?—There is a considerable amount of trouble there owing to football pitches and one thing and another there. There is a lot of trouble about that.

But they don't play football at 1 o'clock in the morning, do they?—No.

Proof for the Crown Closed.

Evidence for the Defence.

T. Lyons

Mr. Cameron—My lord, I propose to call two short witnesses at least to speak to the condition of the accused.

Evidence for the Defence.

Thomas Lyons (41), sworn.

Examined by Mr. Cameron—I live at 58, Norfolk Street, Glasgow. That is Patrick Carraher in the dock; I have known him for some time. I was in his company on the afternoon of Saturday, 13th August, of this year. Carraher called at my house for me.

In what condition was he when he called?—He was quite all right then.

Did you then go together to a public-house?—Yes, to Sweeney's at the corner of Nicholson Street and Norfolk Street. We had some drinks there.

Did you then go to another public-house at the corner of Bridge Street?—Yes, Alexander's public-house. We had some more drinks there.

From there did you go to another public-house in his company? —Yes, to Kelly's in Norfolk Street, where we had some more drink.

Did that bring you to about seven o'clock?—Yes.

I think you then went home, did you?—Yes.

Where did you leave Carraher?—In Kelly's. Carraher left to get something to eat in the "model" he was staying in. He came up to my house again about eight o'clock that evening.

Did you then go out again and go to a public-house at Gorbals Cross?—Yes, McConnell's.

Were you drinking together more or less continuously from eight o'clock until closing time at ten, both in McConnell's and in another public-house nearby?—I don't remember about that.

What time did you get home?—About twenty minutes past ten.

In what condition were you?—Well, I was right out.

Did you have any difficulty in getting home?—It took me all my time to get home.

What condition was Carraher in? Was he much the same?— Well, I was drunk and Carraher must have been drunk too.

Had you and he been drinking more or less drink for drink throughout the afternoon together?—Yes, I quite believe it.

I think you know a man called Patrick Green?—Yes.

Patrick Carraher.

Does he lodge in your house?—Yes, I don't remember seeing him that night.

Cross-examined by MR. WALKER—Does it come to this, that when you left this public-house at ten o'clock you have no clear recollection of events? You were fairly drunk, were you?—Yes.

You have no clear recollection of how you came to leave it, or going home at all?—No.

You don't remember going home, do you?—No. When I get any drink like that I always make for home.

But on this occasion you have no clear recollection of going home at all?—That is so.

And you have no clear recollection of what condition Paddy Carraher was in, or when he left the public-house?—No.

You first saw Carraher about four o'clock in the afternoon of that Saturday?—Between four and half-past four.

Had you had some drink before then?—Yes, I had drink in the morning.

And when you saw Paddy Carraher about half-past four was he sober?—Yes, he looked sober to me, anyway.

PATRICK GREEN (30), sworn.

Examined by MR. CAMERON—I am employed as a labourer, and lodge with the Lyons at 58, Norfolk Street, Glasgow. I know Patrick Carraher. That is Patrick Carraher in the dock.

Were you in Norfolk Street at about a quarter past eight on the evening of Saturday, 13th August, of this year?—Yes, I met Mrs. Lyons there and as a result of a conversation with her I went into McConnell's public-house.

Did you see anybody there?—Yes, I saw Carraher and Thomas Lyons and his brother. They were drunk.

After you had seen them there I think you came out of the public-house and went home for your tea?—Yes.

Did you see Carraher and Lyons later that evening?—Yes, at twenty-five past nine in the public-house.

Did you see them on the street again?—Yes, I saw them about a quarter past ten coming along the road staggering. I was hanging over Mrs. Lyons's window.

Why were you hanging out of the window?—Well, there was a disturbance on the street at the time. Some people were getting taken to gaol.

Evidence for the Defence.

P. Green

What were they being taken to gaol for?—I cannot say.

Had there been a fight?—Yes, outside.

Did you see Lyons and Carraher?—Yes, coming along the road by themselves.

Were they staggering?—Yes, they were staggering from the edge of the pavement to the window.

Taking the whole width of the pavement?—Yes.

Did you go downstairs?—Yes, to the foot of the close.

Did you help either Lyons or Carraher into the house?—I had to take Mr. Lyons, but he was too drunk and I had to call his wife to give me assistance to take him up the stair.

What about Carraher?—He came up at our back, staggering up the stair.

Did he fall on the stairs at all?—He fell twice.

Did he hurt himself?—I cannot say.

Did he come into the room of the house at 58, Norfolk Street? —Yes, he came into the house. He had a good drink.

Had he anything with him in a bottle?—Yes, he had four bottles of beer, and a bottle of wine in his pocket.

Did you see him leave the house?—I never saw him leave the house. I just saw him coming into the kitchen and he left two bottles of beer for Mrs. Lyons's husband and then went out with two bottles of beer and a bottle of wine in his pocket.

Where he went to you cannot say?—No.

He was obviously very drunk and hardly able to take care of himself?—No, he could not take care of himself.

Cross-examined by MR. WALKER—Did you see him leave the house?—No.

What time would it be when you last saw him?—About twenty minutes to eleven.

And he managed to come up the stair?—Yes, he came staggering up the stair at our backs.

You had to help Lyons, but Carraher came up by himself?—Yes.

And how Carraher got out of the house you don't know?—I cannot say.

I think you had gone to bed?—Yes, and after that I cannot say what happened.

Of the drink he had with him, the bottles of beer and the bottle of wine, he left two bottles of beer?—Yes, he left two bottles of beer for Mrs. Lyons's husband in the morning.

Patrick Carraher.

P. Green

As regards your visit to the public-house at eight-fifteen, you went in there and saw Carraher and Lyons?—Yes.

And, I think, Mrs. Lyons?—Yes, the four of us in the room together.

Was the publican still serving them at that time?—Yes, he was still serving.

I think you did not speak to any of them?—No, I just saw them there.

And you are not in a very good position to speak to Carraher's condition then?—He had had a good drink, but I cannot say because I never spoke to any of them.

MR. CAMERON—That is all my evidence, and I close my case.

The Advocate-Depute's Address to the Jury.[1]

Mr. James Walker addressed the jury on behalf of the Crown and said that, while there was no eye-witness who saw the blow struck, he believed that there was a clear inference from the evidence produced in court that the accused, Carraher, had in fact struck the fatal blow. It might well be that Carraher had disposed of the knife by throwing it over the parapet of Albert Bridge, and by so doing had made recovery of the weapon impossible. He requested the jury to return a verdict of murder on the evidence laid before them.

Mr. Cameron's Address to the Jury.

MR. CAMERON—Members of the jury, it now falls to me to discharge what is my most responsible task in this case, and that is to address you on behalf of the accused here. This court has in its day seen very many murder trials in which the issues have almost hourly become more grave until at the end the feeling of responsibility, and indeed the tension, has been so marked as almost to be palpable; but in this case I confess that I have been surprised that the Crown should have seen fit, after the way the evidence has come out, and having regard to the quality of the witnesses that they have led through the witness-box, to ask you to return a verdict of murder, with the unavoidable consequences of that verdict, which you well know. It is true that one life has

[1] Owing to the death of the shorthand writer and the complete lack of report it has not been possible to give Mr. Walker's address in full.

96

Speech for the Defence.

Mr. Cameron

been lost in circumstances of which the mystery has not yet by any means been cleared up; and you are apparently going to be asked by your votes to end another life. Based upon what? Based upon "my theory"—Mr. Walker says—"my inferences". But you are not going to convict a man, far less hang him, upon theories or inferences. Before you are going to take the step that is going to deliver that young fellow to the hangman's noose, aren't you going to be satisfied that every link in the chain of proof is tested? Are you going to hang a man upon suspicion, or conjecture, or upon theories or inferences? That man might be your brother, or your son, and you would judge him in the same way, with no heavier scales and no lighter scales than you would judge the man in the dock. If the man in the dock was one of your own relations you could have no hesitation in the verdict that you would be bound to return upon the evidence that you have heard. He is entitled to the same justice, the same fair play, as your own sons and brothers.

Now, let me remind you, as Mr. Walker has not done, that in every criminal case in these courts, from the greatest to the least, there is one guiding principle, and that is that the burden of proof lies always upon the Crown. It is not for me to say who killed the man; it is not for me to put forward an alternative case; the burden of making out the charges that have been brought lies upon the Crown. The main element in that burden is this—as his lordship will tell you—that no tribunal, whether it be judge or jury, and certainly no tribunal which has to pass upon a life or a death, is entitled in law to convict unless the charge has been proved beyond reasonable doubt. If there be room for doubt, then not only is it your privilege, but in law it is your duty, to give the benefit of that doubt to an accused person and to acquit him.

Now let us see how the evidence stands in this case. I do not propose to detain you at length, because although the issues are grave the evidence lies really in very small compass; and, stripped of its suspicions, stripped of conjecture, I think you will find it comes to very little in the end of the day. There are, as you know, in this indictment two charges made against the accused, one a charge so trivial that it would be more appropriate to a Police Court, and one the gravest that can be brought against any man. Of course, there is no doubt that the reason this first and trivial charge has been brought in is to provide—and this shows how weak the second charge is—to provide at least some kind of justification for the second charge of murder, namely, to bring in

Patrick Carraher.

evidence before you that Carraher had a knife and that he had it
in his hand that night. It appears to have been a pocket-knife.
Well. I have, and I am sure you all have, a knife, very much the
same kind of thing—not a very lethal weapon at all—though I
quite agree that even that would inflict a very deadly wound in
certain conditions. But the mere fact that a drunk man is seen
with a pocket-knife in his hand which he doesn't even attempt to
use—what foundation is that for saying that he is the man who
killed in a murderous attack this young fellow Shaw, whom
apparently he didn't know?

Let us just see what the effect of the two charges is. In the first
place, I am going to submit to you—and I think you will agree—
that they have very greatly confused the issue that you have to
try, because, not content with levelling a charge against this
young fellow upon such a flimsy foundation, the Crown has had
to lean the main weight of its attack upon an alleged confession—
a pretty business!—by a man stupefied with drink who apparently, according to one of the witnesses who spoke to the alleged
confession, was babbling like a child and didn't apparently know
what he was speaking to, or what he was confessing. What was
he confessing? We will see in a moment what was the impression
of the witnesses to whom these confessions were alleged to have
been made, and unless you were absolutely certain that these
confessions—for whatever value they have—related, and were
meant by the man himself to relate, to this second charge, then
would it not be in the highest degree dangerous to place any
reliance upon any report of this conversation in condemning this
man or in taking any steps to bring his life to jeopardy?

Let us see, members of the jury, just how the evidence stands
upon the first charge, because in a way it is an epitome of the
whole. It looks formidable upon paper, but when you begin to
test it the whole story outlined in that indictment just breaks
down and crumbles away. He is charged with assaulting James
Durie, seizing hold of him, taking up a threatening attitude towards him and brandishing a knife at him. Who began it? It
wasn't the accused. It was James Durie who began it. Because
you recollect that Morgan said that it began with James Durie
shoving the accused. There had been an argument about a girl,
whether she was to go a message to Katie Morgan; Carraher was
pulling one arm and James Durie was pulling the other. I don't
suggest that was the most gentlemanly of conduct, but perhaps
the standards of the Gorbals are not the standards obtaining in

MR. JOHN CAMERON, K.C.

Speech for the Defence.

other parts of the world. And what happens next? Then Durie takes the offensive. He shoves him. And in retaliation—and you may very well think justified retaliation—what does the accused do? With one hand he catches the fellow by the lapels of the coat. He makes no attempt to strike a blow at him—strikes no blow. And as for the allegation of brandishing a knife—with the best efforts in the world, the best the Crown can make of that is that it was held in his right hand, which was down by his side; and no attempt was made over the period, which was said to be five or ten minutes, to make use of it. Did you ever hear such a trumpery, silly story of a drunken squabble, magnified into this rather grandiloquent charge in the indictment? Two young fellows scuffling in the Gorbals, and you have been brought here to listen to that! Not even begun by the accused! That is all it is. Donald Cameron, who came on the scene, and who is in many ways the least prejudiced witness of the lot, because after all he doesn't know any of them, said it never occurred to him for a moment that the man meant to use the knife, and he certainly wasn't brandishing it. All he was doing was holding the lapels of James Durie. When Cameron told him to put the knife away, either because he heard the remark or of his own accord he put the knife back in his pocket. What a preposterous suggestion to say that this was an assault in which Carraher was brandishing a knife! At the innocent James Durie, mark you—the little innocent who was attacked by this man. You saw the Duries, and you will be able to form a pretty good idea of what the Durie brothers were like that Saturday night—the fellows who were out for a straight fight, four to one! I think you will have no difficulty in brushing aside this first charge, which, as I say, I am convinced would have found no place in this indictment had it not been that the Crown was so desperate for incriminating evidence that they had to bring in this merely to prove that this drunk man had an open knife in his possession.

How does the case stand upon the second charge? It is an extraordinary case, because nobody professes to have seen what happened. There is no eye-witness who links Shaw and the accused together at the fatal time. That is important. Peter Howard says that he was within two feet—that is his first story and then it became a few yards—within two feet of Shaw when he saw him holding his neck, and he was at that time in a long, straight street, and Carraher wasn't in sight, and nobody suggested he had been running away. Where was he? He certainly

Patrick Carraher.

Mr. Cameron

was not on the scene of the blow at the time the blow was struck, according to Peter Howard, who is the Crown's own witness. In the next place, nobody says where Carraher was at the time the blow was struck. Nobody suggests that he was either in grips with Shaw or in a position from which he could have struck a blow at all. According to Peter Howard's evidence, if there is one person who is not concerned in this crime it is Carraher, because he wasn't even seen—in a street which is straight, as you probably know, and has been shown you, for a very long distance—he wasn't even seen by a witness who was put in as a credible witness by the Crown. And if you don't believe Peter Howard, where is there a case at all? If you do believe him, where is the case at all? If you do believe him, where is the case against Carraher? Because the question you have to try is not, Who killed Shaw: it is, Has the Crown proved beyond reasonable doubt that Carraher killed Shaw? That is the question. Now, the evidence of Peter Howard goes a very long way to absolve Carraher from any complicity in this assault. But there is an even more extraordinary omission than that—one I was surprised to observe. As you know, in these cases it is usual to have medical evidence as to the condition of the clothing both of the dead man and of the man who is charged with the crime, generally because that clothing may or may not show signs of bloodstains, which might very well point in one direction or the other and assist you to come to a determination. Now, you know that you have been sitting here for the past two days, and you have heard all manner of medical witnesses. Professor Glaister and Dr. Garrey have been through the witness-box, but they have not been asked whether they made a report on the examination of the accused's clothing or of Shaw's clothing. Is that not a strange omission? And yet you are being asked to convict Carraher of murder. It is a matter of common knowledge now that scientific methods have advanced so far that medico-legal experts, given a sufficient quantity of blood, are able to identify from which of the various known groups of human blood that blood has come, and therefore very often to narrow down suspicion or clinch proof. In this case—and it is, I think, unique in these courts—the Crown has made no attempt to show whether or not there were blood stains on the clothing of Howard —who was arrested, mark you—or of Carraher who is charged, or what stains were found upon the clothing of the dead man, into what category or group that blood fell, or whether or not stains of the same category or group were found upon the cloth-

Speech for the Defence.

Mr. Cameron

ing of any person concerned in this trial—a most remarkable omission and one which should go a very long way, in my submission, to influence the decision which you will have to come to to-day, and influence it in favour of Patrick Carraher.

What is left? The Duries and Morgan saw nothing, heard nothing and said nothing in the witness-box. As Peter Howard put it—somewhat crudely, I thought—they wanted to know as little as possible about what had happened. All they were concerned to say in their evidence was that they knew nothing about this at all, they weren't there, they didn't know anything about it. Well, we shall see from the evidence of another person who is entirely unprejudiced that that evidence may be open to very grave suspicion. According to the Duries, when they parted at the corner of Ballater Street and Thistle Street, there was nobody in sight. They and Charles Morgan went away up Thistle Street, saw nobody, heard not a sound. The shouting that attracted Constable McCallum apparently fell upon deaf ears in the case of those gentlemen, although they can't have been any further away than the policeman. Howard saw nothing. There was nobody in the street. Shaw, of course, died. Carraher, as you heard, was stupefied with drink and said there was nobody on the street; and the Duries didn't see anyone. Where did the curious gentleman with the handkerchief come from? He is a mystery in this case. Mr. Walker was rather inclined to smile at the suggestion there was any mystery about him, but he is a mysterious figure. He must have been either an eye-witness of the assault—because he appears on the instant—or an eye-witness of what happened immediately thereafter. He comes forward, gives the loan of a handkerchief, and disappears into the Gorbals, never to be seen by mortal eyes again, neither police nor anybody else. Why does James Durie tell lies about that? Because he is lying about it. According to James Durie he never heard anything about a man with a handkerchief until yesterday. According to Morgan the story of the man with the handkerchief was told in the presence and hearing of James Durie that very morning, within an hour of the event, by Peter Howard. Why should James Durie tell lies about it, unless he knows, or thinks he knows, something more than it would be healthy for him to tell? That is the first mystery. Who then was doing the shouting, if there was nobody there? We know perfectly well that Shaw couldn't even speak, and Howard wasn't speaking, he wasn't shouting. Who then was doing the shouting and making the noise that attracted Constable

Patrick Carraher.

Mr. Cameron

McCallum's attention from away along the street? We don't know. Of course, there was no knife found—but I'll come to deal with that later on. If you take the case up to that point, what is there to link Carraher with killing Shaw any more than there is to link John Durie, the drunkard, whom you saw—the fair fighter—James Durie, Peter Howard or Charles Morgan? Not one single iota of evidence—because each and every one of them was as near Shaw as the others—indeed Howard was much nearer—and each and every one of them could have done it. Of course, they all said they hadn't got knives or razor blades. You can believe it if you like. Each and every one of them, Carraher included, apparently had no motive, and therefore they had the same motive—which was none—as Carraher had to do this. If there is a case against Carraher up to this point, there is a case against John Durie, James Durie, Charles Morgan and Peter Howard, equally strong—or even the mysterious stranger with the handkerchief. It is at this point that the confessions, so-called, are brought in to provide at least some kind of basis for proceeding in this charge of murder. Who were the confessions made to? And under what conditions were they made? Mary McCafferty— you saw her—and Robert Howard, the brother of Peter Howard who had been arrested. Remember this, that Robert Howard told us that Carraher was very friendly towards Peter Howard, who was a younger fellow than he was and had been mixed up with the Duries in the earlier episode. Now, let us take McCafferty first. Carraher had only seen her once before in his life. Apparently he doesn't make any remark to her in the journey from Portugal Street over the river; it is only while Robert Howard and the girl Docherty are at the police station that he blurts out, according to McCafferty, a story of having done it with a knife, which he exhibits—said to be a dark-coloured knife. Nobody else has seen a dark-coloured knife. It wasn't the kind of knife apparently which he had at the time of the first charge. Well, now, according to McCafferty it was made quite plain to the accused Carraher, and he well understood it, that what was being enquired into was a very serious assault in which a man had been gravely injured and had lost a lot of blood. That was her story. And you will also recollect that she alleges that Carraher said something about he wouldn't let Peter Howard swing for it. Now, up to that point there had been no suggestion that anybody's life had been lost, so there was no question of swinging for anything. That little exaggeration rather makes one suspect

Speech for the Defence.

Mr. Cameron

that Mary McCafferty—who, after all, is apparently a very close friend of the girl Docherty, who in turn is an equally close friend of Peter Howard—is at least drawing upon her recollection of what we now know happened, that a man's life was lost, and letting that colour her remembrance of what took place. Now, when she was cross-examined it appeared that at that time she didn't know anything about the earlier scuffle with James Durie at Gorbals Cross—not very far away from the scene of Shaw's death, and not very long separated in point of time—but she didn't know anything about the fact that there had been two episodes that night, in one of which Carraher was undoubtedly involved—the first one—and in the other of which Shaw had lost his life, and in which I suggest every one of that group could have been as closely involved as Carraher. At the end of the day she admitted to me in cross-examination that it might possibly have been the first that Carraher had in mind, and for which he thought Peter Howard had been lifted by the police, and he was going to take the blame—as well he might, because it was he and Durie, not Peter Howard—for being mixed up in the first affair. And the matter becomes very much clearer when you recollect that Robert Howard speaks to an alleged confession, not taking place on the way back from the police station but on the way across the bridge when he and Carraher were walking together and the two girls were walking in front. In that connection let me remind you, as just an illustration of the fallacies which memory can create, that according to McCafferty when they went across the bridge the first time and came back they all walked back in a bunch. According to Robert Howard, when they went across from the Gorbals side of the river to go to the Central Police Station they were two by two, the two girls in front and the two men behind. So you see, even in a matter so recent as 13th or 14th August witnesses' memories play them very strange tricks. Well now, that is a small matter, of course, but it does just show you that you cannot always trust recollection or impression.

What does Robert Howard say about it? Howard says that on the way across the bridge—as Mr. Walker has read to you—Carraher quite openly said that a fellow had been cheeky with him and he had scratched him in the face with a knife. I said to Howard, "Would you call being shoved by a fellow cheeky?" He said, "Yes." Durie had been shoving him, and the knife had been out in Carraher's hand, and he had been told to put it away and had put it away, and he had been drunk at that time. Robert

Patrick Carraher.

Mr. Cameron

Howard said it was quite plain to him that Paddy Carraher hadn't the slightest idea that what Peter Howard was in for was anything serious. Now, that is quite contrary to the girl McCafferty's version. According to her, what Carraher was harping on was some little petty scuffle, some very small thing, in which somebody had been cheeky to him and he had had a scrap and scratched him in the face, and it was to that incident that Carraher referred in his conversation; and Howard said—knowing the facts now, that there was this affair with Durie—that it may very well be that it was to that he was referring and not to the later episode. Well now, if we pause there for one moment—these are the alleged confessions and you heard the wording of them. But what are the impressions now, in the witness-box upon oath, of the two witnesses who listened to them? They don't say now that both of those did relate, and were meant to relate, to the second charge. Mary McCafferty says that it may possibly be, looking back on it now, that what he was speaking about was the first episode. Howard says it may very well be what he was speaking about was the first, because it was obvious he was not thinking of anything serious and had no idea that anything serious had happened. That being the impression of the witnesses, are you going to say these are the witnesses to hang this man, when their impressions are not clear? I think you would be taking a very dangerous leap indeed, when they themselves cannot say that it was a confession of murder, but was, "probably" in the one case, and "might have been" in the other, a reference to a petty scuffle and assault which we know took place. The subsequent events, as we know them, seem to me—and you will judge—to bear out the view that I put to those witnesses and to which they assented, namely, that what Carraher had in his drunken mind was this first scuffle. Because, you will recollect, he went to the house of Sutherland, who stays at 12, Portugal Street—it doesn't matter what the number is—and Sutherland observed that he was pretty drunk, as indeed Robert Howard observed. He was then speaking childishly, quite obviously not fully under his own command. What does Sutherland say about it? Sutherland got the news at the coffee-stall—a man had died, whose name he did not know. He said, "I asked Carraher, when I told him that the man had died: 'Is that what Peter is in for?'" It was known, of course, that Peter Howard was under arrest. Sutherland said, "Is that what he is in for?" "I don't know," says Carraher. Doesn't that go a very long way to reinforce the view I have been speaking

Speech for the Defence.

Mr. Cameron

about, that what he had been talking about was not the Shaw affair at all but the earlier minor scuffle in which he had been involved? Then you recollect that he made the comment that he heard that the man was dead—that is all—as if it was some piece of local news, nothing in which he had any concern. And, mark you, this is within a very short time of walking across the Albert Bridge, or whatever bridge he came across. Look at the plan. There is the Central Police Station; there is the building where we are now, incidentally. Apparently he came across the river and he made his way to Portugal Street. Well, it is not very far away even from the police station, and obviously it would not take him very long to get from the Central Police Office to Portugal Street and Sutherland's house. In other words, it was a very short time after he had been saying, "I'll not let Peter stay in prison. I will give myself up." Then he is told the man is dead, and he is asked, "Is that what Peter Howard is in for?" and he says, "I don't know." Obviously there was no connection in that man's mind between the serious injury and death of Shaw and what Peter Howard was in for, and it was what Peter Howard was in for that he was going to give himself up for. In other words, it is quite apparent from the evidence of Sutherland, who was called as a witness of credit by the Crown, that these witnesses who heard the confession did hear a confession to an assault of a minor character which had taken place, in which—as we now know— Durie was involved. Therefore, in my submission, the whole case, which is based upon this alleged confession, simply tumbles to the ground. Because unless you are convinced in your own minds, unless you are certain that your impression is—and it is a true one—that there was a confession of murder and not, as the witnesses who heard it thought, that it might have been very well, knowing what we know now, a confession of minor assault, you would not be entitled to make any use of that in considering your verdict.

Then there are, of course, two subsequent episodes of a minor character. At Mrs. Maguire's house he is still drunk—indeed he is drunk when arrested—and he says, "I had a quarrel with a chap; I don't know what happened." It is perfectly obvious that he knew at that time that somebody was dead, and it is equally obvious, if Mrs. Maguire is to be believed, that he couldn't have associated the death of this man with what he had been doing and what he had been talking about. He said, "I have had a quarrel, but I don't know what happened." Obviously there was no

Patrick Carraher.

Mr. Cameron

association in his own mind with the death of Shaw and his own action; and in my submission there is no proof whatever, and no justification for saying, in this case that this wretched youth—because he is nothing more than a youth—has any proved connection with the death of James Shaw.

If the case had ended there, members of the jury, I would have had no hesitation in asking you to say that this charge has not been made out. But the case does not end there at all, because luckily we have at least one independent witness who was called for the Crown who saw a good deal of what happened, and her evidence traversed the whole story of what I might call the Durie connection—that is Mrs. McLaughlan, who was taking a walk about one o'clock in the morning. You will recollect the lady, a rather stout lady. Now, she is the only independent person, apart from the police officers, who was on the scene either at or shortly after the time of the second, or fatal assault as charged in this indictment. In the first place, she contradicts the story that there was nobody there, and secondly, she makes it appear very plainly that the assault took place in Thistle Street. Now, if I might again ask your attention to this—because it may be of very great importance—Ballater Street runs approximately east from Gorbals Cross, and off Ballater Street there run at right angles various other streets, Hospital Street and Thistle Street. Now, according to the evidence of Peter Howard and the Duries, they walked along with the accused and Shaw and Morgan down Ballater Street, passed the mouth of Hospital Street, until they came to the corner of Thistle Street. At that corner—according to them, mark you—they parted. According to them, when last seen Shaw and Carraher were in the roadway of Ballater Street, and Howard was just at the pavement quite close—in Ballater Street, mark you. Where did Shaw come from when Mrs. McLaughlan saw him? He came from up Thistle Street. Now, we know from Professor Glaister that, with the nature of the wound, the wound in the jugular vein, there would have been no flow of blood until five seconds after the infliction of the wound. Now, five seconds seems a very short time, but if you count "five" slowly you will realize you can cover a fair distance in five seconds. Now, the police officer, Sergeant Johnston, gave you the places and the measurements of the bloodstains, which began some substantial distance up Thistle Street. Is the inference not perfectly clear—indeed I won't call it an inference: is the irresistible conclusion—not this, that, wherever the assault took place, it must have been still

Speech for the Defence.

further into Thistle Street than the beginning of the blood marks, because Shaw was staggering out of Thistle Street into Ballater Street? How did he get there?

LORD PITMAN—I have in front of me the transcript where Johnston says : "The first stage . . . Ballater Street."

MR. CAMERON—That is right, my lord, I am sorry. I thought it was further up.

LORD PITMAN—I thought you must have overlooked that.

MR. CAMERON—Yes, I did. I didn't see the notes last night, but my own note is that the stains began at the corner. Obviously if he had come from Thistle Street, as he was seen coming by Mrs. McLaughlan, the blow must have been struck in Thistle Street. Not only does she say that, but she hears something which is very important. The man who gets the handkerchief speaks to her. Now, I don't want to trust my memory for this, which is important. She heard groans and she is asked: "Q.—What did you see? A.—I saw a chap coming round the corner with his two hands at his neck. There was a chap with a light suit and another one with a dark suit, and the chap with the light suit gave the man with the dark suit a handkerchief. Q.—What state was the man with the dark suit in? A.—Well, I didn't pay particular notice to that. Q.—Were there any other people standing about? A.—There were not very many ; the streets were quite bare."
Then his lordship asked a question: "Q.—Did you see two people standing together or three? A.—There were two at the corner. The chap in the light suit came forward, and I asked him what was the matter, and he told me they had got him through the jugular vein and he had given the chap a handkerchief."
I repeat: "They had got him through the jugular vein and he had given the chap a handkerchief." Now, isn't that rather significant? Who said that? Was it Peter Howard or was it the mysterious man with the handkerchief, who must have been on the scene? "They had got him through the jugular vein." Not "he had got him", but "they". I asked Mrs. McLaughlan about that in cross-examination. I asked her: "Q.—Did you say there were four people whom you noticed standing at the corner of Thistle Street? A.—Yes. There were men talking at the corner of Thistle Street. Q.—How far would that be from the place

107

Patrick Carraher.

where this injured man was when you first saw him? A few yards would it be? A.—About five or six yards."

There was a group of men standing at the corner within five or six yards, and Howard apparently—or the mysterious man with a handkerchief—says, "They have got him through the jugular vein with a knife." I asked her again about it: "Q.—I took you down as saying that one man had told you that they had got him in the jugular vein? A.—Yes. Q.—Who was the man who told you that? A.—The one with the light suit."

Now, there is no doubt about Mrs. McLaughlan's recollection. Who are "they"? She is the one witness in this case who has nothing to hide, who doesn't need to close her eyes or her ears to keep her mouth shut, and she says, far from the streets being utterly bare of people, there were men standing at the corner of Thistle Street, from which direction Shaw came, within five or six yards of him, and she was told by the fellow in the light-coloured suit that they had got him through the jugular vein. Was Carraher ever seen in Thistle Street? Was he ever in Thistle Street? If you accept the evidence of the Duries and Morgan and Peter Howard, who were led by the Crown, he was never there, because they went up Thistle Street and left Carraher, when last seen, in Ballater Street. Now, in face of that evidence where does the whole structure of theory and inference and confession go? Doesn't it just disappear? Here you have the one independent witness, who introduces three elements which simply will not square with the story which you have been asked to accept as being the Crown theory. The first is that the assault took place in a street where Carraher is proved not to have been, and the second is that there were men present, when everybody else is at pains to say there was nobody present. And the third, and the most important, is that the man who makes the only comment on what had occurred uses the plural and not the singular—and we know there were these men standing there. I am reminded by Mr. Wheatley, quite rightly, that the witness you heard this morning, Mrs. Gallacher, who was Shaw's sister, looking from her window, or looking into the street, before the police arrived on the scene, saw a group of people round about the place where Shaw was lying. Of course, that is some distance, I agree, from the place where the fatal blow was actually struck.

Now, I hope I have not gone into this matter in too great detail, but in a case like this, members of the jury, when you are being asked by your verdict to condemn a man to death, you

Speech for the Defence.

Mr. Cameron

must test the whole evidence in detail and see whether the evidence will bear that terrible weight which the Crown has sought to place upon it. In the present case is there not room for doubt now, after you have heard the whole evidence, on two things: in the first place, that you haven't heard the whole story of what took place that night, that there was more than one man involved in it; and in the second place, isn't it abundantly plain that there is no proof, direct or indirect—I say proof advisedly, because suspicion and conjecture are one thing and proof is another—no proof, direct or indirect, that Carraher's was the hand that struck this blow? If you take that view of the evidence—which is not only the merciful view, but, in my submission, the only fair and possible view—then the result, at least as regards the major charge—which is the only one of importance at all—must in my submission be a verdict of acquittal.

But, members of the jury, it is only right that I should put before you another consideration because it is—I trust it won't be—within the bounds of possibility that you might take a different view of the evidence. Supposing you did, the Crown has asked you to return a verdict of murder on the second charge. If you were to think that the evidence showed conclusively and beyond any reasonable doubt that the hand was the hand of Carraher, at the very worst would it be anything worse than a stupid, sudden, unpremeditated act, not committed with the intention of doing any serious injury, far less of killing? Would it not, in consideration of the drunkenness, of which we know, fall rather into the lesser category of culpable homicide rather than in the gravest category of murder? That is a matter for your consideration, but, taking the evidence as a whole, I think you will reach the conclusion without great difficulty that it would not be safe in this case to reach a conclusion on the one question that is put to you: Is it established that Patrick Carraher struck that blow and committed murder?

Now, I have almost discharged my task. I trust I have not tried to exaggerate points that tend in my client's favour or to minimize those which are against him. That is not my duty. My function is, as fairly as I can, to show where there are difficulties, where there are contradictions, where there are gaps in the case for the Crown. I think you will agree that the gaps show themselves at vital points. And when you come, as you must shortly, to deliberate upon this issue, let me remind you that in the one scale is the life of a young man. We know that one has been lost.

Patrick Carraher.

We cannot recover that. In the one scale is the life of a young man; in the other is the evidence you have heard—not merely the spoken word, but the quality and the character of the witnesses themselves. Just think: would you, on what you have seen of those witnesses, feel happy in condemning one of your fellows to death on their word—with their hesitations, their evasions, their lies and prevarications? And yet that is the only material you have to balance against the life of this young man. These courts used in olden days to be the scene of great forensic battles, of speeches full of fire and eloquence. Modern practices and modern habits have tended to produce a much more sober style of oratory. I do not pretend to have any oratorical gift; I am not endeavouring to assail either your minds or your hearts; but remember that you have to judge of the life of a young man. He may have been a fool, he may have been a knave, but I ask you to say that he is not a murderer, and I ask you to acquit him of the charges in this indictment.

Charge to the Jury.

LORD PITMAN—Members of the jury, the serious nature of the charges brought against the panel—or perhaps I ought to say the second charge brought against the panel—requires that you give me your closest attention—not that the principles which apply to a serious charge differ in any degree from those which apply in less serious charges. But a verdict of guilty of any crime according to the law of Scotland is only justified if the jury are satisfied on the evidence and beyond reasonable doubt that the accused has committed the crime charged. Until the Crown has proved a man to be guilty he is in the eye of the law innocent. He has not got to prove that he is innocent; but the necessity for your giving me your undivided attention arises from the fact that the sentence for murder, the inevitable sentence, is one which cannot be reconsidered or modified if once it is carried out. There is one further general remark that I would like to make to you, which is that if you have any reasonable doubt whether the Crown has proved the charges you are entitled to bring in a verdict of Not Proven. That is to say, in the present case there are two charges which must be taken separately and dealt with by you separately. There are three possible verdicts on the first—guilty, not proven or not guilty. The same applies to the second. But although these two charges are included in the same Indictment they must be considered by

Charge to the Jury.

Lord Pitman

you individually, and your decision must be upon the evidence applicable to each of them individually without reference to your decision in regard to the other charge.

Now, as has been pointed out by counsel for the defence, it is very likely, in fact it is almost certainly the case, that the first charge would not have been heard of in the High Court of Justiciary if that had been all. Counsel for the defence suggested that the Crown had included it because of the fact that they were desperate to get a conviction and required the evidence so as to bring the whole matter before you. I cannot think for one moment that there is any foundation for that statement. The reason why a charge of this kind is included is because difficulties always arise when you are telling the story of what happened in the day because objections are taken when the evidence on one charge is being brought; objections are taken that the Crown is not entitled to lead evidence with regard to other charges. And it may have complicated matters if there had been no reference to this alleged assault in the Indictment. But, as I have already pointed out, you must consider the evidence separately. The first point you have to consider and dispose of and not refer to again is whether or not the Crown have made out the first charge of assault, to the effect that on the 13th August the accused did assault James Durie, seize hold of him, take up a threatening attitude towards him and brandish a knife at him. Now, I think you will probably agree that that is a somewhat exaggerated way of describing what took place. I think I am right in saying that in the first instance the threats, if there were threats, came from the other side. The two Duries, as you will remember, were out to find the accused and they wanted the accused because there was an old argument of some kind which they wanted to settle. They wanted the accused to fight and he refused to do so. Well, I am not surprised. He was alone. There was no one there to take his side, and if seconds are required in fights of this kind there was no one there to second him. Whereas the two Duries were there and were quite prepared to take him singly they say, the one after the other. So that one cannot help feeling that the threatening attitude, if there were any threats, started on the other side. The next thing you must remember is that the accused seized hold of James Durie's coat. Now, you must please remember how that came about. The witness Margaret McNicol gave, I think, a very straightforward account of how she had met the accused and how he wanted her to go a message which she was not prepared to do,

Patrick Carraher.

Lord Pitman

how she crossed over to walk to James Durie who had arrived on the scene. She was unwilling, she says, to go for the message; she left him to cross over to where James Durie was standing at the Gorbals Cross with Charles Morgan, and she also said at that time that the accused had had a drink. "The accused then came over to where I was standing, he got hold of me by the arm, James pulled me away, the two got hold of me by the arm, and then Paddy got him by the lapel of his jacket, the crowd gathered and I was put off the road." Then she is asked the question, "What kind of attitude was the accused taking up towards James Durie?" Now, all she says about that is, "He had a knife in his hand. His left hand was on the lapel of James's coat, and the knife in his right hand." "How was he holding it?"—and the answer is, "He was just showing the blade." "Q.—Was anything said? A.—Not that I could say. I got out of the road at the time. James just told him to put the knife in his pocket." And then she is asked, "Did you form any impression as to whether this was serious or not?" and her answer was, "I did not know what he was going to do." Now, that is interpreted by the Crown into adopting a threatening attitude and brandishing a knife at him. Well, I think you are entitled to take the view and say that there technically was an assault, but I do not think it is much more than a technical assault in the eye of the law, the circumstances being what they were; but if you take the view that taking the knife out of his pocket indicates a threat, then I think you are entitled to find him guilty of assault. But it is a very small matter indeed, and really of no importance with regard to the question which you are assembled here to-day to decide; namely whether or not the accused is guilty of murder.

The peculiarity of this case is that there is no evidence at all that the accused and the person who died were really acquainted with each other at all. There is no evidence at all of previous ill-feeling or anything of that kind, and yet there is no doubt that James Shaw lost his life, and the question that you will have to answer before you dispose of the case is, how did James Shaw lose his life? Was it the hand of the accused that cut the jugular vein that caused the death of James Shaw, and, if so, was he guilty of murder or was he guilty of culpable homicide? Now, to begin at the beginning, we have no difficulty whatever in accepting the evidence of the doctors as to the cause of death, and it is not suggested by anybody that James Shaw did not lose his life in consequence of a wound on the left side, which unfortunately—and

Charge to the Jury.

Lord Pitman

I use that word because the doctors even said that it might quite well have not cut the jugular vein—cut the jugular vein, and he died from loss of blood. The question is, what knife caused that wound? Now, James Shaw's first introduction is spoken to by Durie, who says he remembers a young fellow joining the crowd. "—There was a young fellow standing outside the pavement. Q.—Not one of your group? A.—No. Q.—Did he take any part in the conversation of your group?" Now, the conversation at that time was as to whether or not the accused should come out and fight; that is what they were arguing about, and the answer is "Yes." "Q.—Did you know him? A.—No." He heard the accused say that if he had a couple like himself he would come along and redd the corner. "Q.—Does that mean clear up the corner? A.—Yes. Q.—What did this young fellow say? A.—He says to Paddy Carraher, 'You talk like an Englishman,' " and his answer was, "No, I do not," or something like that. Then he said that he and Paddy Carraher started talking. He says, "We did not take any notice of that; it was just a confab," and then they were moved off. And these two kept on arguing until they came to Thistle Street and kept on arguing when they were standing at the street corner. Then he was asked what about, and he said he could not hear the words; they were shouting at one another and talking to one another. Then says James Durie, "My brother told me and Charlie Morgan it is time to get home to bed. Q.—And did you go? A.—Yes, up Thistle Street way. Q.—The three of you? A.—We went straight home, leaving the other three together, that is the accused Patrick Carraher, the fellow Shaw and Peter Howard." Now, those are the three who were left together, and I now come to Peter Howard's evidence of what happened. He gives the same story about Shaw coming up as James Durie gave, and says that when Carraher was asked whether he came from England he said, "What has it got to do with you?" And he says that Shaw was not in the argument with the Duries; he just came walking in and asked Carraher did he come from England, that was all. "Q.—He was not in the argument otherwise? A.—No." Then he goes on to describe how Durie left, saying, "I am going home; it's kind of late." And the three remained at the corner. "A.—I asked Shaw if he was going along the road and he said 'no'. Q.—Did you turn to go along the road? A.—I turned to go. Q.—And did Shaw come with you? A.—No. Q.—Did Shaw remain with the accused? A.—Yes, he remained with Carraher. Q.—Just as you were leaving

Patrick Carraher.

them did you hear anything said between them? A.—Carraher told Shaw to go home and mind his own business, and Shaw wouldn't go away; he said, 'No, I am going to stay here.' Q.—Anything else? A.—No. I just walked on the pavement to go home myself. Q.—Did you look back at all? A.—I just got on the pavement and looked back, and I saw Shaw haudin' his neck. Q.—Did you see anything before that, anything happening? A.—No. Q.—Just tell the ladies and gentlemen of the jury how Shaw was holding his neck? A.—Shaw was haudin' his hand up to his neck, and he was pointing along to Gorbals. . . . Q.—Was he able to say anything? A.—No, he could not speak. Q.—He could not speak, but he was pointing towards Gorbals? A.—Yes." Then he is asked was there anybody else at all near, and the answer is no.

Now, that is very clear evidence which you are entitled to believe if you think Howard was telling the truth. But that evidence is not sufficient in the eyes of the law, because no person can be convicted of a crime on the evidence of one witness alone. That is the law of our country, and therefore the Crown, if they are to get the verdict which they have asked for, have had to lead other evidence, and that, if I may say so, resolves itself into evidence as to what the accused said on later occasions. That is perfectly competent evidence, and perfectly corroborative evidence of Howard's statement, if you believe it. Now, I need not, I think, trouble you with the question as to where exactly the assault was made. The first thing that I think you should satisfy yourselves about is the suggestion by the Crown that the assault was made by the accused. Learned counsel for the defence suggests that it might just as well have been made by either of the Duries or by Howard, but that I think is a somewhat exaggerated suggestion, because they had been gone for five minutes, and there is no suggestion that there was any assault on anybody's part before the Duries went away. The first inkling we have of an assault is Howard's statement that he saw Shaw put his hand to his neck. Nothing was seen, and there is no doubt whatever that the mere fact that he saw Shaw put his hand to his neck proves the fact that he had been wounded, but before you can find the verdict which the Crown have asked for you must be satisfied in the first place that the accused's hand was the hand that did it. Learned counsel for the defence suggested that Mrs. McLaughlan's evidence can be founded on because of what she said with reference to two persons she saw at the Cross. She said, "The

Charge to the Jury.

Lord Pitman

chap with the light suit came forward, and I asked him what was the matter, and he told me they had got him through the jugular vein, and he had given the chap a handkerchief."

Now, of course, in a sense that is not competent evidence at all, because what somebody heard somebody else say is not evidence. But, on the other hand, a person might quite well use an expression like, "Oh, he told me they had got him in the jugular vein," without meaning specifically that more than one person had done it. Nobody suggests two different persons were assaulting him and using a knife. One person did it, and the question is whether or not it was the accused. But I think the suggestion is here that the man who lent the handkerchief and was called a mystery man —I see nothing mysterious in it at all; supposing a man is asked for a handkerchief and he hands over a handkerchief and goes on, he doesn't know the man is dying; all he knows is that he has been asked for a handkerchief. Howard tells us he got a handkerchief from a passing man, and I can see nothing mysterious about it at all. He got the handkerchief and he used the handkerchief in an attempt to stanch the blood, but that does not answer the question as to who struck the blow. Perhaps before I go further I might also tell you that learned counsel for the defence founds upon the fact that Mrs. McLaughlan talks about there being two or three people. Well, if you think that somebody else appeared from the darkness and assaulted James Shaw, or if you think there is any doubt about it, you are bound to give the accused the benefit of that doubt. But up till now all we know is that there was an altercation and an argument going on between the two, and that Howard says there was no one else present at the time. The blow was struck by someone. He inferred, of course, it was the accused, because he was the only person there. The question you really have to decide before saying whether or not the hand of the accused was the hand, is whether or not there is corroboration of Howard's statement. Now that corroboration, if you believe the statement, is the evidence of Mary McCafferty and Robert Howard. The passage has been read to you, but I think it is only right in a case of this kind that you should have it read to you again. The statement of Miss McCafferty is contained in this passage in the evidence, "Q.—You and the accused were left at the Bridgegate while Robert Howard and Kate Docherty went to the police station to see about Peter Howard? A.—Yes. Q.—When you and the accused were standing there did any conversation take place between you? A.—Yes.

I

Patrick Carraher.

Lord Pitman

I asked him was he there when it happened, meaning when th
fellow was injured, and he said, yes, that he had done it. I said t
him, 'You done it?' and he said, yes. I said, 'What for?' and h
says, 'I was arguing with a fellow. He was very cheeky.' I said
'How did you do it?' and he says, 'With a knife,' and he took
knife out of his pocket and showed me it." Now, it was sug
gested in the defence that that had some reference to the firs
charge. The first charge had nothing whatever to do with th
person who was injured. The first charge was a charge of assault
ing James Durie. It is for you to say whether, when she give
this account, the accused was referring to what she was referrin;
to, namely, this serious injury to the man Shaw and the fact tha
they were going towards the police station because Howard hac
been taken there. " 'He was very cheeky,' he says, I said, 'How
did you do it?' and he says, 'With a knife,' and he took out a knif
and showed me it. He took it out of his pocket." She gives
detailed account of the kind of knife it was, "A pocket-knife,
dark pocket-knife." The passage goes on "Do you mean the
handle was dark? A.—Yes. Q.—Did he say whether that wa:
the knife he had done it with? A.—Yes, he told me it was the
knife." Now, of course if you take the view the Crown ask you
to take that is practically a confession by the accused that it wa:
his knife, then I tell you in law there is sufficient evidence corro
borating the evidence of Howard, and in addition to Miss Mc
Cafferty there is Robert Howard who says that when he was going
along Portugal Street the accused Patrick Carraher told him he
had been fighting with a fellow. "Q.—Did he say who the fellow
was? A.—No, he said he had scratched his face with a knife.'
Now, he never was fighting with anyone else except James Shaw.
He could not have been fighting with anybody else. There is nc
suggestion that he was. He had had a quarrel of some kind with
James Shaw and he says he scratched him. Now, it is quite true
that he was referring to something very much less than a murderous assault with a knife. But the answer to that is that this man
was under the influence of drink and really had no notion whatever that he had given such a wound as it turned out to be. And
when he is told that Peter Howard is at the police office he then
comes to himself and says that he would go over and give himself
up and clear Peter's name. That is the expression which he made
use of to Robert Howard. Does not that just mean that it had
come home to him that the assault which he thought was a mere
scratch was a very much more serious matter and he was not

Charge to the Jury.

Lord Pitman

going to allow Howard to suffer because he was the person who had given the scratch and his hand it was that caused the wounds from which James Shaw died?

Now, I am pointing to all this because the first thing you have to determine is whether or not Shaw died in consequence of a wound inflicted by the accused. If you have any doubt about that you are not entitled to find for the Crown, because that is the essential factor. When I say "find for the Crown" I mean find for the Crown under the second charge. The Crown is not entitled to a verdict if you have doubt which is reasonable doubt. On the other hand, if you are satisfied that those two witnesses were referring, and that the accused was referring, when he spoke to them, to an assault of some kind on James Shaw, then you will be entitled, if you believe them, to hold that in fact Shaw died in consequence of wounds inflicted by the accused. That is the first step towards the Crown obtaining a verdict of any kind, but if you have any doubt about that you will find either not guilty or not proven as you choose.

But, ladies and gentlemen, then comes what I think is the most important question with which you have to occupy your mind, and the most difficult question. Is the Crown entitled in the whole circumstances of this case to ask for a verdict of murder? As learned counsel for the defence pointed out to you there must have been many, many murder trials in this court, but I doubt whether there ever has been one in which so little evidence of provocation of any kind has been brought to the jury's notice. It is almost inconceivable that a man who had never met the accused before, and only interferes to tell him that he is an Englishman, should have lost his life in consequence of a quarrel arising out of that. It is too petty for words as the foundation for a charge of murder. And yet the law says that motive or no motive—that never need be proved—if a person uses serious violence with a view to doing serious damage and assaults another man and death results, that is murder. But there are cases in which the crime of murder can be modified to one of culpable homicide depending on what the real attitude of mind of the person charged is towards the person whom he has assaulted.

I ask you to listen very carefully to what I have to say to you now. Murder is constituted by any wilful act causing the destruction of life. It is the malicious or reckless taking away of human life. It is murder if an act by which a life is taken is deliberate or at least committed with the intent to bring about serious bodily

Patrick Carraher.

Lord Pitman

injury. Now, when considering whether the act was done with
the intention to do serious bodily injury you must take the whole
circumstances of the case into account and make up your minds
on that subject. It is a very difficult duty which you are called
upon to perform. You may be disposed to take the view that the
very use of a knife indicates a desire to do serious bodily injury.
On the other hand you may think that the accused had no such
intention. It is for you to make up your mind on the evidence.
I am bound to say I have never heard of a case in which there has
been so little evidence of provocation, and it is usually provocation which results in an intention to do bodily harm. It is tragic
almost to think that a man should have lost his life merely because
he intervened in an altercation between two brothers and a drunk
man as to whether he should have agreed to have what they called
a straight fight. The intervener, James Shaw, butts in, so to speak,
and remarks that the drunk man speaks like an Englishman. You
may take the view, and you are entitled to, that the only explanation of such a happening was the fact that the accused was intoxicated. If you do, I must tell you that it has been laid down by the
Courts in this country that the fact of intoxication may be taken
into view in considering whether an act was done with full
malicious intent or only with culpable recklessness in a minor
degree. The degree of intoxication is of course the determining
factor. If it is such as to preclude the possibility of malicious
intent to do serious injury then a verdict of culpable homicide is
justified. But you must apply your mind to that question, and as
best you can make up your mind to what extent the accused was
really capable of appreciating what he was doing or really had the
intention to do serious bodily injury. I think that comes to this
quite shortly, that you are entitled on one view of the evidence
to acquit a murderer, being of course satisfied that the hand was
the hand of the accused, and return a verdict of culpable homicide.
On the other hand, if you think that the accused deliberately
brought the knife into play to settle his dispute, regardless of the
consequences, and killed Shaw, it is your duty to return a verdict
of murder, a duty from which you should not flinch if that is your
view of the evidence. But that is the question upon which you
have to make up your mind—was the action of the accused
deliberate in the whole circumstances of the case. If you have
any doubt on that matter the accused is entitled to the benefit of
the doubt; that is to say, if you are satisfied beyond reasonable
doubt that the accused's was the hand, but you have doubt as to

Charge to the Jury.

Lord Pitman

his deliberate intention, then it is your duty to return a verdict of culpable homicide.

I shall end as I began by reminding you that the Crown has to prove its case, and it is for you to say whether on the whole evidence, of which you are the judges alone, they have done so, either to the full extent, on which you would return a verdict of murder, or to a partial extent on which you would return a verdict of culpable homicide. I do not think I can say anything more that would help you to decide the question. I have pointed out to you what are the questions upon which the case turns. I need only tell you that you are entitled, if you are not unanimous, to return a verdict by a majority. But I ask you to give your most serious consideration to the questions which you have to consider. I have also to remind you that according to our rules of pleading and the rules under which the charges are brought by the Crown, it is competent when a charge of murder is brought either to have culpable homicide, or, if you take the view, an aggravated assault on the part of the accused; they are minor charges which are covered by the major charge, if that happens to be the view of the jury, remembering always that if you are not satisfied and you have reasonable doubt on either of the charges, you are entitled to return a verdict of not proven.

[The jury retired at 1.10 p.m. and returned at 3.7 p.m.]

LORD PITMAN—I understand the jury want to put a question of some kind?

THE FOREMAN—Yes, my Lord. The jury would like to know what constitutes aggravated assault as a possible verdict, some more information on what exactly constitutes aggravated assault as a possible verdict?

LORD PITMAN—I do not understand what you really want, but what was in my mind when I told you that a conviction of aggravated assault was a possible verdict was a section of an Act of Parliament which in ordinary language means this, that if a person is charged with a serious offence he can be convicted of any lesser offence of the same kind. Therefore it appears to me that there are three characters: there are murder, culpable homicide and aggravated assault; three degrees of assault, one resulting in murder, the other in culpable homicide and the third is merely

119

Patrick Carraher.

assault. That is what was at the back of my mind, but on the other hand if a person commits a serious assault and it results in death, that is culpable homicide.

[The jury again retired and returned at 3.10 p.m.]

Verdict.

THE CLERK OF COURT—Members of the jury, what is your verdict?

THE FOREMAN—Our verdict on the first charge of assault is not guilty; a unanimous verdict. On the second charge our verdict is guilty of culpable homicide, by a majority.

THE CLERK OF COURT—Members of the jury, does this accurately record your verdict:—"The jury unanimously find the panel not guilty under the first charge, and by a majority find him guilty of culpable homicide under the second charge"?

THE FOREMAN—Yes.

MR. WALKER—I move for sentence, and draw your lordship's attention to the one previous conviction mentioned in the indictment.

[Mr. Cameron then spoke in mitigation of sentence.]

Sentence.

LORD PITMAN—Patrick Carraher, the jury have taken a lenient view of this case—because I think their verdict means that they were satisfied that because you were under the influence of drink you had not the deliberate intention that is required in a case of murder. Drink can be founded on in a case of that kind to modify a conviction or a charge, but drink is no excuse whatever for assault resulting in death. The crime of culpable homicide is a very serious one, and the very least punishment that I can inflict is penal servitude for three years.

THE TRIAL

WITHIN THE
HIGH COURT OF JUSTICIARY,
GLASGOW FEBRUARY CIRCUIT

ON

THURSDAY, 28TH FEBRUARY, 1946

Judge Presiding—
LORD RUSSELL

Counsel for the Crown—
MR. DOUGLAS JOHNSTON, Advocate-Depute
MR. K. W. B. MIDDLETON, Advocate

Counsel for the Defence—
MR. J. R. PHILIP, K.C.
MR. H. F. FORD, Advocate

THE CLERK OF COURT—Call the Diet His Majesty's Advocate against Patrick Carraher.

MR. PHILIP—I appear for the accused with Mr. Ford, and the accused adheres to his plea of Not Guilty.

A jury of 15 was then empanelled and sworn.

Indictment.

THE CLERK OF COURT—Patrick Carraher, prisoner in the Prison of Barlinnie, Glasgow, you are Indicted at the instance of the Right Honourable George Reid Thomson, His Majesty's Advocate, and the charge against you is that on 23rd November, 1945, in Taylor Street, Glasgow, near McAslin Street, you did assault John Gordon, junior, 240, Aitken Street, Glasgow, and did stab him on the neck with a wood chisel or other similar instrument and you did murder him, and you have been previously convicted of crime inferring personal violence.

DOUGLAS JOHNSTON, A.D.

Evidence for the Prosecution.

SAMUEL PATON (41), sworn.

Examined by MR. JOHNSTON—I am a detective-sergeant, Eastern Division, City of Glasgow Police, and have 19 years' service. Prior to joining the police force I served an apprenticeship as a draughtsman, and on 26th November, 1945, I was instructed to make a plan of the neighbourhood of Taylor Street and McAslin Street, Glasgow. Production No. 2 is the plan that I prepared, which is drawn to scale and correct, except for a small lane adjoining Canning Place and St. James' Road, which is not shown. The plan shows the area of Glasgow between Parliamentary Road on the north, High Street on the east and Rottenrow on the south. Rottenrow runs roughly east and west, and at the junction of Montrose Street there is a maternity hospital. Continuing along Rottenrow from west to east in the direction of High Street on the south side you pass the junction of North

Patrick Carraher.

S. Paton

Portland Street, Deanside Lane, Hume Street and then Balmano Street. Going along Rottenrow from the maternity hospital on the right side you pass Cathedral Lane, Hopetoun Place and Taylor Street which joins Rottenrow with McAslin Street and Parliamentary Road. Further eastwards we come to Weaver Street, Collins Street, and the Barony Church. Going northwards up Taylor Street from Rottenrow, the first street on the right, that is on the east side, is Gordon Street, then Cathedral Street, then the cross-roads of Taylor Street and St. James' Street, Ronald Street, Parson Street, and McAslin Street. Running parallel with Taylor Street, but further to the east is Stanhope Street and then St. Mungo Street. College Street is off High Street and further south.

Cross-examined by MR. PHILIP—Is there a public-house in Rottenrow named "Thompson's"?—I do not know it by name. There is a public-house in Rottenrow facing Taylor Street, but I could not be sure of the name.

May I take it that you do not know the position of any of the public-houses accurately in that district?—The only one I can be sure about is at the junction of Taylor Street and McAslin Street. That is McFarlane's and is on the south-west corner.

That is not a public-house known as the "Coronation Bar" is it?—I do not know it by that name.

DAVID PHIN (38), sworn.

Examined by MR. JOHNSTON—I am a detective-sergeant in the City of Glasgow Police, and have had 18 years' police service. For the past 13½ years I have been a member of the Fingerprint and Photographic Bureau. On 24th November, 1945, I took certain photographs in the mortuary of the Royal Infirmary, Glasgow, of a man named Gordon whose body was identified in my presence by his brothers. Production No. 3 is a book of two photographs that I took. Photograph No. 1 is a photograph of the head and neck, and Photograph No. 2, the right hand.

Look at Photograph No. 1. You notice a small mark below the ear and above the neck. What is that?—That was an open wound in the neck.

What is the mark on the finger between the nail and the ring on Photograph No. 2?—That was also an open wound on the third finger of the right hand.

Evidence for the Prosecution.

By the Court—When you took these photographs, was the body of which these appear to be photographs a dead body?—It was.

CHARLES GORDON (36), sworn.

Examined by MR. JOHNSTON—I am a plater's helper living at 139, Rhymer Street, Glasgow, and I am a brother of John Gordon. I last saw my brother alive on Monday, 19th November, 1945. On Saturday, 24th November, 1945, I saw my brother's body at the mortuary of the Royal Infirmary, Glasgow, which I attended along with my brothers Joseph and Edward. I recognize photograph No. 1 of Production No. 3 as the back of the head of my brother John.

Cross-examined by MR. PHILIP—Is Rhymer Street where you live in Clydebank?—No, in Townhead.

By the Court—Is your father living?—Yes.
What is his name?—John Gordon.
Was your brother known by any distinguishing name to distinguish him from your father?—No, he was just called John Gordon, junior.

JOHN GORDON (68), senior, sworn.

Examined by MR. JOHNSTON—I live at 240, Aitken Street, Glasgow. John Gordon, junior, was my son. He was born on 29th November, 1905, and had served about 20 years in the Seaforth Highlanders. He served in the late war, was captured at St. Valery, and was released from a prisoner of war camp in 1945.
In November, 1945, was he staying with you on demobilization leave?—Yes, pending discharge.
When did you last see him alive?—At four o'clock in the afternoon of 23rd November.
What was he doing then?—He was in the house all day. My two sons, Joseph and Edward, came up about four o'clock, and he went out with them for a walk. I never saw him alive after that.
Was your son, John Gordon, buried at Dalbeath Cemetery, Parkhead?—That is right.
Look at Labels Nos. 3 and 4. Have you ever seen these before? —Yes, Label No. 3 is John's coat, and Label No. 4 is his cap.

Patrick Carraher.

John Gordon, sen.

Cross-examined by MR. PHILIP—You say that your son John was going out with Edward and Joseph. Were they going to see your son-in-law, Duncan Revie?—No, he didn't say that.

So that if they went to see Duncan Revie they did not tell you that beforehand?—No; I didn't know where he was going. I didn't ask him.

They were in the habit, were they not, of going out with Duncan Revie?—Well, once they left the house I didn't know where they went.

Duncan Revie was a man with no home at that time, was he not?—I know nothing about that.

He was a deserter from the Army and what you call "on the run"?—Yes.

Is it not the case that your sons went out and met him at night and went and visited various pubs?—I know nothing about that.

Which member of your family lives at 139, McAslin Street?—That is Prentice.

Was Duncan Revie's wife living at 139, McAslin Street?—She is there at present.

Have you a daughter, Mrs. Parker?—Yes. She stays in Hinshaw Street, Maryhill, but I cannot tell you the number.

Re-examined by MR. JOHNSTON—Had John Gordon ever been in trouble of any kind?—No; he was 20 years in the Army.

JOSEPH GORDON, sworn.

Examined by MR. JOHNSTON—I am a brother of John Gordon, and am a gunner in the Royal Artillery. When I am at home my address is 240, Aitken Street, Glasgow. My brother had served in the Seaforth Highlanders for $19\frac{1}{2}$ years, was captured at Dunkirk and had been in a prisoner of war camp in Germany until 1945. As far as I know he had never been in trouble with the police. In November, 1945, I was home on leave from Gibraltar.

On 23rd November, 1945, did you and your brother John Gordon go out together?—Yes. We met at the parents' house, 240, Aitken Street, Glasgow; the younger boy, Edward, was also there.

Where did you go to?—We left the house and went to my brother-in-law's, Duncan Revie's, at 139, McAslin Street, where we stayed about five minutes.

Evidence for the Prosecution.

Joseph Gordon

Was Duncan Revie at that time a deserter from the Army?—I believe so, yes.

Where did you go from there?—Went to a public-house, "Coronation Bar" they call it.

You have told us that Duncan Revie's house is in McAslin Street. Between what streets is it in McAslin Street?—I just cannot remember. I have been away a while and just forget the streets.

Is it anywhere near Taylor Street?—Yes, it is the right hand side of Taylor Street. It is about twenty yards along McAslin Street from the junction with Taylor Street.

Whereabouts is the "Coronation Bar"?—Next door to 139; just come out of the close and the public-house is next door.

Did you go into the "Coronation Bar"?—Yes, my brother and myself and Edward; three brothers, also my brother-in-law, Duncan Revie. Four of us went in together. We stayed there till about half-past seven.

When had you gone in?—Gone in there about five o'clock; went in there at five o'clock exact.

How much had you to drink?—Quite a few drinks.

What were you drinking?—Whisky.

Do you know how much John had to drink?—We had the same. We had a round of five or six halfs of whisky, also beer, and we left there.

How much had Duncan Revie to drink?—We had all the same drink.

What sort of state were you in when you left the "Coronation Bar"?—We were all pretty half drunk.

Where did you go from the "Coronation Bar"?—A shop in Rottenrow—Cameron's, they call it. As you go up Taylor Street leaving the "Coronation" it is right up—right opposite in Rottenrow.

Did you go in there?—Yes, all four of us.

That is you, John, Duncan Revie, and Edward?—Yes.

About what time was that?—About half-past seven. We stayed there, as far as I can remember, till about nine o'clock.

How much had you to drink there?—I just cannot remember how much I had there at all.

Do you know how much John had?—I cannot tell you. I lost sight of him.

Do you know how much Duncan Revie or Edward had?—No.

You got into the bar and what happened to you?—Just can't

remember what happened after that; just remember faintly different times. Just remember when we went in the public-house, Cameron's, and remember sitting down at the fire and having a glass of wine and who brought it I couldn't say, but I suppose the other three had the same too. The four of us went in together. I cannot remember much after that, and I don't remember leaving the public-house. I just remember walking down Taylor Street by myself and I remember walking along McAslin Street, but after that I don't remember anything.

When you did start remembering things again where were you?—The first thing I knew I was lying on the floor in Duncan Revie's house. How I got there I cannot say. I should think it would be around eleven o'clock night time or so. I was lying on the floor and I was wakened by a detective and he explained what had happened. I was taken to the police station.

On Saturday, 24th November, 1945, did you attend at the Royal Infirmary mortuary?—Yes.

Did you there identify a body?—Yes, my brother John.

Was that on the morning after the night you and John had spent at the two public-houses you have been speaking of?—Yes.

Look at Label No. 3. Have you ever seen that coat before?—Yes, it is my brother John's.

When did you last see it?—On the night of the 23rd November last my brother John was wearing it in the two bars, in the "Coronation" and in "Cameron's Bar".

Have you seen that cap, Label No. 4, before?—Yes, it is my brother John's. He was wearing it on the 23rd November and the last time I saw it was in Cameron's public-house in Rottenrow.

Do you know a man named Daniel Bonnar?—Yes, I know him pretty well. (Witness identified the witness Daniel Bonnar.)

Did you see him at all on the night of the 23rd?—No, I cannot say I did.

Do you know a man called Patrick Carraher?—No, I don't know him at all, never seen him in my life before.

Cross-examined by MR. PHILIP—Had you been in the Army for a considerable number of years?—Since August, 1940.

Were you just home on short leave?—Twenty-eight days' leave which began on 10th November, 1945.

When you came home you found your brothers John and Edward and Duncan Revie all there?—No, brother John was living with the parents. I was living there myself.

Evidence for the Prosecution.

Joseph Gordon

I suppose you and your brothers and Revie went out a good deal together?—No, I had only seen Duncan Revie once before what happened, and that was the night before.

Was he in hiding?—I could not say. I don't know much about that at all.

You have suggested that Duncan Revie had a house at 139, McAslin Street?—Yes, it originally belongs to a brother of mine.

Had it ever belonged to Duncan Revie at all?—I could not say, I don't know that.

Is it not the fact that Duncan Revie was in hiding as a deserter, and that he was using that house as a port of call?—I could not say anything about that at all. It is none of my business.

You know that he was a deserter?—Yes. Well, I did hear about it when I came home.

On the afternoon of the 23rd when you went out did you tell your father that you were going with your brothers, Edward and John, and Duncan Revie?—Yes.

Was the idea that you would go on to the "Coronation Bar"? —Well, we did not know exactly where we were going.

But you were going out to have a night of it?—Going out to have a drink, yes.

Your father would know that?—Probably would.

You were not just going out for a walk or anything like that? —Well, we went out for a drink, for that purpose.

You reached the "Coronation Bar" at five o'clock; you were there for two and a half hours, and you had at least six glasses of whisky and some beer?—Yes.

You all had the same?—Yes, we all had the same.

Would you agree that even when you left the "Coronation Bar" you were all half-seas over?—Yes.

Indeed, so much so that you have only a very hazy recollection of what happened between seven-thirty and eleven?—Yes.

You do not know whether there was a fight or not during that time?—I never heard anything about that at all.

When you left the "Coronation Bar" did your brother John suggest going to "Cameron's Bar"?—There was somebody suggested it, but I could not say which one it was.

Was it not the case that John was well known in "Cameron's Bar"?—Yes, he was pretty well known.

And it was his idea that you should go and have something more there?—It may have been.

When you got to "Cameron's Bar" do you remember what you

Patrick Carraher.

had?—That is all I can remember. I remember sitting down at the fire in the public-house with a glass of wine.

You remember the first glass, but you do not remember how much more you had after that?—No, I cannot remember much more.

But you were there for two hours or an hour and a half, or do you not remember?—I cannot remember. I might have been there about an hour and a half.

Closing time was nine-thirty, so that you were almost continuously in bars from five until about nine-thirty?—Yes.

And drinking all the time?—Well, I don't know whether we were drinking all the time or not.

As far as you remember?—Yes.

Then when you came to about eleven o'clock, was that because a detective was doing something to you to make you come to? —Yes, I was wakened by a detective.

Was he not giving you something to make you waken up?—I don't know; I cannot remember.

Do you remember being in the company of a man called Keatings that night?—No.

You have no recollection of that at all?—No.

You do not remember being in the company of a sailor who had deserted from the Navy, do you?—No. I remember one chap coming into the public-house during the time I was sitting there and I recognized him. I had been along with him and Duncan Revie drinking the night previous. All I knew him was by the name of John.

Did you know anyone by the name of Joe?—No.

EDWARD GORDON (24), sworn.

Examined by MR. JOHNSTON—I live at 22, Monteith Row, Glasgow, and am a brother of the deceased John Gordon, late of the Seaforth Highlanders. In November, 1945, my brother was on leave and was expecting shortly to be released from the Army.

Did you meet him on a day in November, 1945?—Yes, at my mother's house at 240, Aitken Street. My brother Joseph and my father and mother were also there.

Where did you go to?—We left the house about four o'clock and walked along Duke Street till we came to McAslin Street. My brother John and I stood at the close and Joseph went up for

130

Evidence for the Prosecution.

Edward Gordon

Revie. After about ten minutes he came down and the four of us went into the "Coronation Bar" next door.

Was this house at which you called for Duncan Revie between Taylor Street and Stanhope Street?—Yes, it was No. 139, McAslin Street.

What time did the four of you go into the "Coronation Bar"? —Just about five o'clock. We stayed till about half-past six.

How much had you yourself to drink?—As far as I can remember I had six small whiskies, and three or four pints of beer.

Do you know how much John had?—The same as I had.

When you left about half-past six how many of you were there? —The four of us—John, Joseph, myself and Duncan Revie.

Where did you go to then?—We made up Stanhope Street to Cameron's public-house in Rottenrow.

What did you yourself have to drink there?—Well, the first drink was a glass of wine and a bottle of beer. We all had the same.

At what time did you leave Cameron's public-house?—It was half-past nine when we left it.

When you left it did you leave with the others?—No.

Did you leave alone?—Yes.

When you left were you drunk or sober?—Drunk.

How drunk?—So drunk that I could not walk.

What happened next so far as you remember?—As far as I remember I went up the close next to Cameron's corner. I sat on the stairhead till I felt a little better and I made from there to 139, McAslin Street. When I got up there my brother Joseph was already in the house. Just as I got in Duncan Revie came and told me, "You had better come out, your brother John is on the stair bleeding to death."

When you left Cameron's public-house where was John?—I could not tell you.

Where was Duncan Revie?—I could not tell you.

Where do you last remember seeing John and Duncan Revie? —In Cameron's public-house.

At about what time?—It would be near eight o'clock.

Did they, so far as you recollect, leave Cameron's public-house while you were there?—I could not say.

Now, you told us that you went back to 139, McAslin Street, and found your brother Joseph there. Was Joseph lying on the floor?—Yes.

Was he drunk?—Yes.

Patrick Carraher.

Edward Gordon

What did you do when you got the message from Duncan Revie?—I went down the stair and my brother John was lying on the stair. I asked somebody to go for the doctor. The doctor came and John was taken up to the Royal Infirmary, and we got the verdict that he was dead.

Why did you take him to the Royal Infirmary?—I saw the condition he was in. He was saturated with blood which seemed to be coming from his head and his neck.

When you got to the gatehouse of the Royal Infirmary what happened?—He was taken in to the doctor who examined him and told us he was dead.

On 24th November, 1945, did you attend at the mortuary of the Royal Infirmary?—Yes, I saw the body of my brother John.

Have you seen this coat, Label No. 3, before?—Yes, my brother John had it on on the night of the 23rd November, 1945.

Have you ever seen this cap, Label No. 4, before?—Yes, my brother John had it on that night.

Your brother John was a regular soldier. So far as you know had he ever been in trouble?—No, sir.

Was he a quarrelsome fellow?—No, he was very quiet.

Cross-examined by MR. PHILIP—As regards this particular evening, am I right in thinking that you do not remember anything about your brother John after he went out?—No.

You went to McAslin Street, and you and John stayed at the foot of the close while your brother Joseph went up to get Duncan Revie?—Yes.

Mrs. Revie was living at that house, was she not, but her husband was a deserter and on the run?—Yes.

I suppose he used the house as a port of call?—I suppose so.

And I suppose you and your brother John waited at the foot of the close to see there were no police when Duncan Revie came down?—No.

When you went to the "Coronation Bar" were you not there about seven-thirty?—No.

At any rate, you had six whiskies and three or four pints of beer each at the "Coronation Bar", so when you left there you would be pretty half-seas over?—Yes.

Did not John suggest that you should go on to Cameron's pub? —Yes, it was John's suggestion.

When you went to Cameron's pub at the beginning you had each a round of wine and then some beer?—Yes.

Evidence for the Prosecution.

After that is the position this, that you do not really remember what you had?—No, sir.

But do you remember going to the lavatory at eight o'clock and being sick there until nine-thirty?—Yes.

And then afterwards you were sick again in the close next door to "Cameron's Bar" due to the condition you were in?—Yes.

Is the position just this, that you do not remember very much more until Duncan Revie came and spoke to you at 139, McAslin Street?—Yes, sir.

I think you said that he said that you had better come out, and referred to your brother John?—Yes.

Did you think at first that Duncan Revie was kidding you? —Yes.

Then you went down, and I suppose Duncan Revie was there too?—He came down along with me.

Did some conversation pass between you and Duncan Revie when you were beside John?—Yes.

Did Duncan Revie say anything about Dan Bonnar?—I asked what had happened and he said it was Dan Bonnar.

And he repeated that over and over again?—Yes.

By the COURT—When you went out with Duncan Revie into the close, in what part of the close was your brother John when you first found him?—On the stair head, two stairs up from the close-mouth.

Was that just outside the door on the landing of Mrs. Revie's house?—No, down below.

One stair down?—Yes.

Was John lying on the stone floor on the landing?—He was half-sitting and half-lying on the stair.

Did he appear to be unconscious?—Yes.

JOHN KEATINGS (21), sworn.

Examined by MR. JOHNSTON—I am at present attached to His Majesty's Ship *Victory*, Royal Naval Barracks, Portsmouth. I deserted from my ship on 23rd June, 1945.

Were you running loose in Glasgow until November, 1945? —Yes.

While you were on the run were you staying with the Gordon family?—Yes.

Did you know John Gordon?—Yes, he was in the Seaforths.

133

Patrick Carraher.

J. Keatings

Did you know Edward and Joseph Gordon, and their brother-in-law, Duncan Revie?—Yes.

On 23rd November, 1945, did you meet these four men?—Yes, I met them in Cameron's public-house, Rottenrow, about seven o'clock in the evening.

When you met them were they drunk or sober?—Weren't drunk.

Was John drunk or sober?—He was in between. They all looked much the same to me.

All about in between. Did you have something to drink in Cameron's pub?—Yes.

What did you have to drink?—I don't know.

Were you drunk or sober at this time?—I was sober at that time, but I was drunk when I left the place.

Do you know what John had to drink in Cameron's pub?—No.

Did you join the party?—Yes; I spent the evening with them in Cameron's pub till closing time at nine-thirty.

At closing time did you leave?—Yes.

Who left?—Me and Duncan Revie. I think John had already gone outside.

Did you see him when you got outside?—No.

Did you see Joseph or Edward?—No.

What happened when you and Duncan Revie went outside Cameron's pub?—Had a fight outside the pub with Daniel Bonnar.

Did you know Daniel Bonnar?—No, I had never seen him before.

How do you know it was Daniel Bonnar you had a fight with then?—Just heard his name.

You see that man beside the macer. (Witness Daniel Bonnar brought into court.) Have you ever seen him before?—No.

Tell me about the fight?—Wasn't a fight at all. Just ran after him.

After whom?—Daniel Bonnar, that man that just came in.

You just told me that you had never seen that man before?—No, I know, but that is what I got told down at the police office.

I want you to forget all you were told at the police office or anything. You say you had a fight outside the "Coronation Bar". Do you remember with whom you were fighting?—No.

Could you recognize the man again?—No.

Tell me about the fight. You came outside the "Coronation Bar"?—Cameron's pub it was.

I beg your pardon. What happened then?—I just came outside and I remember running down the road after someone.

Evidence for the Prosecution.

J. Keatings

Why did you run down the road after someone?—I don't know. Must have been doing something to me otherwise I wouldn't have run after him.

Was the road you were running down Rottenrow?—Yes, towards the High Street.

Are you quite sure of that?—Yes.

Were you running alone or was someone running with you? —Duncan Revie was running with me.

Are you quite sure of that?—Yes.

Were both of you running after this man you are unable to identify?—Yes.

Were you dressed that night in civvies?—Yes.

After you had been chasing this unknown person down Rotten-row, what happened then?—My memory is blank. I don't remember what happened. The next thing I wakened up was in the Central Police Office getting my head done. I don't know what time that was.

When you woke up at the Central Police Office were you suffering from anything besides a hangover?—No; well, I felt bruised a bit on my face.

At the present moment you are in Barlinnie Prison?—Yes.

That is the result of being a deserter?—No.

Why are you there?—I don't know. Well, on a charge of breach of the peace.

Cross-examined by Mr. Philip—When you say you are in Bar-linnie Prison on a charge of breach of the peace, do you mean that you have been convicted of breach of the peace? You are, in other words, in prison?—Yes.

And the breach of the peace was the fight outside Cameron's pub on 23rd November?—Yes.

When you said you were at the Victory Barracks, Portsmouth, were they detention barracks?—No.

You have been in detention barracks since because you were apprehended as a deserter?—Yes.

At the time of 23rd November you were on the run in Glasgow hiding from the police?—Yes.

And so was Duncan Revie?—Yes.

Were you going about together a good deal and with the Gordons?—Yes.

And drinking each night together?—Hadn't money to drink.

But you were drinking a certain amount, were you not?—Yes.

Patrick Carraher.

J. Keatings

And John and his brothers would be in the party too?—Yes.

On this particular evening before you joined John and his brothers and Duncan Revie, I suppose you had had some drink first yourself?—No.

Was it what you had in "Cameron's Bar" that made you drunk?—Yes.

Had the others the same as that?—Yes.

Have you any clear recollection of what you had in "Cameron's Bar"?—No. I was drinking beer.

Whatever it was you had it was enough to make you all drunk?—Yes.

When you met the other four, Revie and the three Gordons, would you describe them as half-seas over already?—Yes.

Is your recollection of the fight which took place outside "Cameron's Bar" rather uncertain?—Uncertain.

You think that John went out first?—I think so.

Do you think a fight was going on before you arrived?—No.

And you joined in?—I don't know. I really don't know what happened outside.

I am suggesting to you that the fight was begun either by John or by you, and then that you chased another man along Rottenrow towards the High Street?—I never saw John Gordon outside the pub at all. In fact, I don't think he had anything to do with the fight.

He did go out first?—I couldn't really tell you what happened. I remember being in a fight myself and chasing this other man.

And if you got that other man you were meaning to give him something pretty serious?—With my hands? Only running along with my hands; had my jacket off.

Do you remember if the other man lost his jacket in his flight?—No.

You do not remember who the other man was at all?—No.

Did you say something was told you at the police station?—After questioning. I got questioned at the police station about him.

Were the police annoyed that you could not recognize this man?—I don't know.

Did they tell you that the man was Dan Bonnar?—Yes.

Did they say something like this, "You can take it from us that he was Dan Bonnar"?—I couldn't actually tell you what happened. I know it was Dan Bonnar.

And after what happened did you find that you had your upper

136

Evidence for the Prosecution.

J. Keatings

lip swollen and your nose skinned and all your knuckles on both hands damaged?—Yes.

But you don't remember how that happened?—No.

Re-examined by MR. JOHNSTON—You have told my friend that you were out for a fight that night after you came out of "Cameron's Bar"?—Yes, but the other man must have started it otherwise I wouldn't have looked for it.

Had you any weapon?—No, I don't carry weapons.

Just your two fists?—Yes.

You found that quite good enough?—Always do.

DUNCAN REVIE (25), sworn.

Examined by MR. JOHNSTON—Are you a private in the R.A.S.C.? —Yes.

Are you at present at Barlinnie Prison?—Yes, for breach of the peace.

Was it arising out of a fight you had on 23rd November, 1945? —Yes.

In November, 1945, were you a deserter from the Army, and had you been a deserter for some time?—Yes.

Are you married to a sister of the deceased, John Gordon? —Yes.

Where was she living at that time?—139, McAslin Street. I visited her there from time to time.

On 23rd November, 1945, were you at 139, McAslin Street? —Yes.

Some time in the late afternoon did some of the Gordons come and call on you?—Yes, Joseph Gordon came up to the house and I went down to the closemouth and met John and Edward. The four of us went to the "Coronation Bar" about five o'clock and remained there till near seven. We had a few halfs of whisky and a couple of bottles of beer.

Where did you go when you left the "Coronation Bar"?—We went up to Cameron's pub about seven o'clock and stayed there till about a quarter to nine or so, nine o'clock. I had a few drinks there also. We were drinking beer.

Were you drinking wine?—Yes.

And spirits?—No.

Were you all drinking about the same quantity?—Yes, pretty well level.

Patrick Carraher.

D. Revie

Do you remember a man Keatings coming in?—Yes.

He is a sailor; had you known him for some time?—Yes, I knew him.

He was on the run from the Royal Navy?—Yes.

Did all five of you remain together the whole evening?—Yes.

Who was the first to leave so far as you can recollect?—Eddie and Joseph; they must suddenly have felt sick. I would say they left half an hour before us.

So that left John Gordon, Keatings and yourself in the pub. Did you three all leave together, or what happened?—Well, we walked out at the back of one another. John left first.

Were you drunk or sober when you left?—I had a good drink in me.

Were you able to walk?—Yes.

Did you know what you were doing?—Yes.

What happened when you got outside?—Bonnar came up and challenged us outside the pub to fight.

Whom do you mean by us?—The three of us, John Gordon, Keatings and myself.

Where were you standing?—Just outside the public-house door on the pavement. Bonnar was in the street.

How did he challenge you?—He came running at the three of us and wanted to fight us.

From which direction did he come running?—He came straight across facing the pub. He was shouting, "Come on." He wanted to fight us and was using bad language.

What did John Gordon do?—He never did anything. He remained standing on the pavement.

What did Keatings do?—Well, naturally you are going to fight, aren't you?

Listen to my question. What did Keatings do?—He took his jacket off, and moved over beside us. Bonnar ran away down Rottenrow.

Were any blows struck?—No, he made to make a blow at one of us but he never hit us. I went to fight back just the same.

You have told us that you, Keatings and John Gordon were standing on the pavement outside Cameron's pub, and that Bonnar came up and challenged you to fight. What did you do?——Well, he made a blow at my good-brother John Gordon, and I went to defend him. I went to fight with him. He took to his heels and ran down Rottenrow, and Keatings and I ran after him.

Evidence for the Prosecution.

D. Revie

Did Bonnar ever hit John Gordon?—No.

Did John Gordon ever hit Bonnar?—No.

Did you catch up with him?—Yes.

What happened when you caught up with him?—Well, he had a weapon in his hand and stood in the street, and we never went near him.

What sort of a weapon did Bonnar have?—It was a hatchet.

So you and Keatings saw that and you stopped?—Yes.

Where was John Gordon by this time?—He was standing in the Rottenrow facing Cameron's—just outside Cameron's pub.

What happened then?—Well, he ran down the High Street and Keatings and I went back up Rottenrow.

Did you meet John Gordon there?—Yes. John Gordon and I went down Taylor Street. Where Keatings went I do not know; I didn't see him again that night.

You walked down Taylor Street. Where were you going to go to?—Up to my wife's house at 139, McAslin Street.

What happened then?—We walked down Taylor Street and came to the junction of McAslin Street, and Bonnar and Carraher dived down on the two of us.

By the COURT—You mean two men, of whom one was Bonnar and the other a man called Carraher?—Yes.

Dived down on you?—Yes.

What do you mean by that?—They dived out of a close at us.

You mean they rushed out of a close towards you?—Yes.

Where was the close?—In Taylor Street.

You were still going up Taylor Street just coming to the corner of McAslin Street?—Yes.

Examination continued—You say there were two men, one was Bonnar and the other you have called Carraher. Do you see the second of these two men here to-day?—Yes, in the dock.

Have you ever seen that man? (Witness Bonnar brought into Court.)—Yes, that is Daniel Bonnar.

Had you known them before this evening, 23rd November? —Yes.

You have told his lordship that these two men jumped out of a close in Taylor Street near the junction of Taylor Street and McAslin Street. What happened?—Well, Bonnar dived at me and Carraher dived at my good-brother, John Gordon. Bonnar was

Patrick Carraher.

fighting with me and Carraher had a hold of the good-brother. I saw Carraher's hand up.

You say you saw something in his hand?—Yes. I could not make out what it was.

Look at Labels Nos. 1 and 2. Might the thing which you saw in Carraher's hand possibly have been that?—It could have been.

Which hand was it in?—In his right hand.

By the COURT—Just put yourself into the position with your hand as you remember the hand of Carraher when you say he was holding something. Was his right arm outstretched and was his hand on a level about his shoulder?—Yes. (Witness demonstrates.)

Examination continued—Where was John Gordon?—He was standing at the corner of McAslin Street.

How far away was Carraher from him when you saw this?— The two of them were together. They were just next to one another.

Were they facing one another?—No. John Gordon had his back to Carraher.

By the COURT—What distance separated the two men when you have described Carraher holding up his hand at shoulder level with you thinking something in it? What distance separated him from John Gordon at that moment?—About a yard, I think.

Examination continued—Did you see what Carraher did with his right hand?—No, sir.

What happened after that?—I ran after Bonnar after that down McAslin Street towards Murray Street.

How far did you chase him down McAslin Street?—I ran half way near Murray Street and then I turned back.

Where did you come back to?—To the corner of Taylor Street.

Did you see anyone in Taylor Street?—I saw John Gordon. He was staggering into McAslin Street.

Did you see Carraher?—No.

Why was John Gordon staggering?—There was a wound on the left side of his neck.

What happened then?—I carried him to 139, McAslin Street, and took him up one or two flights of stairs. I then went to the house where my wife was living at that address and roused the other two Gordons who were there, and brought them down to

Evidence for the Prosecution.

D. Revie

where John Gordon was. I took John Gordon down to a taxi and then to the Royal Infirmary. When we got to the Royal Infirmary he was examined and I was told he was dead.

Was there any blood coming from this wound in John Gordon's head?—Yes.

Was it coming from him when you helped him down from Taylor Street into McAslin Street?—Yes.

Was John Gordon wearing this coat, Label No. 3, that night? —Yes.

Are there a number of marks on the coat?—Yes, they are down the left-hand side of the coat, caused by the wound in his neck.

Have you seen this cap, Label No. 4, before?—Yes, the cap John Gordon was wearing that night. There are marks inside it.

Cross-examined by Mr. PHILIP—You were a deserter from the Army from August, 1945, until you were re-apprehended in February of this year?—Yes.

Did you become a deserter through breaking out of the detention barracks at Northallerton in August, 1945?—Yes.

Were you under detention at that time for desertion?—Yes.

So that you had had a previous period of desertion. How long did you desert on the previous occasion?—Once.

Have you been in the hands of the police for crimes of violence? —No.

First of all, you went to the "Coronation Bar", you were there from about five to seven o'clock and you all had about half a dozen whiskies and some beer. Were all of you half-seas over?—Yes.

Then, at John Gordon's suggestion did you go on to "Cameron's Bar"?—Not yet.

I think that he was well known there?—Yes.

Were you hoping to get more drinks there?—Yes.

I suppose you had been going about with John a good deal before visiting various pubs in the neighbourhood?—Yes.

You, of course, were on the run and could only call where your wife was living at odd intervals?—Yes.

And you met John and his brother there, did you, on various occasions and went out spending the evening drinking?—Yes.

That was quite a regular occupation in the evening?—Yes.

At Cameron's pub you had some wine and some beer; may I take it that as regards the later part of your stay in Cameron's pub you have not a very clear recollection at all?—Well, I could mind what I was doing.

141

Patrick Carraher.

D. Revie

Do you remember what you did drink in "Cameron's Bar"?
—Yes.

Do you remember when Edward left you?—I know he left
about half an hour before us.

Is it not the case that Edward spent an hour and a half in the
lavatory of "Cameron's Bar"?—Yes.

When do you say Keatings came?—About a quarter past
seven.

You say that of the three of you that were left, John went out
first, then you, and then Keatings?—Yes.

Do you remember when you got outside Keatings challenging
anyone to fight him?—No.

May that have happened?—I could not tell you.

I suggest to you that Keatings did challenge everyone and in
particular a man called Bonnar, to fight?—I don't mind of that.

And I suggest to you also that John made for Bonnar?—John
Gordon never made for Bonnar at all.

Is the fact this, that you just do not remember very much about
what took place?—I can remember quite well.

Do you remember if Bonnar had something in his hand in the
fight?—Yes, it was a hatchet.

I suggest to you that Bonnar had no hatchet at that point. Is it
not the case that at that time you thought he had something more
like a file?—Maybe I did.

By the COURT—Maybe you did see Bonnar with the file—is that
what you say?—Yes.

Cross-examination continued—Do you admit you have said that
already and said nothing about a hatchet?—Yes.

Well, why are you changing your story now?—If you say it was
a file, I say it was a hatchet.

Is that your evidence?—Yes.

I put it to you that this fight outside "Cameron's Bar" began
through Keatings, you and John Gordon making the attack?
—No, we never made any attack at all.

Then you chased Bonnar away?—Yes.

You had not much difficulty in chasing Bonnar away on most
occasions, is that not so?—No, he ran away.

You were more than a match for Bonnar?—I do not know.

You chased him again later the same evening?—Yes.

Now, later on you came up Taylor Street with John, and when

Evidence for the Prosecution.

D. Revie

you got to the corner of McAslin Street and Taylor Street do you say you saw other men?—Yes, I saw two.

May there have been another man?—There may have been, but I never saw him.

It is a very dark corner?—Yes.

The corner of McAslin Street and Taylor Street is particularly badly lighted, is it not?—Well, I would not say that. You can see all right.

It was a late November night?—Yes.

Is it not the position that you and John were walking on the pavement?—No, walking in the centre of the street.

And that some other men came down the street?—No.

Is it not the case that some other men passed you and they spoke to you after they had passed?—No.

Do you not remember someone passing you and then calling out to you "John" or calling out to you "Gordon", and John recognized him in the passing?—No.

When you saw Bonnar he was the man that you had been chasing before. Did you and John not set out to chase him again and finish what you had attempted to do before?—No.

Was Bonnar carrying anything?—Yes, a hatchet.

Do you remember anyone saying, "Put a hatchet on him, Joe"? —No.

May that have been said?—No.

Were your whole energies taken up with fighting Bonnar?— Yes.

Did John Gordon not come and join in?—No.

I suggest to you that when you are fighting another man who has a hatchet in his hand you have very little time to look round and think about things?—Well, there was not much time in it.

And I put it to you that you have no accurate recollection of what happened to John Gordon at all?—How do you make that out?

By the COURT—That is not the case anyway. Is that what you mean? You have a recollection?—Yes.

And you have told us to the best of your belief what passed? —Yes.

Cross-examination continued—You chased Bonnar?—Yes.

And threw things at him?—No.

Kicked him?—I made a kick, but I never kicked him.

Patrick Carraher.

D. Revie

Is it not the case that you and John Gordon set on the other two and tried to kick them?—No.

Had you not tried to kick Bonnar during the previous fight down at "Cameron's Bar"?—I made a kick at him, but I never kicked him.

I put it to you that your method of attack on both occasions was to try to kick him?—I had to defend myself, hadn't I?

I suggest to you it was you who began any fight?—No, I never began any fight at all; was not looking for fighting.

Do you remember when you chased Bonnar that Carraher was in front of Bonnar?—No.

Do you remember seeing Carraher at all?—Yes, I remember seeing Carraher, but he was not in front of Bonnar when I was chasing him.

Eventually you came back to Taylor Street. Did you not see another man standing about there?—No.

Do you know a man called Watt?—No, I don't know Watt.

May it have been that there was some man unknown to you who was taking part in any fight that there was?—No, I never saw any other man fight.

Eventually you took John up to the stairhead at No. 139, McAslin Street, and went to get Edward down who thought you were kidding him. Eventually he did come down, and did you then tell him that it was Dan Bonnar?—Yes, been fighting.

Is it not the case that Edward asked what was the explanation of this, and you said repeatedly it was Dan Bonnar?—Was the cause of it.

You have no knowledge of what the other man had in his hand at the time of the fight?—No.

Is it not the case that before you met these other men they had come round the corner of McAslin Street into Taylor Street?—No, out of a close.

I am suggesting to you that they had come round the corner of McAslin Street and not out of a close?—No, they came out of a close.

Re-examined by Mr. Johnston—You have told my friend that you told Edward Gordon that Bonnar was the cause of it. What did you mean when you said these words?—He was the cause of the fight. What I mean is it would never have happened only for him.

My friend has suggested that when you were coming up Taylor

Evidence for the Prosecution.

D. Revie

Street three men approached you. Were there two or three men?
—Only two men, Carraher and Bonnar.

Have you any doubt about that?—I have no doubt.

Where did they come from?—Out of a close in Taylor Street.

Did they walk out?—No, they ran out of it towards the two of us.

Who did Bonnar run at?—Me.

Who did Carraher run at?—John Gordon.

You have told us that you were fighting Bonnar. How far away were you from John Gordon?—At the other corner.

Did John Gordon ever join in your fight with Bonnar?—No.

What was John Gordon doing?—He was not doing anything.

Did you ever see him hit Carraher?—No.

What was Carraher doing?—Just as I told you he was doing.

You have told us you saw Carraher's arm raised and that he had something in his right hand. Did you see Carraher strike any blow?—No.

You saw all this while you were still fighting with Bonnar?—Yes.

Did you soon get the better of Bonnar?—He got the better of me.

How long did the fight with Bonnar go on?—Just a couple of minutes; less than that. He just struck me and that was all that was in it.

Did you fall to the ground?—No, I was standing.

After he struck you what happened?—He ran away and I chased him.

Where was John Gordon when you started pursuing Bonnar?—He was staggering.

You saw him staggering before you started to chase Bonnar?—I just ran half-way down and back up again.

I want to get this quite clear. Bonnar hit you, and you started to chase him. At the moment you started to chase Bonnar where was John Gordon?—Staggering in the street.

Where about was Carraher?—I never saw him then.

Did you ever see him after the moment that he was standing beside John Gordon with his (Carraher's) arm raised?—No.

My friend suggests that Carraher was running down McAslin Street towards Murray Street in front of Bonnar?—He may have been.

Did you see him?—No.

Patrick Carraher.

D. Revie

What time passed between you starting to chase Bonnar and the time you got back to John Gordon?—A matter of seconds.

How many yards did you run in pursuit of Bonnar?—About 20 yards down McAslin Street and back.

How far had John Gordon moved in that interval of time? —From the corner of Taylor Street and McAslin Street right out to the centre of the street.

If you come up Taylor Street from Rottenrow into McAslin Street there is a grocer's shop on the corner there?—Yes.

Where was he from that grocer's shop?—About ten yards I should think.

By the COURT—Is that on the right-hand side of Taylor Street as you come up or on the left-hand side?—The left-hand side as you go down.

Re-examination continued—When the fight was on between you and Bonnar where was John Gordon standing?—Right at the corner of the street just next the grocer's shop.

Was he on the same pavement as the grocer's shop?—He wasn't on the pavement, he was on the street.

Taylor Street?—Yes.

Then he had not got into McAslin Street yet?—No.

When you came back after having chased Bonnar where was John Gordon?—In the centre of McAslin Street.

Bonnar struck you with a weapon?—Yes.

What was that weapon, so far as you know?—A hatchet.

What part of the hatchet did he strike you with?—The blunt end of it.

The hammerhead of the hatchet?—Yes.

Not the cutting edge?—No.

So far as you know, had Bonnar any other weapon in his hand that night?—No.

By the COURT—When you described how two men dived out at you and John as you came up Taylor Street and were approaching the corner of McAslin Street, can you tell us on which side was the close from which they came? Was the close on the right-hand side or the left-hand side as you go up Taylor Street to McAslin Street?—A close on the right-hand side.

Was that close situated far from the corner of Taylor Street and McAslin Street?—No, close to the corner.

146

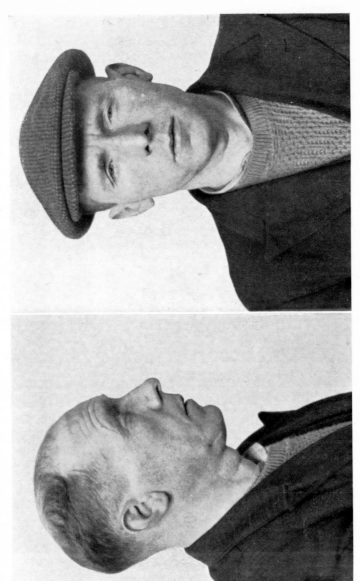

PATRICK CARRAHER IN 1945

Evidence for the Prosecution.

ADAM McDONALD (52), sworn.

Examined by MR. MIDDLETON—I am a painter and live at 130, Keppochhill Road, Glasgow. On Friday, 23rd November last, I went to visit my sister-in-law who lives at 99, McAslin Street. Before going to her house I went into a public-house in McAslin Street near the corner of Taylor Street. It may have been the "Coronation Bar", but it was the first time I had been in it. There I met another painter whom I know called Willie Huie. After leaving the public-house Huie and I stood at the grocer's shop at the corner of Taylor Street and McAslin Street, speaking together. This was about nine-thirty, and we stood talking for about quarter of an hour.

Do you remember some noise?—No, I heard no noise, but I heard talking. That was the first experience I had.

Will you please tell the members of the jury what you can remember happening when you heard that noise of talking?—The first thing I heard of it was I heard a voice shouting, "Put the hatchet on him, Joe." My back was turned to the individual who had said that. He was standing in the middle of Taylor Street. The next thing I heard was, "After him, Harry." When I turned round the person who had been wounded came right forward to me. I took him by the arm. I did not think he was so bad. I saw the wound in the neck. I saw blood and I said, "Come on, chum, I will take you to the Royal Infirmary."

When you saw the man coming towards you, did you see only one man?—No, when I turned round I saw three men running away, running towards the town. It gave me the impression that two were chasing some other man.

You saw four men altogether?—Yes.

As far as you could see was there any other man or any other person except these four about?—No.

When you saw the man coming towards you where was he? —He came right across Taylor Street towards where I was standing at the corner. He was only a matter of ten yards from me, and he came walking towards me.

By the COURT—When you first saw the man approaching you he was coming from where?—From the middle of the cross-roads of Taylor Street and McAslin Street.

You were standing on the pavement at the corner which was nearest to the public-house you had come out of?—Yes.

Patrick Carraher.

A. McDonald

Examination continued—In which street were the three other men you mentioned running away?—They ran westwards away from me down McAslin Street towards Murray Street and the town.

Could you see who they were? Could you see them clearly enough to be able to recognize the three men again?—No.

Where did the voices appear to come from that you heard?—From the middle of Taylor Street.

This was just before you saw the man running away and another man coming towards you?—Yes.

When the man came towards you did you see something?—Yes, blood was coming from the wound in his neck. I took him by the arm and said, "Come on, and I will help you up to the Royal Infirmary." Just at that moment a sailor chap came across the street to give me a help with him. When he saw the blood coming from him he told me to hold him and he would 'phone for the ambulance. He walked so far to the foot of Stanhope Street and he dropped there. We helped him so far and he dropped at the foot of Stanhope Street.

Then you went away did you?—Yes.

Cross-examined by Mr. Philip—Before you heard this shout you did not know what had taken place at all?—No.

When you heard the shout did you turn round at once?—Not at the first shout. At the second shout when I heard, "After him, Harry", I turned round.

Were they just pretty close together?—Yes.

When you looked round the man who came towards you was, as I understand it, at the very head of Taylor Street just where it joins McAslin Street?—Yes, at the junction of McAslin Street and Taylor Street.

He was walking eastwards towards the pavement on which you were standing and the other man would be close, but running away?—That is quite correct.

By the Court—You said that you walked with the injured man as far as the corner of Stanhope Street. Did anyone else join you?—Yes, this sailor chap joined me, but he left the man with me to get an ambulance.

After the sailor had joined you and then gone away, did somebody else join you?—Well, quite a few collected then after the man had dropped at the corner of Stanhope Street.

A few came round the man at once?—Yes, including someone who knew him.

148

Evidence for the Prosecution.

WILLIAM HUIE (61), sworn.

Examined by MR. JOHNSTON—I am a painter and live at 93, Taylor Street, Glasgow. On Friday, 23rd November last, I was standing with a friend of mine called McDonald about 9.30 p.m. on the pavement at the corner of Taylor Street and McAslin Street.

Did you hear something?—I heard a scuffle of feet. Then I saw an injured man coming forward from the other side of McAslin Street towards us. That was the first time I had seen him. There was blood on his coat.

Did you see anybody else?—I saw two men running in different directions.

Which direction were they running in?—One was running in McAslin Street towards me and the other away from me.

You saw these two men and the man who was walking across the street towards you. Did you see anyone else?—No.

Do you know who any of these three men were?—No.

Did you hear anything else?—I heard a voice say, "Get him, Harry."

Are you sure of the words?—Yes. Then another voice said, "You did it."

Do you know who it was that was speaking?—No.

Was it one of the three men you have mentioned, or two of the three men?—I could not say.

Was that the moment you first saw the men running away, or immediately after? Was it after you heard the scuffling of feet?—Yes.

Did you see anything more of the two men you say were running in different directions?—No.

What about the third man, the injured man?—I walked to the other side of the street and went home. I do not know what happened to him.

Cross-examined by MR. PHILIP—Of the two men you saw running, one was running westwards from Taylor Street along McAslin Street, and the other man was running eastwards along McAslin Street?—Yes.

RODERICK MCLEAN JOHNSTONE (44), sworn.

Examined by MR. JOHNSTON—I am chargehand of the public-house occupied by Mrs. Ford at 108, Rottenrow, Glasgow, and I

Patrick Carraher.

R. M. Johnstone

live at 117, Petershill Road. The public-house is on the opposite side of Rottenrow from the Maternity Hospital. Going from the High Street up Rottenrow it is on the right-hand side about 200 yards before the maternity hospital. It is between Taylor Street and Hopetoun Place, and about 100 yards from Cameron's pub on the opposite side of Rottenrow.

Do you remember the evening of Friday, 23rd November, 1945? —Yes. There were a number of people in the public-house.

Do you see anyone here to-day who was in that public-house that night?—Yes, the accused in the dock.

Do you know a man Daniel Bonnar?—Yes.

Was he there that night with anyone?—Well, I just cannot remember whether he was with anyone or not, but he was in certainly that night.

Was Carraher with anyone?—He was in that night too. When you are all together it is a family trade. They all know one another.

Were Carraher and Bonnar together?—Yes, I believe they were.

What time did they arrive in your public-house?—I just couldn't say for sure. I would say maybe round about seven o'clock, and as far as I can remember they were both there until ten past or quarter past nine.

Do you remember who left first, Carraher or Bonnar?—I could not just say. I was clearing the shop out at the time, and they were all going down together. They left about the same time.

Was Carraher drunk or sober?—Sober.

Was Bonnar drunk or sober?—Sober.

Cross-examined by MR. PHILIP—Were there a good number of people in the public-house that night?—Yes.

The public-house is just opposite the entrance to Balmano Street, is it not?—Yes.

I suppose you don't profess to recollect what everyone had to drink that night, and all the people who were there?—Oh, no. Of course, there are two or three waiters.

And you cannot say what Carraher and Bonnar had had before they came there?—No, definitely not.

Do you remember whether there was a man called Watt there? —He was in that night. I just could not tell when he came in.

They would all be sitting about in the pub, or were they at the bar?—Standing about the bar.

I suppose you were not paying very much attention to their

150

Evidence for the Prosecution.

R. M. Johnstone

condition and one thing and another?—I would not just say that. If they are getting a little too much to drink we usually try to get them out.

So far as you could judge from appearances you thought they had not had too much drink to put them out?—That is correct.

That was the only concern you had about whether people were drunk or sober?—I would say well, sober, anyway, but as I say when a person to me as I think is getting a little intoxicated I get them out right away if I thought they were getting that way. You try to keep everyone as sober as you possibly can.

Surely you try to sell as much liquor as you possibly can and then begin putting them out if they get troublesome?—Of course, you sell as much liquor as you can but you have got to conduct the premises as best you can also.

NEIL BRUCE CAMPBELL (17), sworn.

Examined by MR. JOHNSTON—I live at 10, Grafton Square, Glasgow and am now in the Marines. On 23rd November last I was standing at ten o'clock on the corner of Taylor Street and Ronald Street with a man called John Stewart. Ronald Street is the next street to McAslin Street and is about 60 yards from the corner of McAslin Street and Taylor Street.

Did you hear or see something?—Saw them fighting in the street.

Where was the fight?—Corner of Taylor Street and McAslin Street.

How many men were engaged in the fight?—About four. I never saw any more than four.

Do you know who the four men were?—No.

What were they doing to each other, these four men, could you say?—Well, one of the men tried to kick another man and he ran away out into the street off the pavement, and then I saw another man come over and it looked to me as if he was punching him. I saw four men in the street. They were on the pavement, one tried to kick another man, and the one who was trying to kick when he was trying to kick the other fellow this fellow ran away out into the middle of the street, and the other chap went over and it looked to me as if he had punched him.

What was the third man trying to do?—It looked to me as if he had punched the other chap.

Which one, the second one or the first one?—The fourth one.

151

Patrick Carraher.

N. B. Campbell

When you say punched what exactly do you mean by that? Do you mean with his fists?—That is what it looked like to me.

You could not say whether he had anything in his hand or not, could you?—No.

Why did you think that the third man had punched the fourth man?—Because I saw him punching him.

What did the man who was punched do?—Fell immediately.

What about the other three men?—Well, the fellow that punched this other chap started to run down McAslin Street towards St. James' Road.

That is, he started to run west, to your left as you were looking up?—Yes.

That is the man who did the punching. What about the other men. Did they disappear?—Ran down McAslin Street after this man.

That leaves two other men. What did they do?—Well, one went over to see the chap on the ground and then he ran down the street after the other two.

What happened to the man who was on the ground?—When we got down to the chap he was lifted off the ground and was standing in the corner. He was bleeding from the neck.

What happened then?—Told him he had better to go up to the Infirmary and he never answered me.

Did two other men come forward?—Yes. They got hold of the injured man and took him to the Royal Infirmary.

You stayed where you were about the junction of the streets. Did somebody else appear on the scene then?—Yes, the chap that had chased the other two came back again.

How do you know it was the chap that chased the other two?— Well, I took it to be that because he was running up the road and he said where was that chap.

Do you know who the man was that came back?—No.

If you saw him now would you know him?—Yes.

Look at that man. (Witness Duncan Revie brought into court.) Have you ever seen him before?—Yes, I saw him that night at the corner of Taylor Street and McAslin Street. He was the one that chased the other two down McAslin Street.

He asked where they had taken the other man. Did you see him subsequently?—Yes, he ran up round Stanhope Street after the two men who had taken the other fellow away. A minute or two after that he came round again carrying the injured man on his shoulder. He took him up a close in McAslin Street.

Evidence for the Prosecution.

N. B. Campbell

Did you get hold of a taxi?—Yes. The taxi stopped at the close and I went to the close to get the man who was injured. He was lying on the stairs two stories up, and I took him downstairs and put him in the taxi.

Together with that man who was just brought into court?—Yes.

Apart from the man you have just identified you were not able to identify any of the four men who took part in that struggle?—No.

Cross-examined by Mr. PHILIP—Was the first thing that you saw one man trying to kick another one?—Yes.

Had anything been going on before that?—I never noticed it.

You were some 60 yards away. May it have been that there was something going on before you turned round and looked?—No, I was facing down that way.

So that the first thing you saw was one man trying to kick another and the other man retreating out on to the street?—Yes.

Then after you saw that, did one man try to run out and help the man who was being kicked?—I don't know anything about that.

Do you remember any man running east along McAslin Street?—No.

May there have been a man running east along McAslin Street?—I don't think so.

We have had evidence to the effect that there was a man who ran east along McAslin Street. Do you disagree with that?—I don't disagree; I never saw anyone running east.

There may have been a man but you did not see him?—There may have been.

As regards the man who ran out on to the street and attempted to kick the other man did anyone run to the help of the man who was being kicked?—No.

The man who went out on to the street and tried to kick the other man was the man whom you have identified?—Yes.

And all these men were out on the street or on the edge of the pavement?—Well, the one that was being kicked and the one that was kicking were out on the street.

The others were quite close to you?—Yes.

You did not see anyone running out of a close or anything like that?—No.

Is not the position this, that you saw one man going forward to a man on the pavement and then another man run to the pavement as well?—No, I do not remember that.

Re-examined by MR. MIDDLETON—What was it that first called your attention to this fight or scuffle?—I think it was the noise of shouting.

Can you remember anything that was said?—No.

It was pretty dark at the time and you were some distance away?—Yes.

By the COURT—Am I right that you have told us you first heard a noise, looked up and saw a group of four people, and you saw one of the four making to kick another, and the one at whom the kick was made retreated out on to the street?—Yes.

Did someone then come out and chase him, or did someone go off towards the west in McAslin Street?—While this was going on that was then the blow was struck. When the kicking in the street was going on the other one went over to the man on the pavement and punched him.

Were the two who were taking part in the kicking distinct as you saw them from the other two?—Yes.

And was it one of the other two whom you saw who seemed to punch the other?—Yes, that is right.

Was it after the punch that the man who seemed to be punched collapsed to the ground?—Yes.

At the time the punch was delivered and the man who received it collapsed to the ground, were the two who had been kicking separated from the other two?—Yes, the two that were taking part in the kicking were in the middle of the street and the other two were on the pavement.

And it is the two who had been left on the pavement who took part in what you called a punch delivered by one to the other, after which the punched man collapsed on the edge of the pavement?—Yes.

But before you started off to go up to the corner had those who took part in the kicking moved away?—Yes, they ran down west along McAslin Street.

Did one seem to be following the other?—Yes.

JOHN DOUGLAS STEWART (27), sworn.

Examined by MR. MIDDLETON—I live at 130, Taylor Street, Glasgow, and am part owner of a taxi-cab. I was in the Army till

Evidence for the Prosecution.

May, 1941, when I was discharged as unfit. On Friday, 23rd
November, 1945, I was standing at the corner of Taylor Street
and Parson Street with Neil Campbell about ten o'clock. Parson
Street is the next street parallel to McAslin Street to the south.

While you were with Campbell do you remember something
happening?—Yes, there was a commotion at the bottom of Taylor
Street, at the corner of Taylor Street and McAslin Street. There
was some shouting and Campbell mentioned, "There is something up down the street," and when I turned round there were a
couple of fellows fighting in the middle of the street just up a bit
from a junction in Taylor Street.

Did you only see two men?—There were two men in the middle
of the street and one standing on the pavement. I only saw three
men.

About the two men who were in the middle of the street, what
were they doing?—Well, they were fighting in the streets. One
had a weapon in his hand of some sort, and the other was
kicking.

Where exactly was the third man?—He was just standing, staggering about a little bit on the pavement opposite the corner.

Did you and Campbell move down towards the spot?—Yes.
As we got down towards the man that was standing on the pave-
ment, the man with the weapon in his hand ran west down
McAslin Street and the other man ran after him.

What about the third man?—When we walked up to him there
was blood spouting out the back of his neck. We said we had
better get him to the Royal Infirmary and I took him by the arm
towards Stanhope Street. A sailor came along and took the side
I was on and I just followed behind.

Did somebody else come on the scene then?—There were two
or three people came round about.

Do you remember the injured man being lifted on somebody's
shoulders?—Well, the man that had been fighting came back. He
ran after the fellow, then he stopped and came back.

How do you know it was the same man that was running after
the fellow?—I didn't know at the time. He came back, I think,
when he saw the blood. The other fellow was standing down
the road shouting in McAslin Street. I think when he saw the
blood he lost his head and ran after him again.

He seemed to be excited?—Yes.

Do you know who that man is?—Well, I have met him since
that in the police office. I believe his name is Revie.

Patrick Carraher.

J. D. Stewart

Is that the man? (Witness Revie brought into court.)—Yes.

What did Revie do exactly?—Well, he just came back and he just looked at the fellow who was stabbed and he ran after the other man. The next time he came back the fellow was up Stanhope Street, and Revie said to me, "Where have they gone?" I said, "They are taking him to the Royal up Stanhope Street." We just got to the corner, and he ran up and lifted him on his shoulder and carried him back down and up a close.

Then a taxi arrived and the injured man was taken away?—Yes, it came up Stanhope Street. I asked Campbell to go and ask the taxi driver if he would take him to the Royal, and then I just went back to the corner along with Campbell.

Did you go up to a house?—Yes, that was about half-past eleven at night. I was going along Cathedral Street or Stirling Road when I met George Elliott and I was telling him about the thing that had happened.

You told him what you knew. As a result of what you told Elliott did you and he go to look for a certain man?—Yes, we went to find Bonnar.

First of all did you go to a house in Rottenrow?—Yes, there was no one there.

Did you then go to another house?—Yes, in Tarbet Street. I did not know the number at the time—14—but Elliott knew the close.

Did you know Bonnar?—I knew him by sight.

What time was it when you got to 14, Tarbet Street?—It must have been about half-past eleven.

Did you and Elliott go together?—Yes. Elliott knocked at the door and when the door opened someone shouted, "Who's there?" Elliott shouted, "It's me; it's Gasser, Dan." That's Elliott's nickname. There is a long lobby there. We were standing at the end when someone else came and said, "Who's there, who's there?" Elliott shouted, "It's Gasser, Dan." So Bonnar came to the door and said, "It's all right, it is Elliott," so he asked us in.

Did you see anyone else at the door except Bonnar?—No.

On Bonnar's invitation you and Elliot went in. Did you see anyone when you got in?—Yes, there were a few people in the house. There were three men and three or four women.

Look round the court and see if you can recognize anyone here who was in that house at the time?—That man in between the policemen was in the house. (Indicating the accused.)

Evidence for the Prosecution.

J. D. Stewart

When did you first see him that night?—When we walked into the house he was in the kitchen.

There were a number of other people. Did you know any of them?—No, I just knew Bonnar by sight, that was all.

You did not know the accused before?—No, I had never met him in my life before.

Did you and Elliott speak to people in the kitchen?—Yes.

Just say what you told them?—Well, we told them that the fellow was dead.

Did you mention the name?—Yes, Gordon. I did not know his christian name.

Anything else?—There were some people were shouting it was Bonnar did it that night in McAslin Street.

But we want to know what you told the people who were in the room at Tarbet Street. You told them that Gordon was dead. Did you not say anything more?—No, not then.

What happened when you told them that?—They all got excited. There was a woman in bed and she sat up and started talking and she said, "You had better go into the room and say what you have to say," so we all went into the room.

You mean you and Elliott?—Yes, and the accused and Bonnar. I think these were the only ones that went into the room.

What happened when the four men went into the room?—There was not much happened, just talking about what had happened. There had been a fight earlier on in the Rottenrow.

Did you go back into the kitchen?—Yes, we all went into the kitchen.

Do you remember one of the people in the house coming up to you and asking you to speak apart?—Yes, the accused asked me who I was, and I told him it did not matter. He said, "Where do you come from?" and I said, "Over the road."

Where did this conversation between you and the accused take place?—In the kitchen. That was when he asked me, and he said, "Well, come here a minute," and he took me through a door into another room.

Were you alone in that room?—No, there was someone in the bed. I think it was a child.

What happened when you and the accused were in this other room?—He told me that he was having a cup of tea in the house when someone came and told him Bonnar was in trouble in the Rottenrow and he went out and met Bonnar, and the two of them went to a close in McAslin Street, but they didn't see anyone

Patrick Carraher.

J. D. Stewart

there and they went to the corner of Taylor Street and met the two fellows and the fight started.

These were the words as far as you remember—two fellows?—Yes.

Try and recollect the actual words the accused used?—He just said, "I gave one of them a jag and ran away when the fight started."

Did he say anything else about what happened?—No, he did not say anything.

Did you understand from what he said that this took place at the corner of McAslin Street and Taylor Street and that he and Bonnar were engaged with two fellows?—Yes, something like that.

Was anything else said?—No, he did not say anything more.

Did you hear anything at that time in the kitchen about a hammer?—Yes, as I was going out the door there was something said about a hammer by Bonnar.

You described a conversation between you and the accused in a room apart from the kitchen. What happened then after the accused had described the fight to you?—We came back into the kitchen and we were getting ready to go away—I was anyway—and I said to Elliott, "It's time we were going away." The accused put something in my hand and said, "Chip that away."

That was in the kitchen?—Yes.

What did he put in your hand?—I didn't notice at the time, but when I got outside there were two pieces.

Have you seen Labels Nos. 1 and 2 before?—Yes, on the stairs after we got out of the house.

Who had them?—I had them in my hand.

Who had put them in your hand?—The accused.

In the kitchen?—Yes.

You did not look at them until you went out to the stairs?—I did not realize what it was at the time. He just said, "Chip them away."

Were they fixed together?—No, they were separated.

Did he say, "Chip them away" or "Chuck them away"?—Chip them away.

What did you understand that to mean?—To throw them away.

You did not look at what he was handing to you until you got on to the stair?—Yes.

That was the first you had seen or heard of it?—Yes.

158

Evidence for the Prosecution.

J. D. Stewart

Where did you go?—We went down along George Street and into the High Street and stood at the corner.

What happened then?—I said, "What are we going to do with this?" I said, "What is the best thing to do with it?" We stood for a minute or two and we suggested we should put it down the stank, which I did.

Both parts?—One part. The other part wouldn't go down.

Which part did you put down?—The steel part.

That was in George Street?—No, in the High Street.

What about the other part?—That wouldn't go down, so we just walked on and tried another stank and I put my foot on it and pressed it down.

Did it go down?—Yes.

Was this near the first one?—Yes, about a couple up from the first one.

By the COURT—What do you mean by a stank?—A drain.

The iron cover on a street drain with its rib top?—Yes.

Examination continued—On 28th November—that is five days later—were you taken by the police to the High Street and did you point out to them the stanks you mentioned?—Yes, they had one part in the police office.

Which part?—The wooden part, and they were waiting for the Corporation to get the other part.

Did you point out where the other one was?—Yes, the stank.

Did you then identify the two parts and sign the labels?—Yes.

Just go back to the conversation you had with the accused in the room off the kitchen when he said, "I gave one of them a jag", or words to that effect. What did you understand that to mean?—I didn't know; I was not sure what he meant by that at the time.

Cross-examined by MR. PHILIP—When you looked round first of all when you were standing at the corner of Tarbet Street and McAslin Street was there a fight going on?—Yes.

You did not actually see the beginning of it?—No.

And that was at the head of Taylor Street just where it joins McAslin Street?—Yes.

You say you saw only three men?—Yes.

And two of them were in the middle of the street, and one of these men was kicking the other?—That is right.

Patrick Carraher.

J. D. Stewart

That is the man whom you have identified as Revie?—Yes.

Do you say the other one had a weapon?—Yes.

What kind of a weapon was it?—There was a shaft. It could have been a hammer or a hatchet.

Might it have been a file?—It was a very big thing to be a file.

From the distance which you were away, some 60 yards or so, could you see what it was?—No.

Had he that weapon, whatever it was, above his head?—Yes, he was just holding it like that. (Witness indicates towards his head.)

Was he using that on Revie?—That is right.

Then did he run away?—Yes, the man with the weapon.

And Revie chased him?—Yes.

The man on the pavement was standing; he was not lying on the ground?—No.

You never saw him lying on the ground until after?—That is right.

By and by Revie came back and eventually did you go up to the close at McAslin Street where the body was?—Yes.

Did you hear Revie saying anything about Dan Bonnar?—It was not Revie. He had carried him upstairs.

Did you hear a name mentioned?—They said it was Bonnar who did it. "We know who did it. We will get him this time."

Then later you met Gasser Elliott?—Yes.

Why is he called Gasser Elliott?—I don't know.

Is he a bit of a blether?—I suppose so.

He is a friend of Dan Bonnar's?—I believe he knows him very well.

He was walking out with a sister of Bonnar's?—I believe he was at one time.

Did you tell him then that you had heard about Dan Bonnar having done it?—Yes.

When you heard that remark that it was Dan Bonnar who had done it, "We will get him this time" or words to that effect, was that said up the close at 139, McAslin Street?—Yes.

Were the various members of the injured man's family round about the body at the time?—There were two or three people round about, but I did not know any of them.

Did you think Dan Bonnar should be told about it?—That is right.

And was that why you went to Rottenrow first?—Yes.

What you really did was to go and warn Dan Bonnar, and

160

Evidence for the Prosecution.

J. D. Stewart

when you came to Rottenrow he was not in there?—There was no one in there.

Did you think he might be up at his sister's house?—Elliott said, "He may be down in Sarah's house."

At 14, Tarbet Street. You went on there?—Yes.

When you arrived at the door a voice from within asked who was there, and Elliott said, "It is Gasser, Dan"?—Yes.

Did Dan come to the door?—He just shouted, "Come in."

Was Dan not in a bit of a state?—Yes.

Do you remember seeing Dan take off his shirt and throw it away or put it to be washed because it had blood on it?—Yes, he took his shirt off.

Dan Bonnar's shirt had blood on it?—Yes.

When you gave the message which you had to give, you say that that was given to people in the kitchen first of all?—That is right.

With regard to the conversation which you had with the accused, you say that he said something about having a cup of tea. Where was it, Dan Bonnar's house?—I believe it was Sarah Bonnar's.

And you said something about Bonnar being in trouble in Rottenrow?—Yes.

Was that the expression that was used?—I believe it was "trouble".

Was it not something very much stronger than that?—Well, I don't think so.

Was it not something like. "Dan was being murdered in the Rottenrow"?—No, I cannot remember.

May it have been that?—It could have been, yes.

And then you think that the accused next said that he went to a close in McAslin Street and then to the head of Taylor Street and McAslin Street?—Yes, that is right.

You referred to a statement which you said the accused made. Did he say, "a jag" or "a wee jag"?—I believe he said "a wee jag".

Then you said something was said about a hammer by Dan Bonnar. What did he say?—I couldn't tell you. Just wanted us just to take the hammer or something.

He wanted you to hide a hammer?—Take it away, something like that.

Was it after that that it was suggested that these Productions, Labels Nos. 1 and 2, were put into your hands to be taken away?—

161

Patrick Carraher.

J. D. Stewart

Yes, it was just about the same time, just as we were going out the door.

You got the impression, did you not, that Dan Bonnar was in a state of great apprehension when you brought him that news?—That is right.

Can you tell me whether there had been drinking going on either in Dan Bonnar's house or 14, Tarbet Street?—Well, I don't know if there had been drinking or not. I couldn't tell you that. There were some beer bottles in the house.

They had had a good deal, had they not?—I believe so, yes.

Both Bonnar and the accused?—Well, it looked that way anyway.

Re-examined by Mr. JOHNSTON—You said that Bonnar was excited?—Yes.

What about the accused here? Did he appear excited or calm?—Well, he wasn't as excited as Bonnar was, I don't think.

Are you sure who it was who gave you these objects you looked at while you were in the witness-box?—Yes, quite sure.

Who was it?—The accused.

Did you say that Bonnar did speak to you about a hammer and ask you to hide it?—He did not ask me to hide it. It was mentioned about the hammer, to take it away.

Did you see it?—No.

And you did not actually take a hammer?—No.

By the COURT—Did you see the hammer that was mentioned while you were in Tarbet Street?—No.

It was merely a remark passed by Bonnar?—Yes. It was they wanted us to take it away.

Did they never go and get it?—No.

Who was it wanted you to take it away?—Bonnar.

But he did not want it so much that he went to get it for you?—Well, I never gave him the chance to. I said, "I am going away." I wanted out.

It was then you say the accused came to the door with you and handed you the pieces that you have seen?—About the same time.

GEORGE ROSS ELLIOTT (25), sworn.

Examined by Mr. MIDDLETON—I live at 107, Stirling Road, Glasgow, and I am sometimes known by the name of "Gasser."

CHISEL USED BY
CARRAHER IN THE
MURDER OF JOHN
GORDON

Left, the weapon
assembled (actual
size); *right*, the weapon
apart (slightly
reduced)

Evidence for the Prosecution.

G. R. Elliott

I was on my way home on Friday night, 23rd November, last, when I met John Stewart at the corner of Stirling Road and St. James' Road.

Did you learn from him that there had been a fight in the district and that a man had been injured or killed, and also that a man called Bonnar was mixed up with the affair?—That is right.

Did you know Bonnar?—Yes. Along with Stewart I went up to Bonnar's house in Rottenrow, but we did not find him in. It was between half-past eleven and twelve.

When you failed to find Bonnar there did you go to another house?—Yes, to Sarah Bonnar's house in Tarbet Street, along with Stewart.

Did you knock at the door?—Yes.

What happened?—Well, the door was opened by two men, Carraher and Bonnar. I recognize Carraher as the accused here to-day.

Did you notice whether the accused or Bonnar had anything?—They each had something in their hands. It was a weapon, but I could not really swear to say what it was.

What happened when they opened the door and saw you and Stewart?—When Bonnar saw me he said, "It is all right, come in," and we went in.

You were acquainted with Bonnar, and also with the accused at that time?—Yes.

When you went in where did you go?—Into the kitchen; there were a number of people there.

Did Bonnar and the accused come back into the kitchen with you and Stewart?—Yes.

What did you say when you got into the kitchen?—We just told him that the fellow Gordon was dead.

After a time did the men present go into another room?—Yes, Stewart, Carraher, Bonnar, myself and Watt.

Five of you?—Yes.

Did you have some conversation with the other four men in the room?—It was about this man that had been killed.

What sort of state were Bonnar and the accused in? Were they quite calm?—Yes.

You were discussing the matter. How long were you in the room?—A quarter of an hour.

You were talking about this all the time?—Yes.

Then did you and Bonnar go out?—Yes, Watt was out as well.

Patrick Carraher.

G. R. Elliott

So that you mean Stewart and Carraher were left alone while you and Bonnar went back into the kitchen?—Yes, that is right.

How long were you in the kitchen?—A matter of minutes, then Stewart and Carraher came out.

You do not know what passed between Carraher and Stewart? —No.

Did the accused speak to you when he came out?—He addressed everybody that was in the house, not personally to me.

What did he say after he came out of the room with Stewart? —No idea.

Was it anything to do with the events that had happened that night?—All I saw was Carraher putting his hands in his pocket and taking a weapon out.

Do you recognize Labels Nos. 1 and 2?—Yes.

Where did you see that weapon first of all?—In the house is the first time I ever saw it.

Was it joined together then?—Yes.

Where did you first see it?—In Sarah Bonnar's house.

Lying, or in somebody's possession?—In Carraher's possession.

Where did he get it from?—I saw him draw it from his hip pocket.

Was it joined together at that time?—Yes.

Did he separate it into two parts?—Yes.

Was that after you had had the conversation in the room, and after Stewart and the accused had been alone together?—That is correct.

You do not remember any conversation with regard to this weapon at that time?—No.

Do you remember him doing anything when he separated the handle from the other part?—Yes, he took a dish cloth from the side of the window and wiped it with it. I couldn't see anything on it.

Did you see any colour on the towel after he wiped it?—No, never saw.

What did he do with the towel?—Put it back down again after he wiped it.

Then what happened?—Carraher put it in John Stewart's hands.

Did you see a hammer at all?—Not that I mind of.

Or an axe, anything resembling an axe or a hammer in the room?—I never took any notice.

Did you ever hear any conversation about an axe or a hammer?

Evidence for the Prosecution.

G. R. Elliott

—Yes, in the kitchen. Bonnar was saying some of the Gordons had hit him on the head with a hatchet.

What did Stewart do with this other weapon which you have identified?—Held it in his hands, then he put it in his pocket. He was in the kitchen.

Did you and Stewart leave together?—Yes.

What happened when you got out?—Well, we were a bit excited with that weapon in my possession.

But it was not in your possession, it was in Stewart's?—Well, the two of us were together.

You thought it better to get rid of it?—Yes. We went down into George Street and up into High Street and we stopped at a stank and put one part of it down, and then walked on and tried another bit and we had to force the other bit down—the handle part.

They both went down separate drains?—Yes.

Did you go home?—Yes.

Some days later were you shown a handle and blade at the Central Police Office?—Yes, I identified it as what I had seen before.

Did you examine them at the time, before they were put down the drain?—Yes.

You cannot remember the accused saying any more to you about that weapon or about the man who died?—No.

Cross-examined by MR. PHILIP—Are you a friend of Bonnar? —Yes.

Were you at one time walking out with his sister who has since died?—Yes.

You first heard Bonnar's name mentioned by Stewart. Did he tell you that it was being said that Bonnar had done something and that a man had been fatally injured?—Yes.

Did he say anything about friends of the man saying that they would know who did it?—That is correct.

As a friend of Bonnar did you want to go and warn him, and therefore went to his house where you expected to find him?— Yes.

But he happened to be at his sister's house, and you went there? —Yes.

When you came to the door it was Bonnar who said, "All right, come in." Did he appear to be apprehensive?—Well, he was excited.

Patrick Carraher.

G. R. Elliott

Did you think he was expecting an attack?—Yes.

And you gave the message to the people in the house, what you had heard; or was it Stewart who gave it about that time?—The two of us referred to it anyway.

When you mentioned Gordon's name was Bonnar still more excited?—Yes.

Did he say something about getting rid of a shirt that he was wearing?—He took off his shirt in the room.

The shirt had bloodstains on it, had it not, and he wanted to get rid of the bloodstains?—Yes.

Then did he mention anything about a hammer or file or a hatchet?—A hatchet. All I know as regards the hammer is what he said, that he was assaulted with a hatchet.

Did he say whether he was assaulted by Gordon or by whom? —I think it was Gordon he was assaulted by.

Was it following upon that that you and Stewart took away this other Production which you have been shown?—Yes.

Was Carraher quite unaffected in any way?—Yes.

It was Bonnar who was excited?—Yes.

Was the man in the house, Watt, excited?—No.

Do you remember Bonnar making any remark like this, "It is all right. I will take the consequences"?—Yes.

Was that said with reference to the message which you had brought about Gordon's death?—That is correct.

By the COURT—To whom did Bonnar say that?—To Carraher.

At what stage of the proceedings inside the house at Tarbet Street was that remark made?—When we entered the house.

Was it before or after you or Stewart had told them why you had come?—Well, it was just after.

DAVID MACKINTOSH (46), sworn.

Examined by MR. MIDDLETON—I am a detective-inspector, Headquarters Division, City of Glasgow Police, and I have 26 years' service. On Friday night, 23rd November, 1945, I was on duty at the Criminal Investigation Department Headquarters. Some time after 10 p.m. I received a telephone message, as a consequence of which I went to the Infirmary at approximately half-past ten. There I saw Dr. Moore, who took me to the gatehouse where I saw the body of the deceased man, John Gordon. Certain wounds were pointed out to me. In consequence of what I learned

Evidence for the Prosecution.

D. Mackintosh

I went to 139, McAslin Street, with Detective-Sergeant Johnstone and Detective-Sergeant Anderson. There I found a trail of blood extending from Stanhope Street to Taylor Street and up the close two stairs up at 139, McAslin Street. It was on the pavement except that it was on the street at Stanhope Street and Taylor Street. I found a raincoat on the landing two stairs up.

Do you recognize Label No. 3?—That is the coat; it was in that condition when I found it.

Did you then go to the top flat?—I did.

Did you find two men there?—Yes. I had great difficulty in wakening them up. They were very drunk.

Later on that same night did you go to No. 116, Rottenrow, and there interview a man Daniel Bonnar?—I did. We took him into custody.

Then did you go to a house at 14, Tarbet Street?—I did.

Did you find a man there?—Yes, the accused, Patrick Carraher. There were two women there at the time, Sarah Bonnar and Mrs. Daniel Bonnar. The accused was in bed. He was immediately charged with the murder of John Gordon, and cautioned. He made no reply.

Did you then go to the house of a man named Thomas Watt at 146, Rottenrow?—I did, and I took him into custody.

That is, you took the three men, Bonnar, the accused and Watt, into custody on the same charge?—Yes.

On Sunday, 25th November, did you take possession of certain clothing?—Yes, in the Central Police Office; clothing worn by Carraher.

Is Label No. 6 a pair of trousers?—Yes, I took these from Carraher. He changed his clothing that Sunday afternoon. Label No. 7 is his jacket and Label No. 8 is his vest.

On the Monday after interviewing Thomas Ross Elliott, did you go to the High Street and make an examination of some drains there?—I did. From a stank opposite No. 277, High Street, I recovered a wooden handle, Exhibit No. 1. On the Wednesday I was shown a blade, Exhibit No. 2, by Detective-Sergeant Johnstone.

Cross-examined by MR. PHILIP—You have mentioned that you charged the accused?—Detective-Lieutenant Dow charged all three.

They were all charged with murder?—Yes.

Patrick Carraher.

RODERICK ANDERSON (42), sworn.

Examined by MR. MIDDLETON—I am a detective-sergeant, Headquarters Division, City of Glasgow Police, and I have had 22 years' service. On the night of Friday, 23rd November, 1945, I was on duty at the Criminal Investigation Department when a message was received. I went to the Infirmary with Detective-Inspector Mackintosh and saw the body of a man, John Gordon. Later on I went with the Detective-Inspector to McAslin Street and saw blood in Taylor Street, McAslin Street and Stanhope Street, and on the stair at 139, McAslin Street. The blood was on the pavement, but there was also blood on the street at the junction of Taylor Street and McAslin Street. On the second landing and on the third step above the second landing at 139, McAslin Street, there was a concentration of blood and a raincoat, which I recognize as Label No. 3. It was covered in bloodstains. I went up the stair, and saw two men sleeping on the floor of the house. We took them back to Headquarters. Along with Detective-Inspector Mackintosh I went to a house in Rottenrow and took a man Bonnar into custody. We then went to 14, Tarbet Street, and arrested Patrick Carraher on a charge of murder. He was cautioned and charged in the usual way. He made no reply.

Cross-examined by MR. PHILIP—There was also a man Watt who was arrested and also charged with murder?—Yes, but I was not present when Watt was arrested.
Bonnar was arrested and charged with murder?—Yes.
Were the two men whom you found lying asleep upstairs in 139, McAslin Street, Edward and Joseph Gordon?—Joseph Gordon and a man called Keatings.
Was it a drunken sleep?—They had a good deal of drink.

JOHN JOHNSTONE (47), sworn.

Examined by MR. MIDDLETON—I am a detective-sergeant attached to the Headquarters Division of the City of Glasgow Police, and I have 22 years' service. I was present with Detective-Inspector Mackintosh when he went to the High Street to a stank opposite No. 277, and I was present when he recovered something from the gully. Label No. 1 was the handle that was discovered. On the Wednesday I went with an official of the Cleansing Department, James McDowall, to another stank in the High Street and examined it. It was a matter of 30 yards away from the first one

Evidence for the Prosecution.

J. Johnstone

where the knife was got. In the second one we found a steel blade, Label No. 2. I took that blade and handed it to Detective-Inspector Mackintosh.

Would you look at the blade and the handle. They fit one another?—They do, quite easily.

How would you describe that implement with the two parts fitted together?—That is what I regard as a carver's tool. The blade is a little over $3\frac{1}{2}$ inches. It is $3\frac{1}{8}$ inches to the rust. The part wholly covered with rust measures $\frac{7}{16}$ of an inch.

The rusted portion fits into the wooden handle?—Yes.

What distance does the steel part penetrate into the handle?—I did not measure it.

You measured merely the length of the blade?—Yes, that was the length it was going in at that time.

Is it not the same now?—No, it is going in further than that now. It depends on how you put it in.

It is known as a carver's tool. Is it sharpened at the side or only at the point?—The curving towards the tip is the sharpest bit.

Is it sharp at that end?—It is very sharp.

By the COURT—Do you mean the cutting edge is off the vertical and sloping a bit?—Yes.

And do you deduce that has been done in the process of sharpening the cutting edge?—I have no doubt about that.

Cross-examined by MR. PHILIP—Do you agree that the blade of this Label No. 2 is $2\frac{1}{4}$ inches long?—The blade is $3\frac{1}{4}$ inches from the start of the rust.

You see there is what you might call an arm, and then the blade begins beyond the arm?—Yes.

I put it to you that the blade is $2\frac{1}{4}$ inches. Are you prepared to dispute that?—I never measured the blade. I measured from where the blade starts at the handle. I measured it from the end of the handle to the point.

Will you tell me now what is the length of the blade?—The blade is $3\frac{9}{16}$ inches. That is the whole thing together. If we refer to that as the blade then the whole part is $3\frac{9}{16}$ inches.

What I am referring to as the blade is from the point at which the arm widens up to the point?—I took the measurement of the whole part. I did not measure that part you refer to.

Is that not a very important measurement to take?—The most important measurement to me is the part that can be forced into any body.

Patrick Carraher.

J. Johnstone

Does it come to this, you cannot tell the measurement of that? —I can tell the measurement without the wooden handle of the weapon.

Do you agree that the narrower part of the arm upon which the blade itself is placed goes right home into the handle?—That is why I measured it when I took possession of it, because when the weapon is found in a gully it is naturally wet. It has so many hands to pass through before it reaches here that I knew that sooner or later it would get further into the handle of the wood. That was my precaution purely from experience.

You suggest that now it can go further in than it could before? —I have no doubt about it.

Suppose the position be that this had been lying in a wet stank, would not the wood swell and would not the result be exactly the opposite?—It would swell, but it would become softer. The wood swells but it is more easily pierced. You will pierce a wet piece of wood quicker than a hard piece.

If the wood becomes wet, do you agree the wood would swell so as to make the hole smaller?—Wood swells with water, but it becomes softer, and therefore that part of the blade goes further into the handle and easier into the handle.

Re-examined by Mr. MIDDLETON—Is it simply this, that the metal part is $3\frac{9}{16}$ inches, and the length of the steel part which projects from the handle will vary in accordance with the depth to which it is put into the handle?—Yes.

One cannot tell from its present state what it may have been at some previous time?—I say when I recovered it the rust showed the part that had come out of the handle.

So that when you examined it you were satisfied that all but $\frac{7}{16}$ of an inch projected?—I have no doubt about that.

In other words, $3\frac{2}{16}$ inches of the steel part projected?—That is right.

Further cross-examined by Mr. PHILIP by permission of the Court—Is it your evidence that this blade is not in the condition in which it was when you found it?—I see no change in it other than that the rust has been a little impaired through handling.

Is it your suggestion that the rust has altered by handling since you saw this Production?—The Court sees that the knife goes in further now than the $\frac{7}{16}$ of an inch.

Do you suggest there was rust on this blade at the time you

found it and that that rust is not there now?—I see it still, but it is not as clear as it was.

By the COURT—To try and make it as plain as it can be, is this steel portion or iron portion of this carver's tool shaped at one end in the form of a very narrow blade, part of which fits into a handle?—That is correct.

With a hole in it to receive part of the narrow part?—Yes.

Does the remainder of the narrow part plus the wider part terminating in a cutting edge with a point, come outside of the hilt altogether?—I do not understand.

Have you measured in your measurement of $3\frac{1}{8}$ inches that portion of the steel part which, when you got possession of this, was the distance out from the hilt that the whole of the steel projected?—That is correct. It was $3\frac{2}{16}$ inches.

Were these measurements made by you after you got possession of the two parts?—Yes.

JAMES McDOWALL (39), sworn.

Examined by MR. JOHNSTON—I am an inspector with the Glasgow Corporation Cleansing Department, and on Wednesday, 28th November, 1945, I was present when a gully on the west side of High Street, Glasgow, almost opposite No. 243, was drained. That is a street drain with an opening called a stank in the street above. I recognize Label No. 2 as something which was recovered from that drain and taken possession of by the police.

MRS. HELEN JOSEPHINE COLQUHOUN (30), sworn.

Examined by MR. JOHNSTON—I am the wife of a soldier, and live at 107, Rottenrow, Glasgow. For some time I have been employed as a post-woman. My house is at the top of Balmano Brae, and is on the same side of Rottenrow as Cameron's public-house and quite near.

On an evening in November, 1945, were you cleaning your windows?—Yes. My attention was attracted to men fighting in the street in the middle of Rottenrow. I recognized Dan Bonnar. I only saw him fighting with one man whom I did not know; I would not be able to recognize him again.

Would this place where they were fighting be near Cameron's public-house?—Beside it.

Patrick Carraher.

Mrs. H. J. Colquhoun

What time was this?—About nine-thirty in the evening.

What happened in the fighting?—I only saw him fighting one man and then two chasing him down the road.

Who was being chased down the road?—Daniel Bonnar.

Who were chasing him?—I think it was the Gordons, but I am not sure. I know them by sight.

Which of the Gordons was it?—I do not know.

Are you certain it was some of the Gordon family?—Yes.

Were you at your window?—No, I was standing in the street then.

How far down the road did these two men chase Bonnar? —Down about at the Old Men's Home just next door to Cameron's pub was the last time I saw him.

In which direction was Bonnar running?—Towards the High Street.

How far were the other two men who were chasing him behind him?—A few yards.

Did you see what happened after that?—No.

What did you do?—I went down for Sarah Bonnar who stays in Tarbet Street just two or three minutes' walk from Cameron's pub. I found her in her house alone, and I told her her brother was in trouble in Rottenrow. We both left the house and went to Daniel Bonnar's house in Rottenrow.

When you got to Daniel Bonnar's house did you find anyone there?—Yes, Patrick Carraher, whom I identify as the man sitting between the two policemen in the dock.

Did you find anyone else in this house in Rottenrow?—Mr. Watt and Daniel Bonnar's wife, Mrs. Margaret Bonnar.

So in the house there were yourself, Sarah Bonnar, the accused, Watt, and Mrs. Margaret Bonnar?—Yes.

Did you tell anyone why you had come to this house in Rottenrow?—Sarah told Patrick Carraher that Dan was fighting.

What happened then?—Patrick Carraher came out with me, Mr. Watt, and Sarah. Mrs. Margaret Bonnar was in bed.

So the four of you left the house in Rottenrow. Where did you go?—We went down Rottenrow towards High Street. We met Daniel Bonnar coming from High Street and Sarah tried to get him home, but she did not succeed.

Did Daniel Bonnar say anything?—No, not that I remember.

What happened after that?—Nothing, I went home.

Where was Daniel Bonnar when you left the party?—Outside Cameron's pub.

Evidence for the Prosecution.

Mrs. H. J. Colquhoun

Had you walked up with Daniel Bonnar to Cameron's pub? —Yes, along with Patrick and Sarah.

Now, is this what happened, that Sarah Bonnar, the accused and you left Margaret Bonnar's house in Rottenrow, walked down towards High Street and in Rottenrow met Bonnar, and then turned and walked up towards Cameron's pub?—Yes.

The whole lot of you?—Yes.

Was Bonnar wearing a jacket?—Yes, a ladies' costume jacket.

Was he carrying anything?—Yes, a hatchet.

Was Carraher carrying anything?—No.

Cross-examined by MR. PHILIP—When you looked out of the window from your house first of all you saw Daniel Bonnar, did you, engaged with another man fighting?—Yes.

Was there also someone looking on down below watching the fight?—Yes.

Did you think that the other man was going to join in too, and were you afraid of what was going to happen to Daniel Bonnar? —Yes.

Did you go downstairs into the close for that reason?—Yes.

Did you shout to try to get them to stop?—No.

By the time you got down to the mouth of the close Daniel Bonnar was being chased away by at least two other men, and you think that there was a Gordon amongst them?—Yes.

Did you think that Daniel Bonnar was going to come to harm? —Yes.

Was he running away at that time without a jacket?—He had no jacket at all.

Did you see it being torn off his back?—No.

Had he any weapon at that time?—No.

Were you so afraid of what was going to happen to Dan Bonnar that you thought you would go and get help?—I wanted to let his friends know anyway. I wanted to tell his people.

Was that to get help?—It was only to let them know he was fighting.

You first of all got Sarah. Do you know whether you used the expression that Dan was being murdered?—No.

Did you hear that expression being used?—No.

Did you tell Sarah that there were men chasing Dan down Rottenrow?—Yes.

In your hearing did Sarah tell the accused that later?—Yes.

And did the accused go out to help?—Yes.

Patrick Carraher.

Mrs. H. J. Colquhoun

Did you run down Rottenrow?—No, we walked down.

You got some way down Rottenrow and found Daniel Bonnar coming up. By this time he had got on a ladies' costume jacket and was carrying a hatchet?—Yes.

Can you tell me if the reason why he came back up Rottenrow was to get his own jacket?—Yes.

I think that his own jacket was found either inside or just outside a fish and chip shop next door to Cameron's pub?—Yes.

Did Daniel Bonnar go back and get his own jacket there and then turn back down Rottenrow?—I don't know. I left him.

When you left Daniel Bonnar and the accused was Thomas Watt with them?—I think so, I am not sure.

Re-examined by MR. JOHNSTON—You told my friend that when you looked out of your window you saw Bonnar fighting with two men and there was another man standing outside Cameron's pub. Do you know who that other man was?—No.

Was he taking any part in the fight?—No.

You said you expected him to join in the fight. What made you think that?—I did not see him joining in any fight. I only saw him running after Dan Bonnar.

Are you sure that the man who was standing outside Cameron's pub and taking no part in the fight was one of those who ran after Dan Bonnar?—No.

There were two men ran after Bonnar?—Yes.

And there were two men who fought with Dan Bonnar?—I only saw one man fighting with him.

You are quite certain of that, are you?—Yes.

And one man standing outside the pub?—Two men.

Daniel Bonnar ran away. Did the man with whom he had been fighting follow?—Yes.

Did either of the men who were standing outside Cameron's pub do anything?—No.

Did either of them follow Bonnar?—Yes, I think it was three altogether.

Just imagine yourself at your window or at the close, and try and picture what happened that night. You have told us about Daniel Bonnar fighting with one man. Did that one man chase Daniel Bonnar?—That is right.

Were there any other men chasing Daniel Bonnar?—I thought there were other two.

Evidence for the Prosecution.

Mrs. H. J. Colquhoun

What made you think there were other two?—Because I saw two men standing.

How many men did you see chasing Daniel Bonnar that night? —Either two or three; I am not sure.

JOHN FULLARTON (50), sworn.

Examined by MR. JOHNSTON—I live at 2, Moodiesburn Street, Glasgow, and I remember on the night of 23rd November, 1945, there being some trouble in the Rottenrow. I had been in Cameron's pub that night and came out about nine twenty. I was standing at the siver with John Gordon about three yards from the pub when a man approached in a fighting attitude and challenged to fight three men. It was Dan Bonnar, and he came from the direction of High Street.

Was there anyone else standing there?—No.

Who was the challenge to?—I do not know.

Did you do anything?—No.

Did John Gordon do anything?—No, I stopped him.

What happened next?—Well, another man, I don't know who he was, took up the challenge and Dan Bonnar threw off his jacket. Two men took up the challenge and it was settled who was to take him on. Dan Bonnar stepped back and fell over his own jacket, and then he got up and ran.

What happened after that?—Two men pursued him. The whole lot stopped at Weaver Street, and he challenged them to fight.

Who threw out the challenge?—Dan Bonnar. They disappeared then. Dan Bonnar went down the Rottenrow and I don't know where the other two went.

Where was John Gordon at this time?—He was walking down the road with me towards Weaver Street.

Did he take any part in this chasing of Dan Bonnar?—No.

Did you take any part in the chasing of Dan Bonnar?—No.

Do you know the names of the men who chased Dan Bonnar down Rottenrow?—I know one, Joseph Gordon, but I don't know the other.

You and John Gordon were walking down Rottenrow towards Weaver Street. How far did you walk down?—About 300 yards, and then we stopped.

What did you do then?—Turned back.

What did John Gordon do?—He turned back at the back of me.

Patrick Carraher.

J. Fullarton

Where did you go?—To the close next to Cameron's pub.

What did Gordon do?—He was at my back, and he passed right by towards Balmano Street.

Did you see where he went after that?—No.

How long did you stay at the close next door to Cameron's pub?—I lifted Dan Bonnar's jacket at that time. I had seen him take it off.

Was that the jacket he had tripped over?—Yes. I put it in the fish restaurant next to Cameron's pub.

What happened after?—I stood where I was for about a quarter of an hour or twenty minutes, and then Bonnar came back again from the direction of High Street.

Was he alone?—No, Patrick Carraher was with him.

Do you see Patrick Carraher here to-day?—Yes, between the two policemen.

Was there anyone else there?—Watt and two women, one of whom was Sarah Bonnar.

Did anyone speak to you?—Carraher said, "Who was interfering with Dan Bonnar?" I made no reply and gave Bonnar his jacket then, and they went down Taylor Street. That was the last I saw of them.

You had gone into the fish and chip shop to get Dan Bonnar's jacket?—Yes.

Who were "they" who went down?—Carraher, Watt, and Dan Bonnar.

Where did the two women go?—They stood at the corner of Taylor Street and Rottenrow.

Was Dan Bonnar carrying anything?—I never saw him carrying anything.

Was the accused carrying anything?—I never saw him.

Cross-examined by MR. PHILIP—Was John Gordon the one you knew best?—Yes.

Did you meet him in "Cameron's Bar" quite often?—Yes.

Did you often have a drink with him?—No.

But you were quite friendly with him?—Yes, but I never drank with him.

When Dan Bonnar came out of Cameron's pub you thought he wanted to challenge someone to fight?—Yes.

Was he drunk?—I don't know that. I could not say that. He had drink in him.

You found John Gordon standing beside you?—Yes.

176

Evidence for the Prosecution.

J. Fullarton

And did he want to fight Dan?—He was after a challenge thrown out.

There were two people there and they also went to fight him? —Yes.

They were all pretty drunk, were they not?—Yes, they were drunk.

Is it not the case that some of them did not really know what they were doing?—I could believe that.

Do you suggest that all that happened was that Dan made to fight and then fell over his jacket?—Yes.

Do you say there was no blow struck at all?—No; ten yards apart.

If it be the case that one man involved in this incident had quite a lot of bruising, how do you account for that?—Bruising! There were no blows struck at that particular time.

Is it not the case that there was fighting?—Well, I would put it down more as an argument than as a fight.

You do not get bruising in an argument?—Well, that is what it was, an argument; shouting, that is an argument.

I am putting it to you there was fighting?—There were no blows struck.

And that Dan Bonnar was getting the worst of it and that he was chased down Rottenrow?—Yes, he was chased down Rottenrow.

And that you and John Gordon ran after him?—I never ran after him or John Gordon either.

Have you not said on one occasion that you did run after Dan Bonnar?—No, I never said on any occasion. I have no reason to run after Dan Bonnar.

Were you and John Gordon not always beside the other men who went after Dan Bonnar?—No.

When you first saw the accused is it not the case that he was not with Dan Bonnar?—Correct; not at that time.

Why then did you say in your evidence-in-chief that Bonnar came in from the High Street in the east and that the accused was with him?—After. After he had spoken to me.

Is not what happened this, that the accused came from the west and having evidently received some report asked you who was interfering with Dan Bonnar?—Yes.

Why was it you said in your evidence-in-chief that that remark by the accused was after Bonnar and the accused had come from the east?—No. That was before it. Carraher and Bonnar went east to meet him.

Patrick Carraher.

And to help him?—I don't know whether it was to help him or not; they came back with him anyhow.

Do you remember whether there was a fair-haired man who chased after Dan Bonnar?—Never saw him.

Do you know a man of the name of Revie?—No, I don't know him.

DR. JAMES MACADAM MOORE (23), sworn.

Examined by MR. JOHNSTON—I am a Licentiate of the Royal College of Physicians and Surgeons, and in November, 1945, I was house surgeon at the Royal Infirmary, Glasgow. On 23rd November at about ten fifteen p.m. I was on duty at the gatehouse when a man, said to be John Gordon, was admitted. I examined him. On admission he was living, but he died in about one minute. I carried out a superficial examination of the body.

What was the cause of death in your impression at that time? —Loss of blood as the result of a wound behind the left ear.

Was he bleeding on admission?—Yes.

Was the man suffering from any other wound?—There was a small wound on the back of one of the fingers of his right hand.

Was the body later removed to the mortuary of the Infirmary? —Yes. A post-mortem examination was carried out.

Is Photograph No. 1 of Production No. 3 a photograph of the dead man?—Yes.

Do you see a mark below the ear and above the block of wood? —Yes, a small incised wound.

Is it the one from which the blood was flowing?—Yes.

Is Photograph No. 2 a photograph of the right hand?—Yes.

What is the black mark between the ring and the finger-nail? —That is an incised wound of his right ring finger. That is the wound I spoke about.

Cross-examined by MR. PHILIP—Look at Production No. 3, Photograph No. 2. Is that wound on the right hand an angle-shaped incised wound?—Yes.

And the incision is from the top of the finger downwards?—Yes.

Evidence for the Prosecution

Second Day—Friday, 1st March, 1946.

DR. JOHN BLACK (41), sworn.

Examined by MR. JOHNSTON—I am a Bachelor of Medicine and a Bachelor of Surgery of Glasgow University, and I am Assistant Medical Officer, City of Glasgow Police. Acting on the instructions of the Procurator Fiscal of Glasgow, on 24th November, 1945, I made a post-mortem examination of the body of John Gordon in conjunction with Dr. Gilbert Garrey, who died a few weeks ago. Production No. 5 is my report which I made jointly with Dr. Garrey. It is signed by us both and is a true report.

Look at Labels Nos. 1 and 2. Could the wound which you have described in the neck of John Gordon have been caused by that weapon?—I think the wound could have been caused by that weapon.

Is Production No. 6 a report dated 8th December, 1945, signed by Professor Allison, the late Dr. Garrey and yourself?—That is so. (Reads report.)

Is Label No. 6 the pair of trousers of which your report speaks? —That is so.

Are Labels Nos. 1 and 2 the weapon handle and the knife blade which that report speaks to?—That is so.

Cross-examined by MR. PHILIP—You make the blade of that knife only 2¼ inches long?—2¼ inches.

According to your report, Production No. 5, you think that the depth of the wound which you found was 4 inches?—It was 4 inches as it was measured at the time of the post-mortem examination.

Considerably longer than the length of the blade?—There was a difference in the measurement as measured at the time of the post-mortem examination.

What was the length of the wound before it reached the vertebral canal?—The wound just entered the vertebral canal. It just pierced the lining on the wall of the vertebral canal, and it measured 4 inches to that point.

Then the direction of the wound was upwards?—Upwards and inwards.

179   N

Patrick Carraher.

Dr. J. Black

It reached a point, as I understand, above the atlas?—The atlas is the top vertebra; between the atlas and the base of the skull.

The atlas is the top vertebra on which the skull rests?—Yes.

And that is considerably above what appears externally as the neck?—The wound was behind the angle of the jaw. The top vertebra is at the base of the skull.

So far as Label No. 6 is concerned, your spectroscope test revealed no blood?—We did not find any positive trace of blood.

Re-examined by Mr. Johnston—You have told my friend that the blade of that chisel is $2\frac{1}{4}$ inches long. From what point is that measurement taken?—From the point to the shoulder.

You have not included any part of the steel portion which is meant to fit into the handle?—No, none at all. It is from the point of the blade to the shoulder.

How far does the blade protrude from the wooden handle?—When we had them they were separate. Do you mean as it stands at the moment?

Yes?—Roughly half an inch.

So that half an inch would have to be added to the $2\frac{1}{4}$ inches which you have given us, in finding out how much of the blade protruded from the handle?—The instrument could be inserted up to the handle.

In what could the instrument be inserted up to the handle?—Any soft material which would take the blade.

Could it be inserted into a human body up to the handle?—It could be.

How deep was the wound in John Gordon's case?—As measured at the post-mortem examination it was four inches exactly.

Could Labels Nos. 1 and 2 be inserted into a body to a depth of 4 inches?—I do not think this could be inserted to 4 inches, but I say the wound at the time of being measured at the examination was 4 inches; but I don't think this would be inserted up to 4 inches.

Do you mean by that that the wound, when you examined it, was not in the same condition as when John Gordon died?—I think there are certain factors to be taken into consideration in saying the length of the wound was 4 inches at the time of the post-mortem examination. Firstly, the muscles of the neck were infiltrated with blood, which would increase the bulk of the muscle, and secondly, the thickness of the muscles of the neck

Evidence for the Prosecution.

Dr. J. Black

would depend to some extent on the position of the neck, if the muscle was relaxed more than stretched. Again, there is a certain amount of give on the surface tissues, which again decreased the length of the wound necessary at the time of its infliction. I think these factors have got to be taken into account in the length of the wound as measured at the time of the post-mortem examination.

As a layman, what is puzzling me at the moment, and perhaps is puzzling the jury, is this. You have a weapon, the blade of which is $2\frac{1}{4}$ inches long, which protrudes about half an inch from the wooden handle. You have a wound in the neck of John Gordon 4 inches deep, and you say that that weapon could have inflicted that wound. How do you reconcile these two statements? —I cannot see any inconsistency in saying that this instrument could effect the wound for the reasons I have mentioned, for the reason that the length of the track could be increased to an appreciable extent by the facts that I have mentioned by the infiltration of the muscles. It could also be affected by the position —whether the muscles were or were not stretched with any constriction of the wound, and also by any amount of give there might be in the skin from that going in.

So, in your opinion, there is no inconsistency between the length of the blade and the depth of the wound?—I think it is quite consistent with its having caused the wound.

Are you of the opinion that that weapon could have caused the wound from which John Gordon died?—That is my opinion.

Further Cross-examined by MR. PHILIP by permission of the Court—Do you agree that if the head is held in its normal position it would be quite impossible for that blade to go 4 inches, as you found the wound?—In a normal width of neck without any infiltration of muscle. The head was in its normal position the way I saw it. We placed the head in its normal position before we measured the track of the wound at the time of the post-mortem examination.

Do you agree that if the head is held in its normal position it would be quite impossible for that blade to go 4 inches, as you found it?—I think it would be impossible for that implement to go 4 inches in because it is not 4 inches long.

Do you agree that there are all sorts of implements that could have caused that wound?—Oh, yes, I only say that it is consistent with having been caused by this instrument.

Patrick Carraher.

Dr. J. Black

By the COURT—As I understand it, there are three factors that have to be taken into account. Am I right in thinking that post-mortem changes on the tissues of the neck between death and the date you made your post-mortem examination might account for some of the increased length of aperture made by that instrument?—Well, after death occurs the tissues lose their elasticity. They are relaxed and probably it would to some extent.

Then you mentioned a second one. At the moment of impact there will be a certain give in the flesh on the surface of the body which receives the impact?—Yes.

Enabling the blade to go further in than if the head of the weapon handle had stopped leaning against the surface?—Than if the surface had been rigid. It would go further in because of the elasticity of the tissues.

Then is there a third factor which has to be taken into account, the angle at which the neck as it was in this case might be exposed to the weapon at the moment of impact?—The muscles which were involved are the muscles which move the head, and dependent on whether they were stretched or relaxed their width would vary to some extent.

Have you had a good deal of experience in investigating incised wounds by stabbing and the like in the course of your police career?—I have attended quite a number of fatal stabbing wounds and other wounds.

Are you quite confident in giving the opinion which you have given that the wound in Gordon's neck could well have been made by the weapon that you hold in your hand, Labels Nos. 1 and 2?—I feel quite satisfied that is a reasonable opinion.

When you signed the post-mortem joint report did Dr. Garrey sign it in your presence?—No, it was signed before I got it, but I am satisfied that the signature to Production No. 5 is Dr. Garrey's signature which I am familiar with.

Had you collaborated with him in the preparation of that report giving the results of what you found?—I had.

Does the same apply to Production No. 6, the examination of the clothing and the weapon for bloodstains, so far as Dr. Garrey is concerned?—Yes, Dr. Allison, of course, was engaged in it.

PROFESSOR ANDREW ALLISON, sworn.

Examined by MR. JOHNSTON—I am a Bachelor of Medicine and I hold a number of other medical degrees. I am Professor of

Evidence for the Prosecution.

Professor Allison

Forensic Medicine at St. Mungo's College, Glasgow, and I have had very considerable experience in all classes of cases dealing with Forensic Medicine. On the instructions of the Procurator Fiscal for the City of Glasgow I prepared a true report, Production No. 6, along with the late Dr. Garrey and Dr. Black.

You state in that report that the blade of the chisel measured $2\frac{1}{4}$ inches long by $\frac{9}{16}$ of an inch wide at its broadest part. We have been told to-day that the wound from which John Gordon died was a wound in the neck and that it was 4 inches deep. Could a weapon such as Labels Nos. 1 and 2 have inflicted a wound in the neck 4 inches deep?—Yes, if you take into consideration the fact that what was measured was the track of a wound which would be associated with a certain amount of bleeding which may have distended the tissues. In other words, the weapon which produced that wound had not necessarily to pass through 4 inches of tissues to make it, but after it was made bleeding caused swelling.

Do you see anything inconsistent in a wound 4 inches deep revealed at a post-mortem examination being inflicted by that weapon, Labels Nos. 1 and 2?—I see nothing inconsistent.

Cross-examined by MR. PHILIP—I think your view is that the instrument itself, if that were the instrument, could not have penetrated the whole 4 inches?—Two inches, of course, cannot penetrate 4 inches, but you can get, after penetration, a very large amount of swelling due to the blood which is effused, and I have actually tried, by pushing a narrow probe through the neck, to find the distance which would require to be traversed before entering the spinal column, and I have found that that was 2 inches.

Did you ever see this wound?—I did not, but I had certain information concerning it when I was precognosced by the Fiscal. I was asked if it was possible, assuming that there was a surface wound in a certain situation, and that the other end of the wound was on the spinal column, that an instrument of this length could have produced that. I gave it as my opinion that it was possible, and I tested my opinion by experiment.

On a dead body?—Yes, on a dead body.

Supposing you have a flat instrument and one which is not flat. Would a flat instrument penetrate and cause a wound of a shorter length than one which is not flat?—Not necessarily. I don't see why there should be any difference.

Patrick Carraher.

Professor Allison

Would not the difference be this, that if the instrument is not flat the tissues would be torn for a distance further?—If you take an instrument which is pointed, let us say a skewer which is circular, and one which is flat, like that (i.e. the chisel), if they have both a point of equal sharpness and are used with equal force they should penetrate to the same depth.

And if you had an instrument which had not a point of equal sharpness, is it not the case that that instrument would show a deeper wound than an instrument with a sharp point?—A sharp-pointed instrument is likely to penetrate further than the blunt one.

I am taking it, observe, two instruments which have penetrated exactly the same distance, a sharp one and a blunt one. Is it not the case that any destruction of tissue would go deeper in the case of a blunt instrument than in the case of a sharp instrument?—I don't know what you mean by "destruction of tissue". If you mean the mere division of tissue, you get a cleaner division of tissue with a sharp point than a blunt one.

But a blunt instrument would force the tissue apart to a greater extent than a sharp one?—Do you mean you are going to have a certain amount of bruising with a blunt instrument which you will not have with a sharp one?

No, I mean what I said, that the tissue would be forced further apart?—You mean tearing then, as opposed to cutting?

Tearing and cutting together?—With a blunt instrument you are more likely to get a degree of tearing as opposed to cutting.

Would you agree with me that this wound might be caused by all sorts of instruments?—I did not see the wound, but, from what I know of it, I would not say it could be caused by all sorts of instruments.

By the COURT—You have described making an experiment in order to test the opinion you have given us to-day that a wound 4 inches long as discovered at the post-mortem examination, reaching to the vertebral canal having entered at the neck, could have been caused by the instrument Labels Nos. 1 and 2. Is there much variation in individuals in the distance between the surface of the neck and the vertebral canal?—No.

We have been told that the distance from the aperture made by the weapon on the surface of the neck to the vertebral canal was 4 inches, and that the blade of that instrument, Labels Nos. 1 and

Evidence for the Prosecution.

Professor Allison

2, measures $2\frac{1}{4}$ inches, and that there is a further part of the neck of the blade which might emerge from the weapon handle, thus adding to the total length of the iron or steel up to perhaps at least another half inch, making $2\frac{3}{4}$ inches. With these facts before you, do they or do they not alter the opinion that you have given, or do they confirm it?—If you take that additional length which is between the end of the blade and the point which enters the wooden handle, you then have to consider an instrument of $2\frac{3}{4}$ inches before the bulge of the wooden handle would hold up further progress of the blade. That is the first point. The next point is that the wound *that* made, went through the normal tissues of the neck, which I have demonstrated by experiment may be reached by an instrument 2 inches in length. Subsequent bleeding infiltrating the soft tissues of the neck could easily increase the size and make the length as found at the post-mortem, 4 inches. If you take a very simple illustration which I think most people have seen for themselves, just imagine the size of the neck of a child with mumps, how big it gets. The infiltration of blood into the tissues may produce a very similar degree of swelling, and that would account for the increased distance.

DANIEL BONNAR (32), sworn.

Examined by MR. JOHNSTON—I live at 116, Rottenrow, Glasgow. On the afternoon and evening of Friday, 23rd November, 1945, I was drinking in Thompson's public-house in Rottenrow, about 100 yards from Cameron's pub, with Thomas Watt and Patrick Carraher, whom I identify as the accused. I left Thompson's pub with Carraher and Watt about a quarter or half past nine and we went to my house where we stayed about five minutes.

What did you do then?—I went to see a friend. I asked Carraher and Watt could I go for a friend to invite him for a drink of beer and a cup of tea. Mr. Charles McArthur was the man's name. I went alone, and Carraher and Watt remained in my house.

Was anybody else in the house?—My wife, Peggy, was in bed with the kid.

You got down to Rottenrow?—I went to Charlie McArthur's house and knocked on the door. He was not in, so I made for Kerr's public-house in Taylor Street.

Did you get to Kerr's public-house?—I met a chap called Philip Donnelly. I asked him did he see Charlie McArthur. He said he

Patrick Carraher.

D. Bonnar

did not see him, and I invited Donnelly in for a cup of tea and some beer.

What did you do then?—I went forward to speak to Murdoch McKenzie. He was standing with a fair-haired chap at the Old Men's Home in Rottenrow about 10 yards from Cameron's pub. The big fair-haired chap was shouting he wanted to fight.

He wanted to fight with you?—Yes, when I went forward I asked him what was the matter.

By the COURT—You have told us the big fair-haired chap started shouting that he wanted to fight. What happened then?— I took his jacket and put it on and asked him what was the matter. He had his jacket off.

Examination continued—What happened then?—He said he would beat the best man in Rottenrow. I tried to pacify him.

Did you succeed?—No. He grabbed me by the lapel, and pushed me out and pulled me forward. I asked him not to pull me, and he loosened his grip on the lapel of my jacket. He said to me did I fancy a straight fight. That was a fair fight. I accepted his challenge. I walked to the middle of the street and took off my jacket. Then the chap walked towards Cameron's pub and he talked to Revie. I did not know what he said to Revie.

By the COURT—You accepted his challenge to a fair fight. What happened, did you stay or did you go away?—I stayed in the middle of the street and he walked along to Cameron's pub to where Revie was standing and he spoke to Revie. I was left in the middle of the street with my jacket off; my jacket was lying on the ground. Revie came running from the public pathway with his booted foot, but missed me. I jumped back and he fell to the ground, he lost his balance.

Examination continued—Did you ever have the fight?—No, there were no blows struck.

Why did you not have a fight?—The other chap then attacked me, the fair-haired chap. I turned and ran down Rottenrow to my sister's, No. 4 Collins Street.

Did you get a ladies' jacket from her?—Yes, to replace the one I had taken off and left in Rottenrow. I then went back to Rottenrow.

When you came back to Rottenrow whom did you meet?—I met Carraher and Thomas Watt facing Weaver Street.

Evidence for the Prosecution.

D. Bonnar

Did you meet Sarah Bonnar and Peggy Bonnar?—No, I met Sarah. I met Carraher and Watt at Weaver Street and we went up Rottenrow towards Cameron's pub, and it was then that I met my sister.

Did you, Carraher and Watt go somewhere after that?—Yes, we went and made for McAslin Street.

Why did you make for McAslin Street?—We went up to try and get things fixed, to get them put in the right way, to try and get things talked over. We did not want any fighting.

By the COURT—For what purpose did you go up to McAslin Street?—Patrick Carraher and Thomas Watt and I went up to McAslin Street. I knew the Gordon brothers since I was young.

Were you looking to see the Gordons or look for them?—No, I was going to see if I could see them to explain what had happened, that his good-brother had attacked me.

You were going to see the Gordons and tell them Revie had attacked you?—Yes.

Examination continued—Did you tell Patrick Carraher that was the reason you were going to McAslin Street?—Yes.

To what house did you intend to go?—Frances Gordon's house. I don't know the number in McAslin Street, but it is between Stanhope Street and Taylor Street.

Is that the house which Duncan Revie's wife was staying at?—I don't know where Duncan Revie was staying at that time.

You, Watt and Carraher started off towards McAslin Street. How did you go?—Down Taylor Street, along Cathedral Street, up Stanhope Street and turned left and went up the second close along from the left travelling west.

Did all three of you go there?—No, Watt stayed outside and Carraher and I went up the close.

Are you quite sure Watt was with you?—Yes, quite sure.

Now, was the close you went up one where one of the Gordons lived?—Yes, Frances Gordon.

Did you go up to Frances Gordon's house?—No, we went right into the back court and I looked up at the window, and the light was shining from the window. We came out of the close and joined Watt, and we turned from McAslin Street into Taylor Street.

What did you do then?—As we turned, John Gordon and Duncan Revie were coming down. I said to John Gordon,

Patrick Carraher.

D. Bonnar

"John." I was wanting to call him away and speak to him about Revie, but I never got the chance to speak to John Gordon. Revie attacked me with his booted foot and I jumped into the middle of the street. I had a hatchet in my possession.

That is what you were going to use as a peace offering to the Gordons, was it?—No.

By the COURT—Do I understand you to say that you were going to speak to John Gordon, but before you had an opportunity Revie did something to you?—Revie attacked me with his booted foot. He made a kick at me.

You had a hatchet in your possession?—Yes.

You took that in your hand?—No. I jumped to the middle of the street and I let the hatchet slide down. I let it come down my sleeve.

Go slowly. When Revie made a kick at you what did you do?—I jumped back into the middle of the street off the siver and Revie came at me.

So that you and Revie went away from the other two into the middle of the street?—Yes, Revie kept coming to me and I was retreating. It was me that was retreating to the far side of the street.

You were retreating from Revie to avoid the kick?—Yes.

Examination continued—Where was John Gordon at that time?—I don't know where he was. I just left him standing there on the pavement when Revie attacked me.

Where was Carraher?—Carraher and Watt were facing John Gordon.

Are you quite sure Watt was there?—Yes, Watt was definitely there.

What happened then?—Revie kept coming with his booted foot, which he swung and lost his balance. I had reversed the hatchet and used it as the policemen would use the wooden part of the hatchet when the man attacked me.

By the COURT—Revie attacked you?—Yes. I reversed the hatchet. I brought the hatchet from my sleeve and I used it. I was using the handle of the hatchet in the same manner as a policeman would use it.

Examination continued—And you hit Revie?—Yes, he hit me and

Evidence for the Prosecution.

D. Bonnar

I hit him. I asked Revie to wait a minute, I wanted to speak to him. He would not listen to me.

Did you turn and run?—I turned and ran away along McAslin Street west towards St. James' Road. Revie was at my back.

Do you know where John Gordon was at that time?—No.

By the COURT—The last you had seen of him was when you left him on the pavement and retreated out to the roadway with Revie trying to kick you?—Yes.

You never saw John Gordon again?—No.

When you left the pavement you had left Carraher and Watt beside John Gordon?—Yes.

Examination continued—What happened to Carraher while you were running away?—I did not see Carraher.

Did you see Watt?—No.

When did you next see Carraher?—When I got to the top of Canning Place Carraher was waiting for me.

Where was Watt?—I don't know. I never saw Watt after.

Did you go down Canning Place?—Yes, we crossed Cathedral Street, went down Hopetoun Place and turned down Rottenrow. We were going to turn into the pend into my house, but we saw Philip Donnelly. I left Carraher standing at the pend and went into my house.

Whom did you find there?—My wife and sister. I think Carraher came in afterwards. Watt came in after Carraher; he was the last to come in.

Did you have any conversation with Carraher while you were coming down with him from Canning Place to your house in Rottenrow?—No. We were not talking at all.

Did you not discuss what had happened?—When I met Carraher he was standing waiting on me and he told me he was fighting with Gordon. He said he had given Gordon a jag, or something.

Can you remember the exact words Carraher used?—No, I cannot mind.

Your recollection is that Carraher said he gave Gordon a jag. Did he say anything else about the fight?—No.

Did you say anything about the fight?—I never spoke about the fight. I didn't know till Carraher told me that he was fighting with Gordon. I did not know whom he was fighting. I was fighting with Revie.

Patrick Carraher.

D. Bonnar

Were there five people in your house in Rottenrow—Sarah, Peggy Bonnar your wife, Carraher, Watt and yourself?—No, there was also Philip Donnelly and Murdo McKenzie.

Did you get injured at all in the fight?—Yes, just at the side of my head. It was bleeding.

Did you say anything about your injury?—I never mentioned it.

Did Carraher say anything?—No.

Did he say nothing about the fight?—He said he was fighting with Gordon, or something.

Did he say that in the house?—Yes.

Did he say anything about the result of the fight with Gordon? —No.

Did he say anything about how he had been fighting with Gordon?—No.

By the Court—Did you understand what he meant when he said he had given Gordon a jag, or something?—Well, he could have pressed something against him, or something.

Did you understand what he meant when he made that statement?—No.

Did you ask him?—No.

Why not?—Well, I didn't know what he meant the way he spoke.

You had no idea at all, and you did not ask him?—No.

Did you never ask him what he had done?—No.

Examination continued—You have heard the word "jag" before. What does it mean?—Well, something jagged you. He could jag you with a pin or jag you with anything.

What does "jag" mean?—Someone has pressed something sharp against you with a point, something with a sharp edge.

Does it mean cut?—No, it will be pressed into you. Just like a jag, something like a hole.

You were discussing what happened in your house. Did Sarah Bonnar and your wife leave your house?—Yes.

Did you, Carraher, Watt, Murdoch McKenzie and Donnelly stay on for a time, and did you then go to Carraher's house?— Yes.

Who went with you?—Me and Carraher went to the house and Watt went for cigarettes.

Was that to 14, Tarbet Street, where your sister Sarah Bonnar was living?—Yes.

Evidence for the Prosecution.

D. Bonnar

When you got there did you find Sarah and your wife there?—Yes.

Did Watt join you there?—He came up to the house after that.

Did anybody else come to the house?—George Elliott, "Gasser" Elliott. He came with a tall chap whose name I do not know.

Why did they come to the house?—He heard my name being mentioned at the time John Gordon was injured, and he came up to tell me that John Gordon had died.

When they gave that information to you was there anyone else in the room?—He gave me that information in the kitchen when he came into the house.

Who else was in the kitchen?—Me, Carraher, Watt, my sister was in bed and my wife was sitting next to the bed.

Did Carraher hear that bit of information?—Yes.

Did you then go into the room off the kitchen?—I went as far as the room door. My sister was getting up out of bed.

By the COURT—Did all of you men, Elliott, his friend, you and Carraher go out of the kitchen?—We went out of the kitchen to the room.

Examination continued—After a minute did anybody go into the room?—I think my sister went into the room. She got up out of bed.

After your sister had got up did you go back to the kitchen?—Yes, and my wife was still sitting in the kitchen.

Where was "Gasser" Elliott, his friend and Carraher when you went back to the kitchen?—They were in the room. Shortly after that "Gasser" Elliott and his friend left.

After they had left did Carraher say anything to you?—He just said, "That's that away."

What did you understand by that?—Well, he meant that he or Elliott had given the big fellow something.

Shortly after that did you and your wife leave?—Yes.

Later that night were you arrested on a charge of murder?—Yes.

You had a weapon that night, had you not?—I had a hatchet in my possession.

Had Carraher anything?—No, he never showed me anything.

Fit Labels Nos. 1 and 2 together. Have you ever seen that before?—I have seen something like it about three weeks before Gordon was injured.

Patrick Carraher.

D. Bonnar

Where did you see it?—In Rottenrow.

In whose possession was it?—Patrick Carraher.

Cross-examined by MR. PHILIP—Were you detained for some time on a charge of murder?—Yes.

Was the evidence which you have given now first given by you to the police when you were under that charge?—Yes.

Reverting to the very beginning, I think you began that period in Thompson's bar. Had you previously met Carraher at his own house and had Carraher before that been drinking during the day?—Yes.

Did you often drink with Carraher?—Yes.

When you went to Thompson's public-house had he already had a good deal to drink?—Yes.

By the COURT—How do you know? Had you been in his company earlier?—No. My sister said he had been drinking through the day. I was up to my sister's at night. I went up with Carraher. When I went up to my sister's house Carraher invited me for a pint of beer, and I heard my sister say that he had a good refreshment the day; he had been drinking through the day, like.

Cross-examination continued—Were you in Thompson's bar from about six thirty till closing time, a matter of about three hours?—Yes.

Had you both a good deal of drink during that time?—Yes, we had a pretty decent drink.

I think you were pretty drunk yourself, were you not?—I wasn't what you would say drunk; I had a good drink right enough.

Was Carraher a good deal worse than you were?—Yes.

Later on while you were in Thompson's bar did Watt join you?—Yes.

At closing time did you leave, taking with you a considerable supply of drink and go to your own house at 116, Rottenrow?—Yes.

Had you and Carraher each six bottles of beer?—Yes, six small bottles each. Watt had three large bottles.

And then you were going to have a good time there?—We were going to have tea and a drink.

You thought you would get in a friend and so you went for Charles McArthur?—Yes.

When you came back eventually to the front of Cameron's bar

Evidence for the Prosecution.

D. Bonnar

you saw a fair-headed chap after you had spoken to Donnelly?—Yes.

Was he a sailor of the name of Keatings?—The fair-headed chap had on civilian clothes at the time. Keatings, I think his name was, or something.

Was he very drunk?—Yes, he had a good drink.

Were there a group of men with him who were also very drunk?—No. He was with Murdo McKenzie, who was holding the chap by his arms. He was shouting and bawling. McKenzie was trying to pacify him.

Was he wanting to get at you?—I don't know who he was fighting, but he was just shouting, "I'll fight the best man." I don't know whether he was arguing in the pub or not. I wasn't in Cameron's.

At that time did you see Revie?—Yes.

Was he pretty drunk too?—Yes, he had a good drink.

Was there a Gordon there too?—I saw John Gordon, who also had a good drink.

Some conversation passed between you and this fair-headed chap, but did it come to this that when any action was taken it was the fair-headed chap who wanted to attack you?—He wanted to fight me.

And by that time he had his jacket off?—Yes.

You tried to stop him fighting you?—I wanted to take him away. There was a black-headed girl along with him.

It has been suggested that at that time you had a file or some instrument of that kind in your possession. Is that so?—No.

Do you say that the fair-headed chap first turned back towards Revie beside whom John Gordon was standing?—Yes.

Did not both Revie and John Gordon make to attack you too?—No.

Did they not make to chase you?—Revie and the fair-haired chap attacked me and chased me down Rottenrow towards High Street. I ran to Collins Street.

You had left your jacket behind?—Left it in the street facing Cameron's public-house.

By a fish and chip shop close to Cameron's bar?—Yes, there is a close between it and the fish shop.

And when you went down to Collins Street that was to get a jacket, was it not, and to get something else?—I went to my sister because I got chased. I was getting attacked.

You were afraid?—Yes. They were against me. Two to one.

193

Patrick Carraher.

D. Bonnar

Did you think they were going to do you in?—No, beat me up.

And so you went to your sister's house, and did you get anything when you were there?—I asked my sister for a jacket, and she gave me a costume jacket. I said I would have to take something with me in case I was attacked by Revie or someone.

You got a hatchet?—Yes.

That was a sharp pointed hatchet?—Just an ordinary hatchet you break sticks with.

You came back and you felt secure now when you came back with this weapon, is that not so?—To keep them at a distance if they would attack me.

Eventually did you go up near Cameron's bar and get your own jacket again at the fish and chip shop?—Yes.

By that time you had met Carraher and Watt had you not?—Carraher and Watt were along with me.

They had come to help you?—They asked me what had happened.

Then you proceeded up Taylor Street for a bit, and eventually you went along Cathedral Street and McAslin Street round to the house of Frances Gordon?—To a close.

Your idea there was to try and get things right with Revie, to speak to the Gordons about it?—Yes.

Did you see a light in the house?—Yes.

And did you think there might be too many of them there for you?—I thought if I went up to explain, if Revie and the fair-headed chap were in the house and attacked me I would need to defend myself, and if there was a woman in the house it would have put her in a state of fear.

Were you anticipating there might be an attack by Revie against you?—In the house.

Was that by what had happened previously?—Yes.

Watt and Carraher were with you, Watt staying at the outside of the close?—Yes.

Then, when you came down through the close again to McAslin Street you decided to go westwards towards Taylor Street. Was Watt with you there?—And Carraher, yes.

Did you meet Revie and John Gordon at that corner?—No. As we turned the corner John Gordon and Revie were about ten yards from the corner coming down. They were travelling north and we were travelling south.

It has been suggested that you and the accused dived out of a

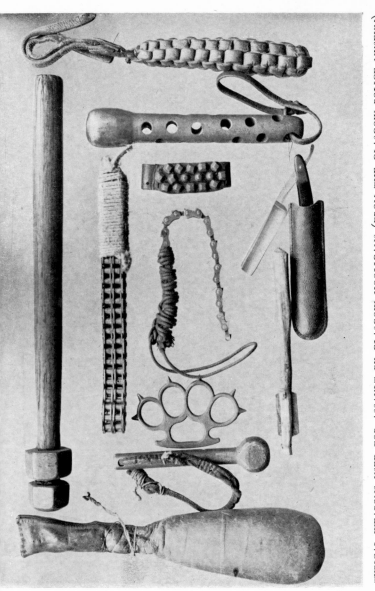

TYPICAL WEAPONS USED FOR ASSAULT BY GLASGOW HOOLIGANS (FROM THE GLASGOW POLICE MUSEUM)

Evidence for the Prosecution.

D. Bonnar

close in Taylor Street and attacked Revie and Gordon. Is there any truth in that whatsoever?—That is not true at all.

The two of you just happened to meet in the street practically at the corner of McAslin Street and Taylor Street?—Yes.

Were you almost past them before you noticed them?—As they were coming down I noticed them. I noticed John Gordon. I know John Gordon from being a kiddie. I said, "John." I wanted to speak to him, take him away and ask him to speak to Revie. But I never got a chance to speak.

Did both of them take up an aggressive attitude?—Revie attacked me right away and made a swing at me and jumped off the siver.

Did Gordon take on Carraher?—I don't know.

You said something about dropping a hatchet. Did you drop your hatchet at one point?—I dropped the hatchet and reversed the hatchet, holding the head of the hatchet in my hand.

Do you remember, at the time you dropped the hatchet, someone shouting, "Put the hatchet on him, Joe"?—No, I never heard it.

Might it have been said?—I never heard it but it might have been said.

Did you hear anyone shouting, "After him, Harry"?—No.

The fight took a little time, did it not?—Two or three minutes.

There would be blows on both sides?—Yes.

I put it to you that you struck John Gordon?—No.

Watt was still with you at the head of Taylor Street and the corner of McAslin Street?—Yes, Watt and Carraher.

Then you went westwards along McAslin Street and you saw nothing of Carraher until Canning Place?—Yes.

Do you know an expression, "a jig"? Have you heard of a "square jig", for example?—Yes.

What does that mean?—A fair fight. Jig is a slang word for fight.

If you said you had a wee jig that would mean a wee fight?—Yes.

Didn't Carraher use the word "wee"?—He said "wee".

Why did you omit reference to the word "wee" in your examination-in-chief?—That is the word Carraher puts to me, "I gave John Gordon a wee jag." I had it down in my statement to the police that Carraher said he gave him a wee jag.

Why did you not say that in your examination-in-chief?—I said Carraher told me he gave him a jag.

Patrick Carraher.

D. Bonnar

You are quite clear the word "wee" was used?—Yes.

Then did both of you go to your house at 116, Rottenrow and have a singsong and talk about the Moscow Dynamos?—We had a singsong and I was asked to sing.

You had rather a bright evening, had you not?—Yes.

And all of you were bright at that point?—Yes.

Then you went on to Tarbet Street and there a knock came on the door and "Gasser" Elliott and Stewart appeared?—Yes.

And you went to the door?—No.

You came along to the door after it had been opened?—I was standing in the kitchen and the door was just like that. (Indicating.)

So you did not need to go along to the door. Did one or other of them say that John Gordon was dead?—Yes.

Is it not the case that from that point onwards your manner was very different from what it had been before?—When I got told that John Gordon had died, and I knew I had been there at the time, and I knew then John Gordon was killed.

Is it not the case that you said at one point, "I will take the consequences"?—No, that is not true.

And immediately you got this information about John Gordon's death did you not at once get rid of your bloodstained shirt?—I took my shirt off and cleaned myself up. I knew I would be arrested.

Did you not at once get rid of your hatchet?—I took the hatchet in my house, along with Carraher, and put it in the bunker.

Was it not after that that there was any talk by Carraher about "That's that away"?—When Elliott and the big chap left I was drying myself, and Elliott said, "I am away," and after this Carraher says to me, "That's that away."

Carraher was quite unconcerned that evening?—Carraher got a fright, the same as me. We all got a fright. We were all upset. The house was upset.

We have had evidence that it was you who were upset and that Carraher was not?—I definitely got a fright because I knew John Gordon so well. I have known him since a kiddie. I went to school with Joseph Gordon. Carraher got a fright, my wife got a fright, my sister got a fright.

Do you remember Carraher saying anything about people "piping" at him?—Yes, I have heard him often. That is just like a man who comes into a public-house and he looks and he says,

Evidence for the Prosecution.

"That man's piping at me." Any man that pipes at you is a man who is looking at you. That is slang for looking.

But looking at you in a suspicious way?—Well, it all depends on how the chap looks at him.

Carraher has used that expression to you as if he was worried about people looking at him, and he has always referred to that as people piping at him?—Yes.

Is the word "piping" commonly used among your pals?—Yes.

Re-examined by MR. JOHNSTON—You have told my friend that the word "jig" means a fight?—Yes, a man saying, "I will have a fair jig," that is a slang word for a fight.

You told me that the word "jag" means to shove a sharp instrument into something?—Yes.

In the conversation you had with Carraher somewhere about Canning Place what did Carraher tell you then?—When I got to Carraher he just said, "I have given Gordon a wee jag."

By the COURT—When you arrived at Canning Place after the fight at the corner of Taylor Street and McAslin Street, was Carraher already there?—Yes.

Whereabouts in Canning Place was he standing?—Up off St. James' Road.

Was he right up at the top of Canning Place?—Yes.

When you arrived there had you come along Cathedral Street and then turned up Canning Place?—I came along McAslin Street and across St. James' Road and up through Canning Place.

And from St. James' Road how did you get into Canning Place?—Up through a passage way, a public pathway. Carraher was standing there when I arrived.

Had you arranged to meet him there?—No.

MRS. MARGARET CASSIDY or BONNAR (26), sworn.

Examined by MR. JOHNSTON—I live at 116, Rottenrow, Glasgow, and am the wife of the witness Daniel Bonnar. I remember the evening of Friday, 23rd November, 1945. My husband went out about the back of six o'clock and returned about a quarter past nine with Watt and Patrick Carraher. I identify Patrick Carraher as the man sitting between the two policemen. My husband then went out again to bring in some friends for a singsong.

197

Patrick Carraher.

Mrs. M. Bonnar

My sister-in-law, Sarah Bonnar, came into my house with Mrs. Colquhoun.

Did Sarah Bonnar give you certain information?—Yes, she said that my husband was fighting in the Rottenrow. She asked if he was in the house, where he was, and she said that he was fighting in the Rottenrow.

What did the accused, Patrick Carraher, do then?—They all just went out then.

Did they go out quickly or slowly?—I was in bed, you see. From my bed you can't see the door. They just walked out, as far as I know. I did not go out.

Some time later that evening did Sarah Bonnar come to your house?—Yes, she was only five or ten minutes out and she came back again and we sat together.

After you had been sitting for some time did someone else come into the house?—Only my husband and Patrick Carraher. It must have been about ten to ten. About five or ten minutes after that Watt came in.

Anyone else?—No, I went out then with Sarah over to her house at 14, Tarbet Street.

Did you leave at your house, 116, Rottenrow, your husband Daniel Bonnar, Patrick Carraher and Watt?—Yes.

Did anyone come to the house at 14, Tarbet Street?—Yes, my husband and Patrick Carraher came in about half-past eleven, and about ten minutes after that Watt came in. Later two other men came in, one of whom was Gasser Elliott.

Why did Gasser Elliott come to the house at Tarbet Street?—I don't know. He was looking for my husband.

Did he say anything?—I heard him say that John Gordon was dead.

Did your husband hear him make that remark?—I don't think so.

Was there anyone else in the room when Gasser Elliott made that remark?—We were all there—Sarah Bonnar, myself, my husband, Watt and Patrick Carraher.

What happened after Elliott told you all that John Gordon was dead?—Well, they were all in a state. They were all excited. Sarah was in bed and she told them to go into the room till she got up, and they did so. After Sarah got up they came back. Gasser Elliott and his friend then left.

After Gasser Elliott and his friend left did anyone say anything?—No, not that I can remember.

Evidence for the Prosecution.

Did Carraher say anything to your husband?—No.

He did not speak to your husband at all?—They were speaking. They could not believe it right. They were talking about that. They could not make it out.

What were they talking about?—They were surprised at what had happened.

Were they talking about the death of John Gordon?—My husband said he could not believe it.

Just before you left did Carraher make any remark to your husband?—Not that I can remember.

Then you and your husband went home and your husband was arrested in the early hours of the morning of the 24th?—Yes.

Cross-examined by Mr. PHILIP—Sarah Bonnar came into your house early in the evening, about nine fifteen, and said that your husband was fighting down in the Rottenrow?—Yes, it would be about half-past nine.

She was anxious that someone should go and help?—No.

Did she say that he was being chased?—She said the other woman said he was being chased along Rottenrow.

SARAH MACFARLANE BONNAR (38), sworn.

Examined by Mr. JOHNSTON—I was formerly married to a man Harvey. That marriage has been dissolved. I live at 14, Tarbet Street, and am a sister of Daniel Bonnar. I am generally known as Sarah Bonnar. About nine fifteen on the evening of 23rd November, 1945, Mrs. Colquhoun, a post-woman, came to my house and told me that my brother Daniel was being chased by the Gordons in Rottenrow. We went to my brother's house at 116, Rottenrow. Patrick Carraher opened the door to me when I chapped at the door, and he and Watt were in the house. Mrs. Bonnar was in her bed. I said to Paddy, "Where is Dan?" and he said, "He is out to get a share of the beer."

You informed him that Daniel Bonnar was in trouble?—Yes, and he and Watt went out.

Did you go down to the Rottenrow too?—Yes, and I saw Carraher speaking to a man next Cameron's pub. I did not see Watt at that time.

Did you see your brother?—No, it was after that I saw my brother.

Ultimately did you see them all in the Rottenrow?—Yes, I

Patrick Carraher.

Sarah Bonnar

stayed in the Rottenrow between Taylor Street and the fish shop and I saw John Gordon and a man come past. John Gordon was lying against the shoulder. I said to the man next to the fish shop, "Where did they go?" because I lost sight of them. He said, "I think they went down the Brae," that is Balmano Brae. I went a bit down Rottenrow and I met my brother.

Did you see Patrick Carraher and Watt?—Yes, the three of them were in company in Rottenrow. They were coming up Rottenrow towards Taylor Street end, and they went into the fish shop and got my brother's coat. They then went down Taylor Street way.

Did you then go up to your brother's house at 116, Rottenrow, and find Peggy Bonnar there?—Yes. I stayed there about fifteen or twenty minutes. It must have been about a quarter to ten anyway.

Did somebody come to the house?—A chap came to the house. I think it was Dan came in first. Paddy came in at his back; that is Patrick Carraher who I see in the dock.

Did somebody come in afterwards?—Yes, a man Watt. Nobody else came when I was in.

Did you and Peggy Bonnar leave 116 then and go to your house at 14, Tarbet Street?—We did.

Did someone come round there?—Dan and Paddy came in at twelve o'clock, and Watt came in after that.

Anyone else?—A chap came to the door, and when the girl went to the door there was no one; when Paddy went to the door he saw two men and asked who they were wanting. They were "Gasser" Elliott and another man whose name I don't know. I was in bed at this time.

Did "Gasser" Elliott tell all of you that John Gordon was dead?—Yes.

Did you tell the men to leave the room while you got up?—I did, and they left the kitchen and went ben the room. When I got up they came ben after a minute or two. "Gasser" Elliott and his friend then left.

Did "Gasser" Elliott have anything in his hand when he left? —I never saw anything.

Did he remove anything from your house when he left?—Not that I saw; never saw anything in his hand at all when he left or saw anything in the house.

Do you know what Labels Nos. 1 and 2 are?—I would call it a chisel or something.

Have you ever seen it before?—No, I never saw it before.

Evidence for the Prosecution.

Sarah Bonnar

Cross-examined by MR. PHILIP—On this evening did Mrs. Colquhoun come to your door and say that your brother Dan was being chased by the Gordons?—She did.

Did she use any other expression? Did she use the word, "murder"?—She came to the door and chapped the door and I went to it and she said, "Sarah, if you don't come up your brother will be murdered by the Gordons."

And did you run for help?—I got my coat and ran up to Rottenrow to see if there was any trouble and I went to my brother's house.

When you went to Rottenrow to see if there was trouble, by that time had they moved down the street?—There was nobody there at all.

You then ran to your brother's house. Was that to get help there?—I just went to see where he was.

Has the accused, Carraher, lived in your house for some time? —He has.

Was he living in your house about 1941?—Roughly.

Recently have you noticed a change in his manner?—Aye. He has been different, somehow.

Is he suspicious?—Very suspicious.

Can you tell me anything about men; suspecting men in the cupboards in the house?—Always coming back with the same thing.

Do you mean when there is no one there?—No one there.

Is that a development since about last summer?—Yes.

Is he a very excitable man?—Yes.

Can you tell me what happened with regard to his army grading? —He wasn't fit. He was bad with his stomach and his chest is bad.

Does he drink a great deal?—He does.

Can you tell me whether he eats on the days that he drinks, or what does he do?—He doesn't eat. That's one thing he doesn't do.

Does he drink the days the bars are open and eat the other days?—No, he doesn't eat at all.

On 23rd November had he been out drinking that day?—He was out from eleven o'clock till half-past two.

That was when the bars were open during the day?—That is right.

Was that his usual practice?—Yes.

Patrick Carraher.

THOMAS CONNELLY WATT (47), sworn.

Examined by MR. JOHNSTON—I live at 146, Rottenrow, Glasgow, and I am usually known in the neighbourhood as "Wee Watt". On the evening of 23rd November, 1945, I was in the company of Daniel Bonnar and Patrick Carraher; I identify Carraher as the man in the dock between the policemen. I went with Carraher and Bonnar from Thompson's public-house to Bonnar's house in Rottenrow, and then Bonnar went out to get some friends in to have a drink.

Did you then hear that Bonnar was being attacked in the Rottenrow?—Yes.

Did you and Carraher then leave the house and go into Rottenrow?—Yes. After a time I met Bonnar in the Rottenrow and told Bonnar to go up to the house, that he had a kiddie lying badly in bed, not well.

You tried to persuade Bonnar to go home because his small boy was not well. Did he accept your persuasions?—He refused. He was determined in the words he used that night. Carraher was there when he spoke.

What did you and Carraher and Bonnar then do?—Came right westwards up the Rottenrow and stopped at the fish supper shop. We then went down Taylor Street to Cathedral Street. Bonnar and Carraher then separated, Carraher going along Cathedral Street and Bonnar along Stirling Road eastwards.

Having got to the corner of Cathedral Street and Taylor Street which way did Carraher turn?—To the right.

Which way did Bonnar turn?—To the left.

By the COURT—Where did you go?—Westwards towards Canning Place.

Did you go with Bonnar?—No.

So all three of you separated?—Yes.

Did you arrange to meet some place later?—No.

Did you meet later?—Not till I arrived back in the house.

Examination continued—Are you quite sure of that?—Yes.

You know that what Bonnar says is that all three of you went up to McAslin Street and went into a close between Stanhope Street and Taylor Street, and that you then came out of the close and went up McAslin Street and down Taylor Street?—No, I know nothing about it.

Evidence for the Prosecution.

T. C. Watt

And that you there met John Gordon and Duncan Revie?—Did not meet nobody. I was on my own at that time when I reached Canning Place.

So that your story is you left Carraher and Bonnar at the junction of Cathedral Street and Taylor Street?—Yes.

Did you see them again that night?—When I went back to the house.

What time elapsed between your leaving them at the corner and getting back to the house?—As near as possible about an hour.

When you got to Canning Place what did you do?—Went up Canning Place into St. James' Road, across to Ronald Street to the top of Taylor Street. There I met a man and a woman and a child, and they told me it was terrible.

I do not want to hear what they told you. Did you see anything?—No.

Did you see anything of Carraher there?—No, I saw nobody.

What did you do after you had spoken to the man and the woman and the child?—I came right down again the same road, across St. James' Road, back into Canning Place, and up to Bonnar's house again.

Why did you go up Cathedral Street, up Canning Place, through the lane into St. James' Road, up Ronald Street to the junction of Taylor Street?—To get away from the two of them, because the determination was there to cause trouble.

Was that the whole evening?—Yes.

What made you think there was going to be trouble that night? —Because of the words that were said, that there was somebody going to get it, using a vulgar word.

Was that your way home, Cathedral Street, Canning Place and so on?—No.

Why did you go that way?—To get away out of their road.

Did you know where Bonnar was going and where Carraher was going?—No.

When you got back to Daniel Bonnar's house in Rottenrow was anyone there when you got in?—The two of them, Bonnar and Carraher, were in the house along with Sarah Bonnar and Daniel Bonnar's wife. After some talk Sarah and Peggie Bonnar left.

Was there any talk of what had happened earlier in the evening between you and Patrick Carraher and Bonnar?—Yes, they got up a discussion explaining how the thing had happened.

Who got up a discussion?—Well, the first thing whenever I went into the house, Bonnar answered the door when I chapped.

Patrick Carraher.

T. C. Watt

He opened the door and I went in. I saw Bonnar looking round about the fireplace and the sink. I said, "What are you looking for?" He said, "A hatchet," so I said, "Where did you put it?" He said, "I left it in the sink." So Carraher turned round and said perhaps Peggie had shifted it. That was the first thing whenever I went into the house, and then the discussion came up after that.

What was the discussion?—About how they used the weapons. Bonnar spoke first, and said he lifted the hatchet and struck him on the back of the head and that he drew it down, but did not know whether he hit him hard enough for to kill him.

Did he say who he had hit on the back of the head?—I didn't hear him say what person he struck, but I don't know how many persons were there.

Did you not ask him?—No, I didn't ask him. I just let him tell the whole story and I just took it all in.

Did Bonnar say anything else?—Carraher came out next.

What did Carraher say?—He said that he did a bit of a toe dance, and showing how he came down with the tool.

By the COURT—When he showed you what he did with the tool what part of his body was he moving?—He was moving his right hand backward and forward that way (indicating).

Carraher illustrated how he had been tip-toe dancing and he showed how his arm came down while he was doing so?—Yes.

Examination continued—Are you quite sure that Carraher carried out this demonstration as you have shown his lordship?—Yes.

Have you any shadow of doubt about your recollection?—Yes, I am sure it happened. That was the demonstration he gave to me.

Had he anything in his hand when he was giving the demonstration?—He had the tool—no, he did not have the tool at that time in his hand. Just the bare fists.

What is the tool you are talking about?—Because I had seen it beforehand. A steel blade, but I did not see any handle. Counting the fists and the tool it came to about 6 inches in length, if there was any handle on it at all.

You had seen a steel blade before?—Yes.

In whose possession was the steel blade?—Carraher's.

When was this?—When we left Bonnar's house to go down to Rottenrow; about twenty minutes past nine.

Was that after you and Carraher had received the information that Daniel Bonnar was engaged in a fight?—Yes.

Evidence for the Prosecution.

T. C. Watt

And you say you saw this blade in Carraher's hand?—He had it in his pocket and said, "This is the very tool for them."

How did you see it then?—Because he showed the blade from the top pocket, he drew his thumb across it like that (indicating).

Did he draw back the lapel of his jacket or anything like that? —No.

Did you see this blade clearly?—I saw the steel part.

Do you remember what that steel part was like?—Sharp at the point and it came down and cut in quick and then down.

Have you ever seen Label No. 2 before?—It was much similar to that.

You have told us about the demonstration Carraher gave you and that he had nothing in his hand. Did he say anything?—Yes, he said he did not know whether he got him down the side of the face or shoulder.

Did Carraher say anything more about the fight?—No.

Did you and Carraher and Bonnar then leave the house?—Yes.

I think you left them for a little time and then joined them again at Sarah Bonnar's house at 14, Tarbet Street?—Yes.

In the early hours of the morning of 24th November were you arrested and charged with murder?—Yes.

Cross-examined by MR. PHILIP—And it was then you gave your first statement to the police?—Yes.

You referred to a remark which was made in the Rottenrow by Bonnar, and then you three—you, Carraher and Bonnar—walked down Taylor Street in the direction of Cathedral Street and stopped at the corner?—Yes.

Do you suggest that Carraher went east, that is to say in the direction of Stanhope Street, and that Bonnar went west?—No, I went west. Carraher went east and Bonnar went east, the two of them.

In your previous evidence you said that one, Bonnar, went left, and the other went right. Does that not mean that Bonnar went along Cathedral Street in the direction of Canning Place?—No, he went the High Street way. Carraher went right along Cathedral Street towards the High Street.

Then they both went in the same direction?—Yes, only separated at the junction by the police box.

Is your evidence that they only began to go left and right when they reached Stirling Road?—Yes.

There is a considerable distance between the foot of Taylor

Patrick Carraher.

T. C. Watt

Street and the beginning of Stirling Road?—I cannot tell you how far they went, because when they separated I turned back.

I put it to you that you went with them, that you went up Stanhope Street, that you stood outside a close in McAslin Street, and that you came round to Taylor Street?—No.

Then if evidence has been given to that effect by Bonnar, is it your view that Bonnar is not telling the truth?—No, he is not telling the truth.

Do you say that you spent an hour between the time when you say you left them until you came to Bonnar's house?—Nearly an hour when I spoke to that man and woman at the top of Ronald Street and Taylor Street.

All you had to do was to go up Ronald Street and back to Rottenrow?—It was to keep out of their way.

But even going round by Canning Place could that not all have been done in a matter of ten minutes?—I could not tell you.

How do you suggest you filled in the time?—Talking to the man and woman and I took my time.

Do you mean you were standing at the corner of Taylor Street and Ronald Street talking to a man and a woman for a considerable time?—That is counting the time going up there and back again.

The walking would not take long. Did you stand for some time at the corner of Taylor Street and Ronald Street?—No, I just got up there when the woman and the man approached me. They spoke to me and said it was terrible using a hatchet. I thought it was down in Parliamentary Road. I said, "You had better get out of the road, Missus. I am going up this way. I am going up home. I have enough trouble at home without this."

They told you it was terrible using a hatchet. Did you then proceed to Dan Bonnar's house?—Yes.

Was that because you knew he had a hatchet?—I proceeded to get my drink. I had a drink in the house at the time.

Was that because you knew Dan Bonnar had a hatchet?—No, I did not proceed to his house because I knew he had a hatchet.

You have told us that after it was discovered that it was Wee Watt at the door, the first thing that happened was that Bonnar was looking round for a hatchet?—Yes.

I suggest to you that the reason why he was looking round for the hatchet was because you having heard a conversation about a hatchet went straight to Bonnar's house and told him about the remark, and that he then proceeded to look for the hatchet for the

206

Evidence for the Prosecution.

T. C. Watt

purpose of getting it out of the way?—No. He was looking for the hatchet before I got in. Both Peggy Bonnar and Sarah Bonnar had just left the house when I went in.

You say Bonnar said he struck someone on the back of the head?—Yes.

You don't know who it was?—No. He told me about drawing the hatchet and striking him on the back of the head, but I don't know who he struck.

With regard to what you called tip-toe dancing are you thinking of someone who was getting into the attitude of defence, such as a boxer?—It was a sort of boxer's attitude and tip-toe dancing.

Do you say that the weapon was lifted high up?—Yes.

Was it a case of stretching?—It was the hand that was used, not the weapon.

Was the hand held, according to you, stretched at its full height? —Just half-way above the head. The arm was bent a little, not in full swing.

How do you say the hand was held?—Shut.

That is to say, with the thumb at the top?—Yes.

Will you just illustrate from that position how far you say the hand was brought down?—He came right down with it. He said he came right down and he did not know whether he got him on the side of the face or the shoulder.

You think when the accused was illustrating it he came right down to his waist?—He came right down and then stood up against the dresser.

Was Carraher quite cool? He was not upset in any way?— There was none of them upset.

Not excited at all?—No.

You did not see any kind of weapon at that time?—No.

And the only time when you say you saw something was earlier in the evening?—That was when we got word in the house.

When you saw a little bit peeping out of Carraher's pocket? —Yes.

You said to the man and woman at the corner of Ronald Street and Taylor Street that you were intending to go home. Why did you not go home?—I said I was going down the road, not home. Well, it was home, according to my way—going down that way.

I put it to you that you were at the top of Taylor Street and the corner of McAslin Street that evening and that you were there with Bonnar and Carraher?—No.

207

Patrick Carraher.

Re-examined by MR. JOHNSTON—I want to clear up the point where you left Bonnar and Carraher. You started off down the Rottenrow and went up Taylor Street. Suppose you turned right in Taylor Street, if you carried on walking on the right-hand pavement you would have come to High Street?—Yes.

Supposing you come up Taylor Street and turned only half-right, you would go up Stirling Road?—Yes.

Is there between Stirling Road and Cathedral Street an island? —There is an island between the two streets and a police box there.

Whereabout was it that you left the accused and Daniel Bonnar? —At the police box.

By the COURT—When did you first tell anyone about the demonstration which you say Carraher gave in the Rottenrow house when you returned that night an hour or so after leaving the other two?—To the C.I.D. at the Central Police Station on the Sunday.

On the morning you were arrested?—The morning I was arrested was Saturday morning at half-past four. I was taken out of my bed, and on the Sunday I was taken down for enquiry.

DR. GEORGE MACDONALD SCOTT (55), sworn.

Examined by MR. JOHNSTON—I am a Bachelor of Medicine, a Bachelor of Science. For about 17 years I have been the doctor at His Majesty's Prison, Barlinnie, Glasgow.

So it would be fair to say that you have a considerable experience of looking after the bodily and mental health of prisoners? —That is true.

Have you had the accused, Patrick Carraher, under your care since he went into Barlinnie Prison?—I have.

Have you seen him frequently?—Almost daily.

Have you formed any opinion as to his sanity?—I have formed the opinion that he is sane.

Have you found in him any sign of mental disease?—I have not.

Have you found any sign that he is a psychopathic personality? —If I could have a definition of psychopathic personality perhaps I could answer that.

Well, how would you yourself define a psychopathic personality?—I have great difficulty in defining it, because there is no set definition, I think, of what a psychopathic personality is. The general opinion would appear to me to be that a psychopathic

Evidence for the Prosecution.

Dr. G. M. Scott

personality is one in which there is a condition of emotional instability which affects the judgment and the behaviour, and in which there is episodically or permanently some mental disorder.

Accepting that definition for the moment, have you seen any sign of that in the accused?—I have not.

Cross-examined by MR. PHILIP—You are not a psychiatrist? —Well, I have a great deal of psychiatric work to do. In the course of my work I have to deal with very many cases of insanity.

May I take it that you do not claim to be a psychiatrist, a specialist in the sense that, for example, Dr. Angus McNiven or Professor William Blyth are?—As I say, I have great experience in these cases, and I am not prepared to say whether I am comparable with them or not.

Psychopathic personality is quite a well recognized medical category?—No, on the whole it is not, because it has been so much confused of recent years.

Would you agree that it is quite well recognized at least amongst psychiatrists?—I think even amongst psychiatrists there is a great difference of opinion; perhaps not so much in essentials as in details.

It is a condition, is it not, which would be described as gross abnormality short of certifiable insanity?—Yes, putting it shortly that could be.

You might perhaps also describe it as disease of the thinking processes?—No, I think not. I think that would be a wrong definition.

Would you agree that it is a disease which is perhaps mainly constitutional, but is also accentuated by environment?—That is really more in the nature of what one would call a constitutional psychopathic inferiority. I think that is more what you would describe it.

Would you agree that it is characterized by emotional instability quite beyond the normal?—Yes, I think that is generally accepted.

And that in any condition of stress, for example, that emotional instability will be further accentuated?—Yes, that is so.

Would you agree that it is characterized by suspicions amounting to a delusional suspicion very often?—No, I should not say that was characteristic of it.

But if you find that, then that is a pretty severe case?—No, I should not say so. That might be associated with it, but that might take you into a different class altogether.

Is it also characterized by defective judgment?—Yes.

Patrick Carraher.

Dr. G. M. Scott

One of the features of a psychopathic person is that he is not able to form a correct mental view of the situation such as a normal person would?—Well, I would rather put it that his judgment is more liable to be upset by his instability.

Supposing you have a psychopathic person suffering from this type of mental disease, would you expect that condition to be accentuated by excessive alcoholism?—Undoubtedly alcoholism would affect it.

And that would affect it in such a diseased person to a much greater extent than in the case of a normal individual?—Yes, I think the emotionally unstable person is always more affected.

But I am talking about a psychopathic personality. Do you agree that that type of mental case is much more affected by drink than the ordinary individual?—Yes.

You know that this particular accused attempted to commit suicide?—Yes, I was there at the time.

Indeed, you have removed any razors or anything of that kind? —I have.

What was the date of that attempt?—1934.

Do you also know that he is medically unfit for war service?—I did not know it.

You will not, of course, have seen the affect of drink upon him while he has been under detention?—No, of course not.

Will you agree a psychopathic person would have a sub-normal appreciation of the quality of his acts?—No, I would not agree with that.

And that he would have less responsibility than a normal person?—Do you mean in these particular instances where alcoholism comes in as well?

Take it generally first, and then give your answer in relation to alcohol?—Generally speaking a psychopathic person, as such, would, I think, be considered less responsible than a normal person.

Is it not a well recognized fact that in periods of strain that diminished responsibility tends to increase?—I am not really prepared to say what the degree of responsibility is in any supposititious case like that.

At any rate, you agree that there would be less responsibility in a psychopathic person than in a normal person?—On the whole I should say so.

May I take it that that lessened responsibility would be increased if the patient was in an alcoholic condition?—If alcoholism reduces responsibility, yes.

INTERIOR OF NORTH COURT, GLASGOW, SHOWING THE WITNESS-BOX, DOCK, AND COUNSELS' TABLE. ON THE EXTREME RIGHT IS THE JURY BOX, AND THE BENCHES ON THE LEFT ARE FOR THE MAGISTRATES OF THE CITY OF GLASGOW

Evidence for the Prosecution.

Dr. G. M. Scott

What I want to get quite clearly is this: is it not a characteristic of the case of psychopathic personality that alcoholism does still further accentuate the disease?—Yes.

Did you learn anything about the accused having searched in cupboards to find men who were not secreted there?—No, he has never mentioned that to me, and I had no history of that.

Did you see traces of a persecution mania?—I did not.

Having regard to the charge which was hanging over the accused did he appear to have the appreciation which a normal person has of such a charge?—Yes.

I suggest to you that he had not?—In my opinion it was definite.

And that one of the features of this accused is that he had no appreciation?—No, I don't agree.

Re-examined by Mr. Johnston—My friend has put a number of questions to you all based on the assumption that the accused is a psychopathic personality. Has he or has he not in your opinion a psychopathic personality?—In my opinion he has not.

By the Court—On how many occasions, approximately, had you the opportunity of considering and examining the state of the accused recently?—Well, I have seen him practically every day since about 25th November, and I have also had him watched during all that time in case any such symptom of mental disorder should arise.

I understand you have been unable to discover any traces whatsoever of mental disease or mental disorder?—That is so.

Did you discover any traces suggestive of alcoholism affecting his mental processes?—No.

From what you saw would there be any justification for suggesting that he is a man who is on the border-line of insanity?—I do not think so.

That he is affected by partial insanity?—No.

What is called unsoundness of mind or aberration of mind. Were you able to discover any traces of the conditions described in either of these terms?—No.

Are you satisfied that there are no traces which give rise to the description which could be applied to him in these terms?—I am absolutely satisfied.

Mr. Johnston—That is the case for the Crown.

Patrick Carraher.

Dr. A. McNiven

Evidence for the Defence.

DR. ANGUS MCNIVEN, sworn.

Examined by MR. PHILIP—I am a Bachelor of Medicine and a Bachelor of Surgery of Glasgow University, a Fellow of the Royal Faculty of Physicians and Surgeons of Glasgow; Fellow of the Royal College of Physicians of Edinburgh, and I hold the Diploma of Psychological Medicine of London. I am Physician Superintendent of the Glasgow Royal Mental Hospital, Gartnavel, and I am lecturer in Psychiatry at the University of Glasgow and Honorary Consultant Psychiatrist to the Glasgow Western Infirmary.

Have you conducted an examination of the accused?—Yes, I first saw him on 21st February, 1946.

Have you seen him again since?—I saw him to-day and also on Wednesday.

Are you familiar with an expression, "a psychopathic personality"?—I am; it is a well recognized clinical condition and is described in text-books.

Have you considered the condition of the accused with reference to that clinical condition?—I have. I am inclined to place him in that category.

Would you tell me whether that is a constitutional or environmental disease, or both?—I think it is constitutional.

May it be accentuated by a particular environment?—It might be.

Is it a condition of gross abnormality?—It varies in its manifestations, but it is a condition in which there is an inability on the part of the person affected to adapt himself to ordinary social conditions. That is putting it very broadly.

It is a mental state which is something less than certifiable insanity?—Yes, it is usually less than certifiable insanity.

Is it associated with emotional instability?—Yes.

In this particular case what did you find with regard to the accused's emotional stability or otherwise?—During my examination of the accused he did not show any particular emotional instability, but I thought that his attitude was very abnormal. I thought that he had no appreciation, or very little appreciation, of the gravity of the charge against him, and that he was concerned with what seemed to be trivial matters considering his situation.

Did you ascertain something about his childhood?—From himself.

Evidence for the Defence.

Dr. A. McNiven

Would you look at Production No. 1 for the Defence. Is that a report dated 21st February, 1946, signed by you on soul and conscience?—Yes, it is a true report. It reads as follows:

21st February, 1946.

"On the instructions of Miss Brash, Solicitor, 105, St. Vincent Street, Glasgow, I examined Patrick Carraher at H.M. Prison, Barlinnie, Glasgow, on 21st February, 1946.

"The accused is a single man of 39 years of age. His father is alive. His mother died when he was a child.

"There is said to be no history of mental illness in his family.

"I found the accused to be clear in his mind. His memory is not impaired, and he seemed to me to be a man of average intelligence. He was able to give me a clear account of his life history. He states that after his mother's death, and when he was about 4 years of age his father re-married. His second wife did not live long, and he married again. The accused states that his stepmother did not like him, and that she constantly complained to his father about him, and that in consequence of this he was frequently ill-treated by his father, so that he often slept out of the house in lobbies and other places.

"He went to school until he was 14 years of age, and he attained to the Supplementary Standard. He says that he was an average scholar.

"The accused has never been in regular employment except for very short periods. For many years he has drunk heavily, and he states that he was drunk on the night on which the offence with which he is charged was committed. In 1934 he attempted to cut his throat.

"During my examination of the accused I failed to elicit any symptoms of mental disease in the ordinary sense of the term, but, in my opinion, the accused cannot be regarded as normal. Throughout his life he has shown a gross lack of moral sense, and a complete lack of any social responsibility. He has shown himself to be emotionally unstable, and at times violent in his behaviour, and with very little capacity to control his actions.

"During my examination of him he failed to show any signs of normal appreciation of the seriousness of his present position. His chief concern when I saw him seemed to be not

213

Patrick Carraher.

Dr. A. McNiven

the consequence to him of the charge against him, but the fact that he is under close supervision in the prison. This he resents strongly, and he complained to me about it, saying that he was sane, and yet he was being treated as a person of unsound mind, and he appealed to me to put an end to what he considers to be an injustice to him.

"The accused is sane and fit to plead, but, in my opinion, he is not a normal person, in as much as that throughout his life he has shown a lack of moral sense, and regard for his own safety or for the safety and well-being of others. These characteristics lead me to regard him as a psychopathic personality, which is a recognized clinical condition, in which are included these persons who from childhood or early youth show gross abnormality in their social behaviour and emotional reactions, but who do not as a rule show a degree of abnormality amounting to certifiable insanity.

"This report is given on Soul and Conscience.

"(Sgd.) Angus McNiven, M.B., F.R.C.P.E.""

Do you regard him as a person of diminished responsibility? —Well, it depends on what is meant by responsibility. If it means does the accused know the difference between right and wrong intellectually, does he know that if he commits a wrong act he is liable to punishment, then he is responsible; but if it means that he has a proper appreciation of his social responsibility, that he is capable of resisting temptation and capable of exercising control over his actions, then in my opinion he is not as responsible as a normal person.

At the time you saw him, of course, he had not had drink for some time. Would alcoholism accentuate the condition of the consequences of psychopathic personality you found in him?—It would lower any capacity for self-control he had.

And that capacity in your view, is less than normal?—Yes.

I think since you made that report you have learned that he has certain suspicions?—Yes. I interviewed Sarah Bonnar, the woman with whom he has been living for some years.

In consequence of what she told you what opinion did you form?—I found that he was intensely suspicious, so far as I could make out, without reason.

Would you regard that as another manifestation of his psychopathic personality?—Yes.

Evidence for the Defence.

Dr. A. McNiven

Cross-examined by Mr. Johnston—Am I right in thinking that in the branch of medicine in which you are a specialist the greater the opportunity you or any other doctor has of examining a patient the better is more likely to be your diagnosis?—Yes, I admit that as a general proposition.

You only had the advantage of seeing the accused on three occasions?—That is correct.

Apart from the statement made to you by Sarah Bonnar, you have had to rely for the facts in the first part of your report on the statements made by the accused himself?—Not entirely. My judgment of the accused's condition is based mainly on his record, on his life story.

And the accused has given you his life story?—Yes, that is correct.

Have you been able to check that life story independent of the accused's statement?—No, I have not been able to check it except through the information I was given by Dr. Scott of Barlinnie Prison.

You say he is of average intelligence, and you also state in your report that you failed to elicit any symptoms of mental disease? —Yes, I said that in my report. By that I mean disease amounting to insanity, disease in the sense of what is called a psychosis, as distinct from abnormality in his personality. You refer to certain conditions as being disease conditions, and other conditions are recognized as being disorders of the personality.

Do I understand you to say that this psychopathic personality is a disorder?—Yes, a disordered personality rather than a diseased.

The reason you think he suffers from this psychopathic personality is, I understand, from the last paragraph of your report, first, that he has a lack of moral sense?—That is one, yes.

Am I not right in thinking that a large number of people lack moral sense?—An appreciable number of people but surely not a large number, otherwise society would not be able to hold together. If there was even an appreciable number of people showing a lack of moral sense of the degree the accused has, it would not be possible to carry on social life at all.

Well, should I put it this way, that the moral sense of people varies?—Oh yes, tremendously.

By the Court—Would you say that people who habitually act dishonestly or commit acts of housebreaking are psychopathic

Patrick Carraher.

Dr. A. McNiven

personalities?—I am sure some of them are, but I would not say all of them are or that they are necessarily psychopathic personalities.

But all of them surely display a lack of moral sense and of social responsibility?—Yes, they do in certain directions, but I think it is a matter of degree.

So that the more widely a man displays a lack of moral sense or a lack of social responsibility the more inclined you would be to classify him as a psychopathic personality?—Yes, exactly, that is it.

Cross-examination continued—Now, let me come to the next factor that you point out, that he has got no regard for his own safety? —Perhaps I used the wrong word there. I prefer to use the word "welfare" instead of "safety".

But very many people have little regard for their own welfare? —A considerable number.

Would you regard all people who have little regard for their own welfare as being psychopathic personalities?—No, I don't think that you can single out any particular symptom. As I have mentioned, you have got to take them altogether.

But you would say that if a person has no regard for his own welfare that is one of the symptoms?—Yes, that is one symptom along with others.

So that a completely unselfish person who was willing to sacrifice himself for others would be showing one sign of psychopathic personality?—I don't accept that for a moment.

By the COURT—Thriftlessness plus lack of moral sense, these two combined in one individual, in your view, show him to be a psychopathic personality?—I did not get the first word.

Thriftlessness, lack of regard for one's own welfare ——?—And the welfare of others.

Plus lack of social responsibility?—Yes.

Are there not a good many people in the community to-day throughout the length and breadth of the United Kingdom who would fit into that category?—Yes, unfortunately there are many who would fit into it.

Would you then say that all fall into the category of psychopathic personalities?—I would not like to make a general statement of that kind, but I should think that many of them do. It is an unfortunate thing that there are so many of these people and they constitute a serious social danger.

Evidence for the Defence.

Dr. A. McNiven

Cross-examination continued—Would you say that a selfish, thrift-less person who showed a lack of moral sense was a psychopathic personality?—No. I do not think really that one can limit it in that way. These are all symptoms that go to make up a psychopathic personality. I think that you must have other things as well.

The three adjectives I have used, selfish, thriftless, a person lacking a sense of moral values, are the three which you used to describe the condition which you found in this man here?—Yes, but you would agree that these adjectives would be used to describe various degrees of these conditions. I mean a person might be described by one as thriftless whereas he would not be so regarded by another. It is entirely a question of the man's total reaction to life and his responsibilities and the way he has behaved. You have got to review his life history; how he has adapted himself to life generally. And if that is done in this case, in my opinion one would find that this man has reacted in a very abnormal way.

But, surely, a very large number of people unfortunately go through life being most selfish, being most thriftless and showing a great lack of moral sense?—Well, I hope not a very large number.

Would you say that all those persons are psychopathic per-sonalities?—No, I would not say that. I think one of the char-acteristics of a psychopathic personality is that they are unable to withstand frustration of any kind. They behave somewhat like children. If they want anything, no matter what it is, they must have it by hook or by crook. The ordinary person is able to tolerate a certain amount of frustration. If you put him in a situa-tion which is uncongenial to him he tends to make the best use of it, but these people simply won't do it. It emerged very clearly in the Army, for instance, where the average person, although the conditions under which he was living were very different from those under which he was living in civil life, and although they might be very uncongenial, yet he was able to adapt himself to them. Well, these people you could not do anything with, and no disciplinary measure or any other measure had any effect upon them.

So you would classify as persons having psychopathic per-sonalities and therefore wholly abnormal, all that class of person who in the Army were so selfish as to be unwilling to undergo the rigours of Army life?—Well, no, I think many were unable to undergo the rigours of Army life because they were suffering from other forms of mental illness. But that is a different condition.

217

Patrick Carraher.

Dr. A. McNiven

By the COURT—These people who were unable to adapt themselves to the environment in which they found themselves in Army life; would you say that was because they lacked the capacity so to adapt themselves they must be considered psychological personalities?—No. Many people were unable to adapt themselves to Army life because they suffered from neurotic conditions.

I am excluding the neurotics. Your answer would be, excluding the neurotic types, yes, they would be psychopathic personalities? —Yes, and excluding the mental defective. There again, a large number of these people had to be discharged from the Army because they were psychopathic personalities.

Cross-examination continued—And you would classify all persons whom the ordinary army sergeant major referred to as skrimshankers or shirkers, as psychopathic personalities?—I do not say I would classify all of them, but I do know that many of them, I should say the majority of them, were of that type.

And would you exclude them from all responsibility for their actions?—No, I would not exclude them from responsibility for their actions, but the point is that it was found—correct me if I am wrong—that one can do little or very little with them. They were demoralizing everybody else; they were a disintegrating force, and these people are, wherever they are, whatever group of society they are in, a disintegrating and demoralizing force.

Re-examined by MR. PHILIP—It has been suggested to you that the only factor that you found was a lack of sense of the man's own welfare. Am I right in thinking that you took all the symptoms which are referred to in your report together?—Yes, one must take everything together.

It is quite easy to take one symptom and separate it up from another symptom?—Yes.

But when you get the symptoms together you, as a psychiatrist, arrive at the result that this man is a psychopathic personality? —Yes.

You mentioned also emotional instability?—Yes, emotional instability in a sense that he is impulsive. He does not seem to be able to take time to consider things. Speaking generally, if these people want anything they just must have it, no matter in the face of all opposition or all moral law or regard for other people's welfare.

Evidence for the Defence.

Dr. A. McNiven

And also you regard the lack of appreciation of his own position?—Well, I thought that was very remarkable. He was quite jaunty in his attitude. He described the events of the night when the offence was committed as if he were just describing a frolic and not a very serious matter.

Do you regard that as pointing to defective mental judgment? —I think it is a defect in moral sentiment. I think it is an inability to feel like other people, to appreciate what the normal person feels about these things.

And you place him in the category not of psychosis, which I understand would be certifiable insanity?—Yes.

But in the category of diminished responsibility, psychopathic personality?—I have already answered the question of diminished responsibility.

By the COURT—What was your answer?—My answer is this, that if by responsibility is meant the ability to say when a proposition is put to him that an act is either right or wrong and to say that a certain act is punishable by law, then I think he is responsible. At least I have no reason to think he is not responsible.

You found nothing to suggest he is not responsible in that sense?—No; but if responsibility means to have moral sentiments and to have a desire to do what is right and be able to withstand temptation, then I think that this man's responsibility is diminished in that sense, to be able to control his actions.

So that the desire to be a law-abiding citizen plus the capacity of self-control is typical, you think, of the person with the average moral sense?—I do.

But the yielding to temptation not to be law-abiding and the failure to exercise self-control, you say, is symptomatic of a person with a psychopathic personality who is not fully accountable for his actions?—If you find it in an extreme degree.

What determines the extremity of the degree in respect of a person who has manifested symptoms of not being a law-abiding person and not exercising normal self-control? How do you differentiate degrees among people who are in that class, the people who are not law-abiding citizens and the people who do not exercise control? You decline to assent to the view that all these are psychopathic?—Yes.

What determines the line of demarcation?—Well, I can only say you have got to judge each case on its merits. But I think if you review a man's life and find that throughout his life he has shown

Patrick Carraher.

Dr. A. McNiven

this instability to abide by the law in spite of punishment, and he has shown no capacity for doing useful work and maintaining himself, I think that these are the points that one would take into account, combined, of course, with his attitude to the whole situation. An important point I think is the absence of a real moral sentiment. It is not just so much that he does these things; it is that really in himself he does not seem to have any feeling that it is wrong.

I thought you rather suggested he knew that it was wrong, but was not able to control the impulse to do wrong?—Yes, I am sure if you said to him, "Is it wrong to steal?" he would tell you that it was wrong to steal. But one gets the impression when talking to him that he has no real feelings, if you understand. He has an intellectual appreciation of it but no emotional feeling that the thing is wrong. His whole attitude is that he is casual and jaunty about the whole thing, about his whole life indeed. He has no normal sense of shame or regard for other people's opinion of his behaviour.

Would you describe it as a somewhat callous outlook upon society?—I think that would describe it.

I understand you made three examinations. How long did the one on 21st February last?—I suppose about half an hour.

The second one on 27th February?—A few minutes.

And the third one to-day?—A very short time.

And the decisions you have arrived at in your own mind and the description given of them are based upon these three occasions; you never having seen the man at any other time?—Yes, that is right.

Did you find him clear and rational in the statements he made to you?—Indeed he was most clear and rational.

Was his recollection apparently good?—Perfect.

Did he seem to have any delusions or hallucinations about himself?—None during my first examination of him, and I would not say that he had actually delusions at any time when I examined him.

You have indicated that you were informed that he had appeared to cherish suspicions that were not quite well founded?—Yes. I did not know of the existence of these symptoms when I examined him the first time, but the second time I examined him I questioned him about them. He was very evasive. He denied the statement that had been made, but when I pressed him he admitted that he did have these suspicions.

Evidence for the Defence.

Dr. A. McNiven

Was there any history of previous illness that you could ascertain?—Mental illness—none.

No organic or brain diseases of any kind?—No, I do not think so. If I am right in my diagnosis this condition is not associated with any organic or brain disorder. It is more a twist of the personality.

A twist of the personality demonstrated purely objectively by the conduct of the individual. Is that it?—Yes, I would say that.

And occurring in a person with regard to whose mental powers there is neither diseases nor symptoms of unsoundness?—Well, I think one would have to regard it as unsoundness but not in the sense that he belongs to the category of a definite mental illness, a psychosis or neurosis. It is more a constitutional condition, something that has been there either from birth or from a very early age. It is not something which has been acquired like an illness, like a melancholia or a neurosis.

What material have you for thinking that the accused acquired this psychopathic personality at an early age?—Well, at the age of 14——

He was at school up to the age of 14, so he told you, and was a normal scholar?—Yes. Of course, there is no suggestion that this man's intelligence is impaired, so there is no reason why he should not be a normal scholar. He mentioned his inability to submit to discipline at home, or rather, complained about discipline at home. I think that whereas he puts the blame on the home conditions it may well be that the fault was with himself. I do not know which view is the correct one.

Is there a definition of the term "psychopathic personality" which makes it intelligible to the lay person like myself or members of the jury?—I can quote the definition in my report.

Please do. I did not know you had defined it. What you say in your report, if I may read it is: "A recognized clinical condition in which are included persons who from childhood or early youth show gross abnormality in their social behaviour and emotional reactions, and who do not as a rule show a degree of abnormality amounting to certifiable insanity"?—Yes.

That is to say, a man who is not insane but who from childhood or early youth has shown gross abnormality in his social behaviour and emotional reactions?—Yes.

Did you state in your examination-in-chief that the accused showed no emotional instability?—Yes.

Then it is the case that during your examination he displayed no

Patrick Carraher.

Dr. A. McNiven

emotional instability?—No emotional instability—that he was in the one mood, but in my opinion he did show an emotional disorder in as much as he did not show the emotion appropriate to his situation.

PROFESSOR WILLIAM BLYTH (38), sworn.

Examined by MR. PHILIP—I am a Doctor of Medicine of Glasgow, hold the Diploma of Medical Psychology of London, am a Fellow of the Royal Faculty of Physicians and Surgeons of Glasgow, and am Professor of Psychological Medicine in the Anderson College of Medicine, Glasgow. I am also physician in charge of the Department of Nervous and Mental Diseases of Glasgow Royal Infirmary, and I have been a specialist in psychological medicine in the Emergency Medical Service, and I am Honorary Consulting Psychiatrist to Falkirk and District Royal Infirmary.

Did you examine the accused?—I saw him on 25th February, 1946.

Is the expression "psychopathic personality" a well recognized medical term?—It is a well recognized clinical entity or group well known to psychiatrists.

What is your opinion with regard to the accused's condition in relation to that clinical condition?—As the result of my examination I was of the opinion that he displayed a psychopathic personality.

Is that associated with various symptoms?—Yes. It is a condition characterized by a defective judgment and a tendency to abnormal behaviour.

When you say a defective judgment, do you mean that the patient is unable to judge as a normal person the quality of his acts?—Yes.

By the COURT—Do you mean that he does not know the distinction between right and wrong?—He knows the distinction between right and wrong.

Well, why do you say he does not appreciate the quality of his acts? Surely right and wrong form the qualities of the action? —He does not appreciate fully the consequences of an act as a normal person would.

Examination continued—Is there also lack of normal control?—In certain cases there is.

222

Evidence for the Defence.

Professor Blyth

Did you form the conclusion as to whether or not the accused was of diminished responsibility?—I considered he was of diminished responsibility.

Did you find evidence of progressive mental deterioration? —No, I could not say I did.

Did you ascertain whether he had suffered from certain kinds of suspicion?—Yes, he was suspicious during the examination and he gave a history suggestive of suspicion.

Did you regard these suspicions as real or delusional?—I regarded them as delusional.

By the Court—Were you able to check the accuracy or otherwise of his suspicions?—Beyond seeing his wife on the same day and separately from the prisoner, I had no further means of checking the veracity of his statements.

Examination continued—Did you consider whether he suffered from some kind of persecution mania?—That was my opinion.

An irrational sense of imaginary persecution?—Yes.

Did you consider whether or not in his case there was alcoholic tendency?—He gave me a long history of alcoholism.

Did you have any reason to doubt the veracity of his history? —No.

In a person suffering, as you consider him to be, from this psychopathic personality how would this alcoholic tendency affect his mental condition?—I consider that it would aggravate it.

Would it aggravate the defect of judgment?—In my opinion, yes.

Did you consider him stable or unstable emotionally?—I would say he was unstable.

By the Court—Is that because of any aberration or disease of the mind?—It is a disease of the mind.

What symptoms of disease, if any, did you find?—His general conduct at the time of my examination, while not definitely insane, was abnormal.

And from his abnormal conduct did you diagnose mental illness?—I diagnosed a psychopathic personality.

Examination continued—You expressed the opinion that that amounted to mental instability. Having formed that view, were you confirmed by learning that he had attempted to commit suicide?—That was one fact that led to the diagnosis.

223

Patrick Carraher.

Professor Blyth

Cross-examined by MR. JOHNSTON—Were you told that it was a number of years ago that he attempted to commit suicide?—Yes, he told me that himself.

You have had to rely for all your information on the accused and Sarah Bonnar?—Yes.

And you have accepted his account of his past life?—Yes.

You believed what he told you?—As far as it would fit in with the history. I mean, I cross-checked his statements with Dr. Scott of the prison after the examination.

You said that he had a defect of judgment in that he did not appreciate the consequences of his acts. Has he got enough judgment to appreciate the fact that if he strikes a blow and hits another person the other person is likely to be hurt?—He has.

And that if he strikes a blow and wounds that other person that other person will be wounded?—Yes.

And that if he strikes a blow at a vital place in that other person that other person might die?—Yes, he appreciates that.

Then what sort of consequence is he not able to appreciate will follow from his acts?—His general mode of life, according to his own statement, shows that he does not appreciate fully his responsibilities in life.

Surely that is quite a different thing. He may appreciate the consequences of his acts and yet fail to appreciate that he has got any responsibility?—Yes, that is so.

Does that not simply amount to this, that he is selfish and careless of what the consequences to others are?—Yes, that is so.

The next thing you told us was that his behaviour was abnormal. Was it abnormal when you conducted your examination of him?—In my opinion, yes. He did not show what I would consider to be normal reaction of a man with a serious charge hanging over him.

How many men have you examined who had serious charges hanging over them?—Possibly about 200.

Have you ever been in a position where you could see a large body of men together, the whole of them being threatened with a common danger?—I think so.

Did you serve in the last war?—No.

Would you agree with me that in a situation like that no two individuals, or hardly any two individuals will behave alike?— Yes, I agree with you.

Well, does that not roughly indicate that there is in a moment

Evidence for the Defence.

Professor Blyth

of danger no normal behaviour?—In an immediate and threatened danger, yes; in a case such as quoted at present, no.

Let us take a danger, not an immediate danger, but a danger which is to come within a few hours, or a few days, which threatens a large body of men; have you ever seen men in that condition?—Yes.

Would you not agree with me that no two of these men will react to the threatened danger in the same way?—Yes, I agree.

Is there any normal behaviour as a reaction to danger?—There is a normal anxiety.

But unless what you term that normal anxiety is manifested by some outward action you have no way of estimating, have you? —No.

How can you then say that there is an anxiety of danger or an apprehension of danger?—I can say that there is normal conduct in circumstances such as have been quoted. At the time of my examination this man was more interested in his suspicious ideas than he was in the charge against him. I considered that abnormal.

May it not be that he simply preferred for the moment to consider his suspicious ideas rather than the position he was in? —Well, he preferred to do that for close on an hour while I was conducting my examination.

You say he had lack of control. How did that manifest itself when you were examining him?—That was my opinion from the history which he gave me relating to his past life.

By the COURT—Does that mean that his past life showed that he was a man who had a very poor capacity to exercise self-control?—That was my opinion.

There are a good many people in the country who in the last year or so have displayed a similar lack of self-control?—There are.

Would you class them all as psychopathic?—No.

If along with that they displayed a lack of moral sense would you class them as psychopathic?—I think I would.

That would cover a fairly large per cent. of the population? —Yes, it would cover possibly about 2 per cent.

Cross-examination continued—Then you said he was suspicious. Of what was he suspicious?—Mainly of his wife's behaviour.

May that suspicion have been well-founded?—It might have been.

Patrick Carraher.

So that if it was well-founded it was no delusion?—No.

And the only person whom you were able to question with regard to these suspicions was Sarah Bonnar, the woman with whom he was living?—Yes.

You say he was suffering from a persecution mania; who did he feel was persecuting him?—Mainly the legal authorities.

Was that the authorities in the prison?—No, it was directed against the law generally, not against an individual.

Well, that probably means, does it not, that most criminals have got a persecution mania?—Most criminals have somewhat the same idea.

You say he suffers from mental instability. What led you to believe that?—The history which he gave. His inability on the one hand to appreciate the effects of alcohol and yet his unwillingness to do anything to remedy it.

Was that the sole reason why you thought he was mentally unstable?—That was one of the reasons.

By the COURT—Added to his failure to resist over-indulgence in alcohol you had regard to what he told you about what had happened in the past?—I would agree with that.

The two combined?—Yes.

But how far was he suffering from alcoholism at the date of your examination?—He was not suffering from alcoholism.

Do you know what a dipsomaniac is?—Yes.

Was there any suggestion in the evidence you received that this man was a dipsomaniac up to November last?—He could quite possibly have been a dipsomaniac.

I do not want the possibility, it is the fact?—He differed from a dipsomaniac in the fact that he did not have intervening periods of sobriety.

Was the information you got from him that he was never sober? —No, that he was always under the influence of alcohol but at certain periods very markedly under the influence.

Cross-examination continued—That was the opinion you received from the accused. Did you see any clinical signs when you examined him?—No, there were no signs of alcohol.

You said you thought he was suffering from diminished responsibility?—Yes.

That is, of course, largely a question of law, but what led you to think that he was suffering from diminished responsibility?

Evidence for the Defence.

Professor Blyth

—His general previous history, including his domestic and working life, was in my opinion abnormal.

Do you mean his life as he told it to you, and as you have been able to verify it from Sarah Bonnar, shows that he was a person who was careless of the rights of others?—Yes, I would agree.

Do you mean by diminished responsibility anything more than that?—I mean that he fails to appreciate his duties as a citizen and as a man and does not fit into the social category of any citizen.

By the COURT—That is a condition, is it not, that may be found in quite a number of people who come before the courts charged with offences in this country?—I would agree.

Would you say that they, judged by the same test, would give indications which would justify you in saying that they have diminished responsibility?—Yes.

Re-examined by MR. PHILIP—You have been asked various questions to which you have given answers based upon the accused's history. That is how a psychiatrist forms his diagnosis, by taking a history?—That is the main way, yes.

Am I right in saying that it necessarily has to be so, in relation to mental conditions?—There is no other method.

Had you any reason to doubt the accuracy of the information which the accused gave you upon which you based your opinion? —None in the least; he was very truthful with regard to his own shortcomings.

Was he incapable of exercising self-control or was he merely failing?—No, in my opinion he was incapable.

By the COURT—An opinion derived from the fact that he had not exercised it?—Yes.

Post hoc ergo procter hoc, is that not what it comes to?—Yes.

That means, that because in fact he has failed to exercise self-control it is because he is incapable of exercising self-control due to something in his make-up which diminished his responsibility. Would that summarize it?—Yes, I agree.

Re-examination continued—If you get a certain number of instances can you draw, in your view, any inference of incapacity from that?—Yes. I think the normal man learns by his own errors, and the person who keeps repeating those errors to his own detriment is abnormal.

Patrick Carraher.

Professor Blyth

And is it your evidence that this man is abnormal mentally?
—That is my evidence.

By the COURT—Do I understand you just saw him once?—Yes,
last Saturday.

And during what period were you in his company?—About an
hour and a quarter.

Would you agree that some of the features which you have
founded on for the opinion you have expressed could have been
better tested if you had had more than one opportunity of con-
versing with and examining the outlook of this patient?—Very
definitely, yes.

Does it amount to this, that, generally speaking, in forming a
diagnosis of anything like instability of mind, psychopathic personality and the like, the greater the number of occasions one can
be in the company of the patient the more likely one's diagnosis is
to be correct?—That is correct.

MR. PHILIP—My lord, that is the case for the defence.

The Advocate-Depute's Address to the Jury.

MR. JOHNSTON—Ladies and gentlemen of the jury; you are
charged with a very solemn duty, for the man before you, Patrick
Carraher, is accused of one of the gravest crimes known to the
law, the crime of murder. I am charged with an almost equally
solemn duty, for it is my duty, as counsel for the Crown, to lay
before you those facts and circumstances which point to the guilt
of Patrick Carraher, the accused.

You have listened and, I am sure, listened with great care, to a
mosaic of evidence which is rather like the disconnected pieces of
a jigsaw puzzle. Some of it may have from time to time seemed
almost incomprehensible to you, particularly in its sequence. What
I propose to do is to take you through the events of Friday night,
23rd November, 1945, and then go back over those events and
point out the facts which, in my submission, must lead you to the
irresistible conclusion that John Gordon was murdered by Patrick
Carraher.

You will be told and very properly told by his lordship and by
counsel for the defence, that the burden of proving the case
against the accused lies on the Crown. That burden is to satisfy

Speech for the Prosecution.

Mr. Johnston

you beyond reasonable doubt—not fanciful doubt, but reasonable doubt—that the accused did the acts complained of.

Let us turn to the events of Friday, 23rd November. The first thing that happened was that John Gordon of the Seaforth Highlanders, a regular soldier waiting to be discharged, met his two brothers, Joseph and Edward, in his parents' house. They went to a house in McAslin Street in order to meet there Duncan Revie, a brother-in-law of Gordon and a deserter from the Army. The three Gordons and Revie went to the "Coronation Bar", which was almost next door to where Revie was living. They spent the early part of the evening there, and there is no doubt that all four of them had a considerable amount to drink. Somewhere about seven o'clock the four of them went down Taylor Street into Rottenrow and into Cameron's pub. They there spent the evening, or what remained of the evening, and they were there joined by Keatings, the rather good-looking, upstanding sailor. The five of them were all drinking there. Joseph Gordon and Edward Gordon were both overcome by the amount of alcohol they had drunk and they both went out to be sick; and we need bother with them no more. That left Duncan Revie, Keatings, and Gordon in the public-house. The three of them came out of the public-house, and we leave them there for a moment and turn our minds to the other public-house—Thompson's I think it was called—further up Rottenrow. There, Daniel Bonnar, Watt and the accused had been spending the evening. They had left that public-house at about a quarter to nine and gone down to Daniel Bonnar's house in Rottenrow. There, Wee Watt and the accused remained. Daniel Bonnar left that house in order to find some friend, so that they might have a sing-song and a party. Outside Cameron's pub he met the people whom we left standing there, John Gordon, Duncan Revie and Keatings. A fight started, though how much of a fight it was does not seem very certain. What is certain is that John Gordon took no part in that fight. Daniel Bonnar turned, ran down Rottenrow, and was followed by Duncan Revie and the sailor Keatings. After these two had chased him a little they returned to John Gordon, and then sailor Keatings disappears from the scene. Daniel Bonnar ran on to his sister's house in Tarbet Street.

Now another person comes on the scene, Mrs. Colquhoun, the postwoman, who was leaning out of her window in Rottenrow. She saw this fracas or fight—call it what you will—in Rottenrow. She knew Daniel Bonnar was the person running away. She left

229

Patrick Carraher.

her window, ran down to Tarbet Street where Sarah Bonnar was living. She and Sarah went up to Rottenrow to Peggy Bonnar's house—that is, the wife of Daniel Bonnar—and there found Peggy Bonnar, Wee Watt and the accused. Sarah Bonnar and Mrs. Colquhoun told the three persons there that Daniel Bonnar was in trouble. Immediately Wee Watt and the accused left and went down to the Rottenrow. They there met—not immediately, but shortly thereafter—Bonnar, who had returned from his sister in Tarbet Street. John Gordon and Duncan Revie had by this time turned up Taylor Street and were walking up Taylor Street towards McAslin Street. The accused, Daniel Bonnar and Wee Watt went up Taylor Street; and after that what happened? For a little time after that it is not quite certain what happened. According to Watt's account, he himself went left along Cathedral Street and up Canning Place. According to Bonnar all three of them went up to the junction of McAslin Street and Taylor Street. It is quite certain that the accused and Bonnar got to McAslin Street. The route does not matter and it does not matter where Wee Watt was. Then the accused and Bonnar went along McAslin Street, turned into Taylor Street, and there met John Gordon and Duncan Revie.

There is no doubt whatsoever, in my submission to you, that Duncan Revie and Bonnar had a fight; a very short fight, for Bonnar ran away. There is no doubt, in my submission, that the accused and John Gordon had a fight, or at least had to this extent a fight that the accused struck John Gordon on the left of the neck with a chisel and gave him a fatal wound.

What happened after that? Daniel Bonnar ran along McAslin Street. From there he went to Canning Place. At the junction of Canning Place he met the accused, and it was there that the accused told him, Daniel Bonnar, that he had given John Gordon a jag, or a wee jag. They then went down from there to Bonnar's house in Rottenrow. Sarah Bonnar was there and Peggy Bonnar, and Wee Watt came in. Sarah Bonnar and Peggy Bonnar left and went into the house at Tarbet Street. There was some discussion of the fight, and it was there that the accused demonstrated to Wee Watt how he delivered the fatal blow at the junction of Taylor Street and McAslin Street. Do you remember Wee Watt describing the accused as dancing like a boxer, and his statement that he had his right hand up as if there was something in it? It is true there was nothing in his hand when he demonstrated, but Wee Watt had seen a steel blade protruding from the breast pocket of the accused earlier in the evening, and at a most suspicious time earlier in the

Speech for the Prosecution.

Mr. Johnston

evening, when the accused was going down into Rottenrow to rescue his pal Daniel Bonnar.

After that, the three of them, not together, went to the house at Tarbet Street where Peggy Bonnar and Sarah Bonnar were. About midnight two other people come into the scene; one, who was known to them, was "Gasser" Elliot. The other was a man Stewart. They had come with the news that John Gordon was dead. Sarah Bonnar was in bed. She asked the men to go out to the kitchen. They went out to the kitchen. Some of them came back, but two of them did not come back immediately. The two were the accused and Stewart. And it was then that the accused told Stewart what had happened earlier in the evening. Stewart and "Gasser" Elliot left, but before they left, the accused handed Stewart the weapon which is Labels Nos. 1 and 2. There can be no doubt about that whatsoever. And he gave Stewart this instruction, "chip it"—get rid of it, in other words. And Stewart carried out his instructions, for the weapon was taken apart and he put one part in a stank in the High Street and another part in another stank in the High Street. Later that night Bonnar, Watt and the accused were arrested. Now, ladies and gentlemen, I think that was a fair reconstruction of what happened that night.

In order that the Crown should prove its case beyond reasonable doubt, it is necessary to prove two things; first, that John Gordon died of a stab wound on the neck on the night of 23rd November, 1945—and there can be no doubt about that whatsoever. The next thing that the Crown must prove is that beyond reasonable doubt the man who delivered that wound was the accused.

Now, let me just review parts of the evidence which point, in my submission, irresistibly to the accused and which must lead you beyond all reasonable doubt to the conclusion that the accused was the man who delivered this blow. First of all, let us start off with the first sight of the weapon, or rather, of a weapon. I put it no higher than that. There is no doubt, on Watt's evidence, that the accused was in possession of a weapon when he came down into Rottenrow from Sarah Bonnar's house. And is there any doubt that he intended to use that weapon? I think I am right in saying he drew the attention of Watt to that weapon. Then is there any doubt at all that when he and Bonnar met, they went to McAslin Street for no peaceful purpose? Bonnar was armed, we know. They went to McAslin Street in order to meet John Gordon and Duncan Revie. It is perhaps a little sinister that they did

Patrick Carraher.

not take the straight road up Taylor Street but carried out an out-flanking movement through other streets, in order that they might get to McAslin Street before Duncan Revie and John Gordon. And they did get there. The evidence that they did get there before, is the evidence of Bonnar and Duncan Revie.

Let me say this about the evidence of Bonnar—Bonnar was charged with this crime, and you will be told that Bonnar is not a person to be believed. You will be told that Bonnar is trying to save his own skin. All those things are there, and you must test his evidence carefully, but, test it as you will, you will find that his account of events is corroborated in almost every particular. What about this meeting? There is Duncan Revie's account of this meeting. He described how the two men jumped out of the closemouth; he stated that one went for him, and the one that went for him was Bonnar. He was engaged in fighting Bonnar, but he was able to see that the accused approached and was standing near, within a yard of John Gordon. He states that when the accused was standing within a yard of John Gordon he had his hand raised and something in his hand. What that something was he was not able to say, but he said it might have been the weapon which is here. That account is to some extent corroborated by an entirely independent source, the witnesses Campbell and Stewart, who, you will remember, were standing together at the junction of Taylor Street and Ronald Street, or Parson Street, and were looking down towards McAslin Street. Just let me turn to their evidence. His lordship asked Campbell this question: "Q.—Am I right that you have told us you first heard a noise, looked up and saw a group of four people, and you saw one of the four making to kick another and the one at whom the kick was made retreated out on to the street? A.—Yes. Q.—Did someone then come out and chase him, or did someone go off towards the west in Mc-Aslin Street? A.—While this was going on that was when the blow was struck. When the kicking in the street was going on the other one went over to the man on the pavement and punched him." And his lordship asked this question: "Q.—And it is the two who had been left on the pavement who took part in what you called a punch delivered by one to the other, after which the punched man collapsed on the edge of the pavement? A.—Yes." That is Campbell's evidence. They both thought they saw a punch delivered, but it was such a punch that John Gordon died from it.

It is proper to say that neither Campbell nor Stewart can say

Speech for the Prosecution.

that the man who delivered that punch was the accused. They can, however, say that the man who was punched was John Gordon. And there is the evidence of Duncan Revie and Bonnar that they were engaged in a fight, that is, that they were two people on the street and that one ran away and the other followed. That leaves one man, one possible man of the four who, so far as we know, were there. That is the accused.

Going from there, let us see what happened. The next point is the meeting between the accused and Bonnar. When the accused explained to Bonnar, "I gave him a jag," or "I gave him a wee jag," to whom did he give a wee jag? I suggest to you that you must draw the irresistible conclusion that the person to whom he gave the jag was John Gordon. What is the next bit of evidence? The next bit of evidence I suggest to you is the evidence of Sarah Bonnar and Peggy Bonnar, both of whom told you that after having left the accused and Bonnar together in Taylor Street, the accused and Bonnar were absent for a period and then came back to Rottenrow to the house there. Now, is not the conclusion that these two had been together the whole time almost irresistible, and does it not provide another little bit of corroboration? Then there is Watt again, who described how the accused discussed the fight with him, demonstrated how he had struck the blow, and said the accused said, "I am not sure"—I don't pretend these are his real words—"I am not sure if I struck him on the cheek or on the shoulder." Has that not got a ring of truth in it? "I am not sure whether I struck him on the cheek or the shoulder"; that, and the demonstration which Watt gave you in the witness-box.

We go on, and the next bit of evidence is the evidence of Stewart, who, you remember, with "Gasser" Elliot went to the house. And you remember that Stewart was given this (Labels Nos. 1 and 2) by the accused and told to "chip that away". Why did the accused want that "chipped" away if it was not an incriminating object? Is there any reason whatsoever for throwing away a perfectly good tool, unless the tool had some connection with the crime of which you have just heard? So far as we know, there was only one man wounded with a cutting weapon that night. That man was John Gordon. Is that the cutting weapon? I submit, ladies and gentlemen, that you must come to the irresistible conclusion that that is the weapon which was used.

Then again, there is the evidence of Bonnar who said—and this to some extent corroborates Stewart—that the accused had told him that "That's that away." What did he mean by "That's that

Patrick Carraher.

away"? Did he mean that the fatal weapon had been got rid of? Now, as I said, there is a very heavy onus on the Crown in a case such as this. The onus is to prove to you beyond reasonable doubt, not fanciful doubt, but beyond reasonable doubt, that the fatal blow was struck by the accused, that John Gordon was murdered by Patrick Carraher. In my submission there is only one possible conclusion you can come to on the evidence which you have listened to for the last two days, and that is that the accused murdered John Gordon. On the Indictment, which is an Indictment for murder, it is possible for you to bring in a verdict of culpable homicide, but in a case such as this there is no possible room for a verdict of other than murder.

Now let me say one word about the defence which has been suggested to you by the medical evidence, which is the defence known to the law—though not well known to the law—of diminished responsibility. I should say, first of all, that I shall submit in a moment to his lordship that there is no evidence whatever which is sufficient in law to establish that defence. Does the medical evidence which is led by the defence come to anything more than this, that the accused is a selfish person who has little regard for the comfort, convenience or safety of others? I suggest that there is nothing more than that, and that does not diminish the accused's responsibility, his criminal responsibility. I would remind you that, if you should have to come to consider this evidence—and I shall submit to his lordship that it is not a matter for your consideration at all—you must weigh the evidence of the two doctors who were led by defending counsel against the evidence of the doctor, Dr. Scott, led by the Crown. You must remember that Dr. Scott has seen the accused almost every day since about 26th November, and that of the two doctors for the defence, one has seen him on one occasion and the other on three occasions only. It will be for you, if the matter ever reaches you, to decide which evidence you prefer. But, as I said before, I shall submit to his lordship that that is not a question for you at all, and that the only question which should be submitted to you is this: Did the accused commit the crime of which he is charged in this Indictment? I submit to you, ladies and gentlemen, you would be lacking the courage which is proper and fitting for a jury of the citizens of Glasgow if you brought in any other verdict than a verdict of guilty as libelled.

I would ask your lordship to direct the jury that there is not sufficient evidence. . . .

Speech for the Prosecution.

Mr. Johnston

LORD RUSSELL—Well, sufficiency of evidence is for the jury. You mean that there is no legal evidence upon which a reasonable jury could hold . . .

MR. JOHNSTON—That there is, in law, no evidence on which a reasonable jury could hold that the accused was suffering from such an aberration or weakness of mind that would in any way diminish his responsibility for his acts. I would refer your lordship to the case of *H.M. Advocate* v. *Savage*, which was reported in 1923 J.C. 49, and the more recent case of *H.M. Advocate* v. *Braithwaite*, which was reported in 1945 S.L.T. 209. I do not know if your lordship wishes me to quote the cases.

LORD RUSSELL—I think you should give from the reports such attempts at definition of the condition which should support a finding of impaired or diminished responsibility.

MR. JOHNSTON—I quote from Lord Justice-Clerk Alness's judgment at page 51, where the Lord Justice-Clerk says this: "And I think one can see running through the cases that there is implied —as Lord Stormonth Darling in terms said in the case to which the Lord Advocate referred—that there must be some form of mental disease. Well, ladies and gentlemen, that is a very difficult region of law. I have told you the kind of thing that is necessary, aberration or weakness of mind; mental unsoundness; a state of mind bordering on insanity although not reaching it; a mind affected so that the responsibility is diminished from full responsibility to partial responsibility. That is the sort of thing that must be proved in order to establish that the crime which would otherwise be murder is only culpable homicide."

LORD RUSSELL—Is it your submission that the words to which importance and weight must be given in the passage you have read are "some form of mental disease" and the words "bordering on insanity"?

MR. JOHNSTON—I think so.

LORD RUSSELL—Mental disease resulting in a condition which borders on insanity.

MR. JOHNSTON—That is my submission.

Patrick Carraher.

LORD RUSSELL—Assuming that, I would respectfully agree with the Lord Justice-Clerk's definition. Is it supplemented in any way in *Braithwaite*?

MR. JOHNSTON—*Braithwaite* affirms the case of *Savage*, and the case of *Savage* is quoted with approval. Lord Justice-Clerk Cooper quotes Lord Justice-Clerk Alness's opinion. He says this: "The Solicitor-General read a passage from the Charge of the Lord Justice-Clerk in the case of *H.M. Advocate* v. *Savage* and I am going to read a sentence or two again, because it seems to me to give as explicit and clear a statement of the sort of thing which you have to look for as I can find. He says 'It is very difficult to put it in a phrase'—and I respectfully agree—'but it has been put in this way; that there must be aberration or weakness of mind; that there must be some form of mental unsoundness; that there must be a state of mind which is bordering on, though not amounting to, insanity; that there must be a mind so affected that responsibility is diminished from full responsibility to partial responsibility'."—Aberration or weakness of mind, some form of mental unsoundness. My lord, this state of psychopathy and the evidence led in support of it in my submission comes far below that which Lord Justice-Clerk Alness and Lord Justice-Clerk Cooper say is necessary before there can be any diminishing of the responsibility for a criminal act.

LORD RUSSELL—You say it is so far below it that the judge is entitled to withhold from the jury the decision of the question whether or not there exists diminished responsibility or impaired responsibility?

MR. JOHNSTON—In my submission that is so. I say they are so far below it that the evidence which we have heard to-day in my submission bears not at all on, and indeed that there is no evidence of, mental aberration or disease of the mind such as is required; that the evidence which we have heard to-day belongs to another category altogether, and I so move your lordship to direct the jury.

Mr. Philip's Address to the Jury.

MR. PHILIP—Ladies and gentlemen of the jury, the charge which you have to consider is the gravest known to our law, and

Speech for the Defence.

Mr. Philip

a conviction on that charge carries the penalty of death. I approach the question, as I am sure you do, with a sense of grave responsibility and a determination faithfully to discharge one's duty. At the outset, let me remind you, though it has been mentioned already, of your proper approach to this question. The burden of proof is upon the Crown. There is no rule, no principle, better established in the law of this country than that an accused is presumed to be innocent, unless and until he is proved to be guilty. Moreover, it has often been said that, where the charge is one affecting the life of the accused, that onus is all the heavier, and a man on trial for his life is entitled to the benefit of every doubt. Therefore your approach should be this, that you can only return a verdict contrary to the one which I shall ask of you if you think that every link in the chain is established. If one link breaks down the whole chain is broken.

Now, ladies and gentlemen, the first question which I ask you to consider is this: Has the Crown proved that the hand of the accused inflicted the neck wound found on the deceased? I shall submit to you upon the evidence that the Crown has entirely failed in that proof. Indeed, I can hardly recall a case in which the direct evidence was so confusing and so uncertain in its inferences. Let me just remind you of such evidence as there is bearing upon that question. At the outset the Crown tender the witness Revie. Revie was one of a party who had first of all gone to the "Coronation Bar", where they had had six half glasses of whisky each and three or four pints of beer, and, on leaving, it is admitted that they were all "half-seas over". They had all had the same. They were then joined at another bar, "Cameron's Bar", by Keatings, and Keatings, with what he drank at the second bar only, was in such a state that he had to be forcibly roused afterwards by the detectives who found him; but all the others, the Gordons and Revie, had been at the "Coronation Bar" first. Thus, Revie arrives on the scene of the alleged crime in a condition which you must take to be comparable to the condition of the others. That is the man whom the Crown in the first place tender as a witness. Now let me examine what he suggests. First, that the accused and Bonnar dived out of a close. No one else suggests that. It is inconsistent with the evidence of another witness tendered for the Crown, Bonnar himself, who says that he and Carraher came round by Stanhope Street, along to McAslin Street. It is inconsistent with such evidence as one gets from eye-witnesses. Campbell speaks to the first thing that was seen being Revie kicking

Patrick Carraher.

Bonnar. Accordingly, right at the outset in the suggestion which Revie alone makes, a suggestion that the attack was precipitated from the other side, Revie stands alone; and he is, in my submission, discredited. Now the next thing that Revie suggests is that the accused's hand was up. He does not say that he ever saw the accused strike any blow. Observe this, ladies and gentlemen; no single witness says that he saw the accused stab the deceased, but Revie says that he saw the accused's hand up like this. Now how can that be true? How can it be true if the other evidence is, as it is, that Bonnar was retreating backwards across the road with Revie following? Revie would necessarily be turned the other way, and, accordingly, that really does not enable you to arrive at any conclusion as to who struck any blow.

Now apart from that, keep in view what Revie said immediately after the incident. Edward Gordon, who after all would have no goodwill towards the accused, states that, after Revie had called him down from upstairs: "I asked what had happened." That was in the close. "I asked what had happened and he said it was Dan Bonnar. Q.—And he repeated that over and over again? A.— Yes." That is the record of what Revie said at the time. Revie tries, when he comes to give his own evidence, to suggest a variation of this; his suggestion is, not what Edward Gordon says that he said, namely that it was Dan Bonnar, but that Dan Bonnar, according to him, was the cause of it. He tries to put a gloss on the whole matter. But that won't do, ladies and gentlemen, because one finds that there is corroboration of Edward's remark; Stewart, who had gone up the close and reached the body at the time when one of the Gordons and others had come down, heard the remark, "It was Bonnar who did it and we will get him this time." Now the importance of that is that that is the contemporary record, and a record which originated with Revie. That is the contemporary record of Revie's impression. Then there is another very significant point about Revie's evidence and it is this. You remember the witness McDonald, the painter, who had no interest whatsoever in the matter, heard a remark, "Put the hatchet on him, Joe." I put that to Revie and I gave him the chance of admitting it, admitting that the remark had been made. Revie did not say that he did not hear it. I think that is the significant thing. Revie denied that the remark was ever made. Now why should he deny it? In my submission, ladies and gentlemen, a very natural explanation why he denied it is this, that that remark was made by him, and the reason why I suggest it was made by him

Speech for the Defence.

Mr. Philip

is because of the reference to "Joe". Who was Joe? Who, there, had a name like Joe?—John Gordon. When one considers that Revie was engaged in a fight, and we know the kind of man Revie is from the number of fights that he seems to be in, and when we know that his whole energies, as he himself admits, were absorbed in the fight, I ask you to place no reliance on his accuracy as to what happened.

Well, what is the other evidence? I take first of all the people who may have seen some fragments of the fight. McDonald comes next. He does not identify anyone. What he does say is, first of all, that his attention was attracted by the remark, "Put the hatchet on him, Joe." You will remember, I think, a rather significant fact, that Bonnar, when he was in the witness-box, said something about letting a hatchet drop. Does that not suggest to your minds that it would be at that point that Revie would think, "Well, here is the hatchet coming into action", and Revie would call out, "Put the hatchet on him, Joe"? The next thing that McDonald says is that he heard, "After him, Harry." Now, no one seems to have been able to offer any explanation of what that remark would mean. It seems to me a possible explanation—it came after the other remark—that, if Revie had said, "Put the hatchet on him, Joe", then the other antagonist with Revie, Bonnar, would try to stop that happening and would call out to the accused, not "Harry", but "Paddy". That may be the explanation. But this man McDonald does not identify any of these men. He simply sees or hears men running off, as he thinks, westwards along McAslin Street.

The next witness tendered by the Crown is Huie. He was McDonald's companion, you remember. They both came out from the corner of Taylor Street and McAslin Street. Huie brings in a rather interesting and I think important element which has not been mentioned before. He heard a scuffle. He saw a man on the road—and by that he means not Taylor Street but McAslin Street. As he saw him the man was not in Taylor Street but in McAslin Street and coming over towards him; that is to say, the man had been out somewhere in the middle of McAslin Street and Taylor Street. He sees two other men only, and the significant point is that they were running in different directions, one going west along McAslin Street, and the other going east along McAslin Street. Who was the other man? I think, ladies and gentlemen, that if you cast your minds round to consider who the other man was it can only have been Watt, because Bonnar speaks

Patrick Carraher.

about Watt and the accused coming up Stanhope Street and along McAslin Street, and Huie, who has introduced this other man, must be referring to someone in the group who was present, and I suggest to you that that can only have been Watt. If so, then Watt also was on the scene at this particular time.

The next witness is Campbell. Now Campbell gives a very significant piece of evidence. In the first place, when he was asked what was the first thing he saw, he says it was not men darting out from a close; it was not the people whom he could identify attacking others. It was a man whom he afterwards identified as Revie kicking another man. That is how he saw the thing start, and you will remember that he was standing at the foot of Taylor Street, where Ronald Street crosses it or Parson Street crosses it, and he says he was looking up at the time. Therefore if there had been anything else happen before that surely he would have seen it. That shows the attack came from the side of Revie. Then he says he saw a man giving a punch. There is no suggestion of any weapon at all. He thinks he saw a man giving a punch to a man on the pavement. He cannot identify that assailant at all. It may have been Watt—one does not know. It is left quite indefinite who that man was. There is one point which quite frankly puzzles me, and I think it will puzzle you too. If Huie and McDonald saw the man who was afterwards the deceased crossing the street on to the pavement, how can he possibly be the man who was on the pavement at the time when he was punched?

The last witness of this group is Stewart, who was also, like Campbell, standing at the corner of Taylor Street and Parson Street. He did not even see four men. He saw only three, and he says that one had a weapon and another was kicking. Now that surely was Bonnar with the weapon and Revie kicking him. Then he says that he saw a third man standing on the pavement. I think that is again significant, because the man whom Campbell had seen had, according to Campbell, fallen after the punch, and yet Stewart sees a man on the pavement standing. Is it not quite clear that the man whom Campbell saw was not the man who was afterwards wounded? Even if it was, how can it possibly be said that that was a blow which ultimately caused his death? How can it be said that it was the accused who struck the blow?

LORD RUSSELL—I think Mr. Stewart said that the man standing on the pavement was staggering. You said standing.

Speech for the Defence.

MR. PHILIP—The reference I had was: "There were two men in the middle of the street and one standing on the pavement."

LORD RUSSELL—It goes on: "What was he doing? A.—He was standing, staggering about a little bit."

MR. PHILIP—I am obliged. As regards Bonnar, Bonnar was the last person who gave evidence about being at the actual scene. Bonnar says that he saw nothing of any blow struck at the deceased. Bonnar is quite clear that Watt was there as well as the accused.

Now that is how the matter stands upon the evidence of persons who were actually at or about the scene of the incident, and one is only in the region of suspicion, one is only in the region of conjecture. But you have got to say yes or no to the question: was it the accused, on that evidence plus what I will come to in a moment, was it the accused who struck the blow which inflicted the neck wound? So far as the eye-witnesses' evidence is concerned, ladies and gentlemen, my submission to you is this, that that evidence could not possibly be accepted as adequate to discharge the onus or anything like it.

Now let me turn to the next type of evidence dealing still with the question of whether it was the accused's hand that inflicted the neck wound. What is the next stage? It is suggested first of all that there was a conversation in Canning Place between the accused and Bonnar. The suggestion is that the accused made a remark something like this. He referred to giving a wee jag, or something of that kind. I must confess that when I heard Bonnar in the witness-box using that expression it sounded very like the other word jig. However that may be, I want to take it on the footing that what the accused said to Bonnar—if Bonnar is to be believed—was that he gave him a wee jag. Ladies and gentlemen, just test this statement. Assume for the moment that it is truthful evidence. I am going to ask you to consider whether it is truthful evidence or not, but meantime test it on the assumption that it was truthful. I have not heard a word on this point from the learned Advocate-Depute. The Crown has entirely ignored the fact that the deceased had two wounds. It has all along just been assumed by my learned friend that the accused struck the major blow. If you look at the photographs and consider in your own minds which of these two wounds—assuming jag means piercing or cutting or something of that kind—which of these two wounds

241

Patrick Carraher.

Mr. Philip

answers to the description of "a wee jag", can there be any doubt at all? It would be the one on the finger. Again, Stewart gives evidence. He also uses the expression "a wee jag". Ladies and gentlemen, just to illustrate how dangerous it is to press evidence of this kind beyond where it should go, my learned friend took from them both that the expression was a "jag"; but they both agreed at once, when the expression "a wee jag" was put to them, that that was the correct expression. Well, can "a wee jag" mean anything? If it does, can it mean worse than just such a jag as one might get on the finger?

Now, there is one other statement, in fact a kind of dramatic exhibition, which is spoken to by the witness Watt. Again I say nothing in the meantime about whether Watt is a credible witness or not. I am going to take the matter on the assumption for the moment that he is credible. I will have something to say in a moment about credibility. He gave a dramatic display in the witness-box, and what he said was, "The hand", according to the accused, and he spoke to him about it, "The hand was above the head, the thumb upwards, and he brought it down to his waist." I wanted to get just exactly what it was and that is the way in which he described it. Now, how could a blow of that nature possibly cause such a wound as was found on the deceased's neck? The medical evidence is that the wound is a short distance behind the left ear and that it goes upwards so that it penetrates somewhere above the atlas, which is the top joint of the spine which holds the scalp. Such a wound could be caused only by some kind of upward thrust. How could it be caused by a downward blow to the waist? But might not such a blow cause injury to a man's finger? His finger would be just about the level of his waist. Accordingly, if one is considering the probabilities, an injury to a finger is the natural and likely result of such a blow. If this evidence is true that the blow was struck downwards, and downwards to the waist, then it might naturally have caused injury to a finger. That is entirely consistent with the other statements, if they are to be believed, that it was "a wee jag".

I have for the moment asked you to consider the effect of these statements on the assumption that they were all true. I wanted to test them on the evidence as it was given. But seriously, ladies and gentlemen, are you going to accept the evidence of two men like Bonnar and Watt who in the first place disagree with each other, and in the second place are both men who gave their statements while they were under custody for the same alleged crime?

Speech for the Defence.

Mr. Philip

What is the natural reaction of men in that position? It is surely to take every means to try to exculpate themselves. Observe also how poorly their evidence consists together. Take one crucial point. Bonnar says the accused, himself and Watt went up Stanhope Street, came along McAslin Street, looked into the close at No. 139 where Frances Gordon's house was, saw a light on, I think from the back garden or from the back of the close, saw a light on and decided not to go in, came back, Watt having stood at the mouth of the close, and then went back along Taylor Street. That is Bonnar's account. What is Watt's account? Watt's account is that he left Bonnar and the accused at the corner of Taylor Street and Cathedral Street. Then, it is very difficult, although he says he went by degrees up to the corner of Taylor Street and Ronald Street and then back eventually to Bonnar's house at No. 116, Rottenrow, it seems to me almost impossible to imagine how he filled in the period, an hour he says, between the time when, according to him, he left Bonnar and the accused, and the time when he got back to Bonnar's house. Which of these two stories are you to believe? My learned friend does not offer any explanation of these discrepancies. He does not say, "Well, I think you should accept this one account and I think you should reject the other." Ladies and gentlemen, there is a conflict here. You cannot believe both. How can you decide which you are going to believe in that state of matters? I think the true explanation of this matter is that those two men, Bonnar and Watt, are each out to save their own skins.

Now I dealt with one point upon the medical evidence. I dealt with the point that the medical evidence showed that the neck wound was caused by an upward thrust, and, as I have indicated, it seems to me that one cannot possibly fit that in with the evidence of Watt, if it is to be believed. There is one other curious point on the medical evidence and that is with regard to the length of the wound in the neck, 4 inches, and the length of the blade of the carver which has been produced. Well, the medical evidence, of course, on that matter never attempted to do more than this, to suggest that the neck wound may have been caused by that instrument. The medical evidence does not attempt to affirm that it was caused by that instrument. It simply attempts to suggest that it might have been caused by that instrument. What I have to ask you to consider is this. One may explain away this and that, one may say if you hold the head in a certain position you shorten the four inches. One may say if there was blood flowing into the

Patrick Carraher.

wound it would enlarge the wound. One may make this or that conjecture as to how one finds a four inch wound alleged to have been made by a two-and-a-quarter inch blade plus at the most half an inch beyond it. One may have a conjecture about that, but the point I ask you, ladies and gentlemen, to have in view is this, that that is not proof. It is the contrary of proof. It is the kind of thing which one gets in fiction, but it is not proof.

That is the body of evidence which has been put before you by the Crown to suggest that it was the accused's hand which inflicted this neck wound. One further point related to the disposal of the carver. Now observe how that occurred. Upon the evidence, Gasser Elliot and Stewart go to the house and say Gordon is dead. Now, ladies and gentlemen, my recollection of the evidence is this, that what next happened was, not that the accused suggested getting rid of that, but that Bonnar began to concern himself, and the first thing that Bonnar did was to remove his shirt which had blood on it. Where had that blood come from and why did he want to remove it? Bonnar wanted to get rid of that shirt. Bonnar wanted to get rid of the hatchet which he had. There is no doubt he had the hatchet. Then that having been suggested, as every single one of us would have done in similar circumstances, the accused said, "Well, get rid of this too." Now it is very significant that it was Bonnar who first tried to dispose of his obviously incriminating shirt, because it means that the idea came first into the mind of Bonnar, and it was only the idea as it came into the mind of Bonner that later suggested itself to the accused as well. It is upon that evidence that the Crown asks you to find that the accused inflicted the neck wound. But, in drawing an inference from evidence, one is not in the region of conjecture, one is not in the region of suspicion. One is considering whether there is proof or not, and to decide a matter of that kind upon the evidence produced would, in my submission, be not a discharge of your duty but a breach of it. You have got to weigh very carefully whether there is proof beyond a reasonable doubt upon this matter, and I think you will find it very difficult to understand a great part of the evidence which has been tendered by the Crown, particularly the evidence of the alleged eye-witnesses. It seems to me that one is here left with only the fragments of a fight. One gets a little glimpse of it from one witness and a little glimpse of it from another, but one does not get a consecutive account of what actually took place. In these circumstances I ask you, and I ask you with confidence and in all seriousness, to find, in the first

Speech for the Defence.

Mr. Philip

place, when you are considering your verdict, that the Crown has not established that the accused inflicted the wound on the neck of the deceased.

But, I am not going to leave the matter there. This is a case where, as I said, there are a whole series of links, each one of which has to be considered. Let me for the moment assume, against my previous submission, that the accused's hand did inflict this wound. You will never reach that conclusion if I am right in my first submission, but let me go on to consider the next submission, the alternative submission. His lordship will direct you upon the quality of an act which is necessary to cause the act to be labelled murder, and, subject to what his lordship may direct you, first of all I remind you that homicide is not of itself murder, that there may be various kinds of homicide, with some of which one is not concerned in this case. There might, for instance, be justifiable homicide, but there are other kinds of homicide, and some of those are murder and some of them are not. The typical murder is a wilful and malicious intention to kill, no doubt with elements of premeditation. Just look at the circumstances in this case. In the first place you have two sides who ultimately came to this scene at the top of Taylor Street. You have two sides—it is not too much to say—well certainly the Revie-Gordon side—sodden with drink. I am not going over that evidence again, but you remember that they had been "half-seas over" when they left the "Coronation Bar", and three of them were so drunk by the time they were half-way through their stay in "Cameron's Bar" that they do not clearly remember what happened afterwards. On the other side you have Bonnar and the accused and Watt, and the evidence with regard to the accused is that he had been drinking in the morning between eleven and the time when the pubs closed, and not merely that but he was drinking steadily all the time. There was evidence of that both from Sarah Bonnar and from Daniel Bonnar himself. Then at about five or six o'clock he goes to "Thompson's Bar" with Bonnar, and the way in which Bonnar puts it is something like this, that he had a good deal and the accused had more.

These are the two groups which by chance converge, along with Watt, as I submit, at the point at the top of Taylor Street and its junction with McAslin Street. Then again this is not just an ordinary meeting. There had been a previous incident. Various witnesses have given different accounts of how it started. You remember Mrs. Colquhoun said that the fight in Rottenrow had

Patrick Carraher.

Mr. Philip

started through an attack on Bonnar. I think Fullarton on the other hand rather took the opposite view. It does not really matter how that previous fight started. What is significant is that Bonnar was chased down Rottenrow by the Revie party, some say Revie and Keatings. My learned friends observed that no one had said that John Gordon had gone, but my recollection is that one witness does say so. However, it does not really matter. The point is this, that there was a previous incident when Bonnar had been scared for his life and had gone off to College Street to his sister and had got, as he said, a hatchet there. Well, it is in that situation that these parties met.

Now the only independent evidence is that, so far as one can get at any start at all, whatever started at the top of Taylor Street started with Revie kicking. Even if the parties were in separate groups one cannot compartment this fight. It was certain men on the one side and certain men on the other. One cannot compartment it, and it is perfectly plain to you who know human nature that if one side is attacked first, well then the other side naturally are thrown into the position of supporting their own company. I think that that view is very much supported by those remarks to which Huie spoke to and to which I referred at an earlier stage, because it seems to me—if one could reconstruct this at all—that the sequence would be something like this. Revie kicks Bonnar. Bonnar somehow drops a hatchet. Revie calls out "Put the hatchet on him, Joe", referring to John. Then Bonnar shouts "After him, Harry". I am not concerned to say that that was how the things happened. It is not for me to say how it happened. It is for the Crown to prove its case. What I do say is that here is an entirely intelligible explanation of the sequence of events and my learned friend has not offered any alternative explanation of these various shouts or remarks. I suggest to you that that is an entirely natural and reasonable explanation. If that be so, then I submit, and his lordship will direct you with regard to this matter, that there was at least either provocation or a reasonable question as to whether there was not provocation. His lordship will direct you on the question of provocation, but my submission is that if there is a doubt as to whether a particular act which led to a fatality was provoked, then you would not be entitled in that view to return a verdict of more than culpable homicide.

I have so far said nothing about the question of diminished responsibility. Before I pass to that let me just summarize what I have said already. In the first place, I ask you in arriving at your

Speech for the Defence.

verdict to consider whether the Crown has proved that the accused's hand inflicted the neck wound. On that matter I ask you to answer no. In the second place, supposing for any reason you take a different view, well then I ask you to hold that the act did not amount to more than culpable homicide. But, in the third place, if the position be that the accused's mental condition is or may have been such that at the time of the act charged he was not fully but only partially responsible for his actions, then, subject to his lordship's direction, I submit that you are not entitled even on that view to hold more than culpable homicide. Putting it shortly, diminished responsibility reduces any crime which would otherwise be murder from murder to culpable homicide.

Now with regard to the question of diminished responsibility I would ask you to note at the outset two points. In the first place two of the most eminent psychiatrists in Glasgow have taken the view that this man is a psychopathic personality. They have given their opinion that he has diminished responsibility, but what I think is very significant, too, is that Dr. Scott, and please do not forget this evidence, while his opinion was that the accused was not a psychopathic personality, also took the view that if he had been a psychopathic personality his responsibility would have been diminished. So that if you reach the view that this man is a psychopathic personality then, as to the consequences, all the doctors agree. The only difference between them is whether or not this man is a psychopathic personality. It is a very remarkable position. I do not personally recall a situation like this before. The difference is between two of the most eminent psychiatrists on the one side and the prison doctor on the other. Well, ladies and gentlemen, in face of that how could you possibly reach the view that this accused was not a psychopathic personality and was not of reduced responsibility? After all there is no region more difficult to assess than the region of the mind. It is not a case where one can go through a physical examination and detect outward symptoms. It can only be done by a history, and these doctors, these eminent psychiatrists, have come forward and given their opinion.

In face of that opinion I respectfully suggest that it would be really assuming the functions of psychiatrists yourselves to reach an opposite view. Just let me remind you, however, of the various factors. In the first place Dr. McNiven in his report describes this, if I may just quote his actual words, as a form of gross abnormality. It is not a case of just a little abnormality or anything of that kind,

Patrick Carraher.

but he regards this man as falling into the category of a psychopathic personality, a case where there is gross abnormality, though a degree of abnormality which falls short of certifiable insanity. Of course if the degree of abnormality had amounted to certifiable insanity that would be a case of psychosis and then the accused would be unfit to plead. It is just because it falls below certifiable insanity that he is fit to plead, but he has nevertheless a diminished responsibility. Just remember, too, the facts which we know about the accused. His childhood was, according to the history obtained by Dr. McNiven, unusual in this respect, that it was in an environment which was calculated to accentuate any kind of abnormality which he had. A step-mother rightly or wrongly put him out into the street. He was frequently ill-treated and he often slept out of the house, in closes and other places. Again in 1934, it is in evidence that he attempted to commit suicide. The evidence also is that he was so addicted to alcohol—and this is after all the Crown evidence; it is the evidence of Sarah Bonnar and the evidence of Daniel Bonnar—that he only eats to any extent on the days when the bars are not open. Then there was the evidence given by Sarah Bonnar that he has these delusional suspicions. He imagines that there are men in the cupboard when there are not men in the cupboard, and Dr. McNiven—and this was the expression that he used—was of the view that it involved a defect in his judgment, that he had not the capacity to form the judgment which a normal man would form and Dr. McNiven also was of the view that, if such a man were taking drink to the extent to which the accused is proved to have been taking it, that would accentuate his defect of judgment.

Dr. Blyth is of the view that there was, to use his own words, a mental abnormality, and it having been suggested that was this not just a failure to control his actions, Dr. Blyth was quite definitely of the opinion, and he is better able to judge than we are, that it was an incapacity or a lack of capacity, not just a failure, a lack of capacity, to control his actions. My learned friend sought to suggest to you that the position simply was that the accused was thriftless and callous. Well, ladies and gentlemen, a man in these categories does not harbour delusional suspicions. A man in these categories does not attempt to commit suicide—very much the reverse. A man in these categories would be perfectly alive to the situation in which he was if a murder charge was hanging over his head. The extraordinary thing is that these doctors consider this man does not appreciate to the full the seriousness of the

Speech for the Defence.

Mr. Philip

charge which hangs over his head. In that situation, subject to what his lordship may direct you, I would respectfully submit that there is only one possible conclusion to which you could come on this matter and that is that the accused is a man of diminished responsibility. Accordingly my submission to you is that, after you have considered the whole evidence, you will find the accused not guilty or the charge not proven; that alternatively, if you consider that the accused's hand inflicted the blow which was struck at the deceased's neck, your verdict will be culpable homicide; and in regard to that you will have regard both to the fact that this incident, if it did take place, took place in the course of a drunken brawl, and also to the fact that the accused is, on any view, a man of diminished responsibility.

My lord, upon the questions of law in this case, my submission is, first of all, that with regard to the question of diminished responsibility your lordship should direct the jury that there is evidence upon which they are entitled to hold diminished responsibility; and further that, if the jury consider that the accused's mental condition was or may have been such that, at the time of the act charged, he was not fully but only partially responsible for his actions, then they are not entitled on any view to return a verdict of more than culpable homicide. Upon that matter I found on the cases which have been cited by my learned friend. The Lord Justice-Clerk in *Savage's* case, 1923 J.C. 49, referred to a variety of things which may constitute diminished responsibility or which may be an element in diminished responsibility. It is not necessary that each one of these should exist. It is sufficient that that kind of thing should be found. Your lordship will find the passage at page 51. The Lord Justice-Clerk says " I have told you the kind of thing that is necessary", and then his lordship gives a list of them such as "Aberration or weakness of mind", or for example, "A state of mind bordering on insanity although not reaching it." In my submission that is exactly how Dr. McNiven puts it in his report. Or take another example, "A mind affected so that the responsibility is diminished from full responsibility to partial responsibility." Upon that matter I would ask your lordship to have in view that Dr. Scott himself has given evidence that, if there is a psychopathic personality, then there would be diminished responsibility. Therefore the only difference between the doctors is whether or not there is psychopathic personality, and not whether that type of personality involves diminished responsibility.

Patrick Carraher.

Mr. Philip

Then, in the second place, I would ask your lordship to give a direction to the jury as follows: that if the jury consider that the accused's mental abnormality was accentuated by drink they are entitled to take into account the evidence of drink in considering the degree of his responsibility. My lord, may I just explain my position upon that matter. I accept it—it was laid down of course last year, in *Kennedy* v. *H.M. Advocate*, 1944 J.C. 171 at page 177— that, in the case of a normal man, the test is whether the condition of drink is such that the panel is at the time incapable of forming the specific intent required to constitute the crime charged. That is the case of a normal man, but the direction I have asked your lordship to give is one relating to accentuation of a mental abnormality already existing, and in my submission your lordship should give that second direction.

Then I also ask your lordship to give this direction to the jury: that, even if the jury were to reach the view that the accused's hand did cause the neck wound in the deceased, yet were in doubt as to whether the act was or was not provoked, then they are not entitled to find more than culpable homicide. Of course these points may be taken together or they may be taken separately, but they are separate matters of law. Upon the last point I would refer your lordship to *Woolmington* v. *The Director of Public Prosecutions* —a case which your lordship remembers went to the House of Lords—[1935] A.C. 462, the Lord Chancellor, Lord Sankey, at pages 481 and 482. In my submission that vouches the direction which I have asked your lordship to give.

LORD RUSSELL—This was on provocation. What is the effect of the direction?

MR. PHILIP—The effect is this, that if the jury are in doubt as to whether the act was or was not provoked then they are not entitled. . . .

LORD RUSSELL—The Crown has not discharged the onus?

MR. PHILIP—Yes, that is the point, the Crown has not discharged the onus. It is, of course, the position which very frequently arises in cases of fights.

LORD RUSSELL—I do not quite follow. Could you just give me Lord Sankey's observations?

Speech for the Defence.

MR. PHILIP—Your lordship remembers *Woolmington* was a case where there was a young couple. The wife had left the husband and had gone to live with her mother . . .

LORD RUSSELL—I only want the dictum of the Lord Chancellor. I do not want to take up more of your time than is necessary. Can you refer me to the passage on page 481?

MR. PHILIP—It begins at page 481: "Throughout the web of the English Criminal Law one golden thread is always to be seen, that it is the duty of the prosecution to prove the prisoner's guilt subject to what I have already said as to the defence of insanity and subject also to any statutory exception. If, at the end of and on the whole of the case, there is a reasonable doubt, created by the evidence given by either the prosecution or the prisoner, as to whether the prisoner killed the deceased with a malicious intention, the prosecution has not made out the case and the prisoner is entitled to an acquittal. No matter what the charge or where the trial, the principle that the prosecution must prove the guilt of the prisoner is part of the Common Law of England and no attempt to whittle it down can be entertained. When dealing with a murder case the Crown must prove (*a*) death as the result of a voluntary act of the deceased and (*b*) malice of the accused. It may prove malice either expressly or by implication. For malice may be implied where death occurs as a result of a voluntary act of the accused which is (i) intentional and (ii) unprovoked. When evidence of death and malice has been given (this is a question for the jury) the accused is entitled to show, by evidence or by examination of the circumstances adduced by the Crown, that the act on his part which caused death was either unintentional or provoked."

LORD RUSSELL—But that does not bear out quite the proposition you gave me. I understood you were saying that where evidence led as to provocation leaves the situation in doubt as to whether or not there was provocation, the jury must hold that there was provocation.

MR. PHILIP—I do not say that they must hold that there is provocation. I say, if provocation is expressly proved. . . .

LORD RUSSELL—Yes, that is trite law.

Patrick Carraher.

MR. PHILIP—But "If the jury are either satisfied with his explanation or, upon a review of all the evidence are left in reasonable doubt whether, even if his evidence be not accepted, the act was either unintentional or provoked, the prisoner is entitled to be acquitted." In my submission, in this particular case, one is left in reasonable doubt.

LORD RUSSELL—I follow. That is to say really that, on any topic on which the burden of proof rests upon the Crown, if at the end of the day there is reasonable doubt in the minds of a reasonable jury as to whether the burden of proof is discharged, then the Crown has failed. That is so. I thought there was something special as regards provocation.

MR. PHILIP—Well, that is applied with regard to provocation in the passage I have quoted.

Charge to the Jury.

Lord Russell

Third Day—Saturday, 2nd March, 1946.
Charge to the Jury.

LORD RUSSELL—Members of the jury, it is now my duty to address you on this case and give you such guidance and directions on the law as fall within my province. You have had the privilege of hearing two addresses, one from Crown counsel and one from Mr. Philip for the defence, in which the points on which they rely for their respective submissions have been placed before you. So far as anything they said meets with your approval you will give it consideration, but you are the masters of the facts here, and it is your province, and your province alone, to come to the conclusion on the facts which you think the evidence warrants. Now, you have been told twice, but nonetheless I am going to repeat it a third time; in this case as in every case the Crown is bound to prove the guilt of the accused beyond reasonable doubt. It is what is called in law the burden of proof. The burden of proof rests on the Crown. That means this, that if, after having considered the evidence on any question of fact which you have to determine, you are left in reasonable doubt as to whether or not the fact is proved, then it is your duty to give the benefit of the doubt to the accused. It means the Crown has failed to discharge the burden of proving that fact, but remember, the doubts which will lead to such a result in your decision must be reasonable doubts founded upon reason.

Now, so far as the facts are concerned you are the persons who must judge of such matters as the credibility of the witnesses you have seen passing through the box. For example, it was suggested to you yesterday that certain witnesses perhaps are mistaken in their recollection and you are not to accept their evidence as true or as accurate; or it may be suggested that a witness is dishonest and you are not to accept what he says as accurate. Well, that is all a matter for your consideration. You saw those witnesses pass through the box, you heard what their story was, and if you think that they are honest and that their recollection is to be trusted as reasonably accurate you are quite entitled to accept their evidence. Remember, witnesses speaking to events that are in the past, as we know from experience in the Courts of Law, are very apt to differ in details quite honestly from one another, because at the moment which they are describing one has per-

253

Patrick Carraher.

haps observed one factor in the situation which was not noticed
by another, the other having noticed some factor which was not
noticed by the first person. You get these discrepancies in detail,
but, after all, the questions which will have to be considered by
you in this case are the broad questions of how the deceased John
Gordon met his death, and if you are satisfied by the medical
evidence that he met his death on the night of the 23rd November
last from hæmorrhage caused by an incised wound in his neck
that was put there by a man who assaulted him, assaulted him wilfully or with reckless indifference as to the consequences, then you
will come to the conclusion that John Gordon was murdered. I
do not think there has been any suggestion to the contrary in the
able speech you heard for the defence. Gordon was murdered on
23rd November last. Now, that is merely the introduction. The
Crown puts forward for your acceptance that the person whose
hand held the weapon that caused that fatal wound is the accused,
and the evidence they have led is suggested as supporting and
proving that it was the accused. Well, you have heard a summary,
a résumé, of the evidence in the speeches that you heard from the
two counsel, and I do not intend, and it is never really the function
of the judge to rehearse again to the jury the whole of the evidence. I propose, however, for your help and guidance to mention
one or two of what appear to me might be important matters for
you to consider. If in the course of these remarks I appear to give
you any impression as to what I think might be proved, please
remember that it is not binding upon you; it is for you to consider
and for you to decide what you think is proved.

Now, you remember the evidence which has traced the movements of the deceased John Gordon from the early evening until
the moment when he left the foot of Rottenrow and proceeded
northwards along Taylor Street on his way to the corner of Taylor
Street and McAslin Street, where the fatal assault took place.
You have heard the evidence of the witness Revie who accompanied John Gordon on that journey along Taylor Street.
Similarly, you have heard from the witness Bonnar the movements
of himself and the accused Carraher when they set off also from
the corner of Taylor Street and Rottenrow and made their way
by a kind of circular route up into McAslin Street, first to the
house where Revie lived and where it was thought they might
find the Gordons, and not entering that house but proceeding
westwards to the corner of McAslin Street and Taylor Street
where that couple met the other couple. Now, you have heard

the story given by Revie and by Bonnar, and there is one point that was not mentioned to you in the course of the speeches which I think I might remind you of. You remember the witness Watt, who gave evidence yesterday, was in the Bonnar house in Rottenrow about twenty minutes past nine on the night of 23rd November when word came that Dan Bonnar was fighting in Rottenrow, or was in a mêlée or in a mix-up, and you remember Watt told you how he and the accused Carraher, who was in that house at that moment, went out to look for Dan Bonnar, and Watt told us that when these two left to go out to look for Dan Bonnar and find him, the accused, as they were going out, showed a blade in his pocket and made the remark, "This is the very tool for them"—and he described the tool as similar to the chisel which we had produced in court. I mention that for this reason: Bonnar had been asked by his sister to come away in home and stop this fighting after they met and after they learned that there had been a scrap in the road opposite "Cameron's Bar"; but you remember they said Bonnar would not come home. When Bonnar and Carraher and Watt met and Bonnar refused to come home and when these three went up and proceeded to go round—whether Watt left them or not does not appear to be very material, but you will consider that—when Bonnar and Carraher set off on that road, you know, as Bonnar told us, that Bonnar had a hatchet which he had got from his sister's house previously after having been in the first fight near "Cameron's Bar", and presumably Carraher had this weapon which Watt saw in his pocket and about which Carraher the accused had made the remark, "This is the very tool for them."

You have the description of the meeting between these two couples at the corner of Taylor Street and McAslin Street, and as it is two days since you heard the evidence of what Revie said, I am just going to read you a few sentences to recall how Revie described what happened when these two couples met. Having described how he and John Gordon were arriving at the corner, he is asked: "Q.—What happened then? A.—We walked down Taylor Street, came to the junction of McAslin Street, and Bonnar and Carraher dived on the two of us. Q.—You mean two men, one of whom was Bonnar and the other was a man called Carraher? A.—Yes. Q.—Dived down on you? A.—Yes. Q.—What do you mean by that? A.—They dived out of a close at us. Q.—You mean they rushed out of a close towards you? A.—Yes. Q.—Where was the close they rushed out of? A.—In Taylor Street.

Patrick Carraher.

Lord Russell

Q.—Were you still going up Taylor Street, just coming to the corner of McAslin Street? A.—Yes." And then he identified Bonnar who was brought into court, and he identified Carraher, the accused, as the other man, and then later on he described how "Bonnar dived at me and Carraher dived at the good-brother. Q.—That is John Gordon? A.—Yes. Q.—Well, go on, tell us what happened? A.—Bonnar fought with me and Carraher had a hold of the good-brother. I saw Carraher's hand up. Q.—Do you say you saw something in his hand? A.—Yes. Q.—What did you see? A.—I could not make out what it was. Q.—Look at Labels Nos. 1 and 2. Might the thing which you saw in Carraher's hand possibly have been that? A.—It could have been." And then, asked to demonstrate the position in which he recollects seeing Carraher's hand at the moment when he was holding Gordon, he demonstrates, and he is asked, "Was his right arm stretched out and was his hand on a level about his shoulder? A.—Yes." Now, that is the gist of the statement. You will remember the rest of his evidence; he is cross-examined about it, and you will remember the evidence of Revie as to the circumstances which occurred when he and Gordon arrived at that corner.

Now, that is the one eye-witness. Revie never saw a blow struck. In the passage I have read to you he describes all he did see, because you remember he explained how he and Bonnar got out on to the centre of the road, and Bonnar finally made off running westwards along McAslin Street and Revie followed, and it was not until Revie came back and found Gordon injured that he realized what had happened. The other person who might be represented as an eye-witness of it is the witness Bonnar, but Bonnar is not able to throw very much light on the position either. If I may just remind you in a word, he said that he and Carraher did not dive out of a close in Taylor Street upon Revie and Gordon, but his account is that he and Carraher came along McAslin Street and he said Watt was there too, and they met just at the corner, and you remember his description of it is—"As we turned the corner Revie and John Gordon were coming down. I was going to speak to John Gordon, but Revie came at me to kick me, and I went out into the middle of the street with Revie after me. I left Gordon standing on the pavement. I do not know what happened to him. Carraher and Watt were facing Gordon when I retreated to the street"—and then he explained how he ran off, followed by Revie and got away. Well, there is evidence that

Charge to the Jury.

Lord Russell

at the moment, as you heard from other evidence, at the moment immediately before John Gordon is seen to have been wounded with blood spouting from his neck, he and Revie had met Bonnar and Carraher under the circumstances that Revie and Bonnar tell you.

Now, there is the picture, Revie saying, "Carraher had a hold of John Gordon and his hand out," Bonnar saying, "When I retreated from the pavement with Revie after me Carraher and Watt were facing John Gordon." Very well, 60 yards or so, according to the witnesses' estimate, further down Taylor Street from the corner of McAslin Street were standing two men at the time of this occurrence, Campbell and Stewart. You remember Campbell was the young marine, and he describes how, having his attention directed up to the corner, he saw four men apparently engaged in a scrap, one kicking another man on the street, and the other man who was being kicked then turning and running off west. That was one couple of the four that he saw. His description of the other two was—"Of the other two on the pavement one gave a punch to the other and the punched man fell." Campbell went up to the corner and by the time he reached there the man who fell had got up, and he saw he was bleeding from the neck. Stewart on the other hand can only recollect seeing three men, and it may be, of course—it is for you to judge—that Stewart's attention was only drawn to the occurrence after Bonnar had run off down McAslin Street and would be out of sight. At all events, there is Stewart's description, and he says a man was on the pavement when he looked, staggering, and when he went up with Campbell this man who was staggering was bleeding from the neck. Then you have the evidence of the two painters, you remember, who were at the corner. Their evidence was just that, hearing scuffling and hearing some things shouted out, they turned round and saw a man coming towards them bleeding from the neck. They cannot identify anybody; neither can Stewart nor Campbell. Well, there is the position. Stewart and Campbell so far corroborate, if you accept their evidence, corroborate the story of Bonnar and Revie that a fracas such as we heard described did occur at the place and at the time described by Bonnar and Revie, that one of the fights was taking place accompanied by kicking out in the street, and that on the pavement there occurred something which Campbell thought was a punch, causing the punched man to fall on the pavement, and when Campbell got up to him the punched man was bleeding

Patrick Carraher.

from the neck. Well, if you accept that evidence, it is, if you think it credible, evidence which in essence corroborates the story of Revie and Bonnar so far as it goes, without of course identifying either of the men. Campbell does not identify any of the four men.

The next thing on which there is evidence which you may find to be corroborative is that of Stewart, the witness, a taxi driver who had been with Campbell and who had gone up to the corner 60 yards or so. Stewart later that night meets a friend of his called Elliott and, telling Elliott about what had happened at that corner and that he had heard that Bonnar was involved, he and Elliott set off to find Bonnar and to tell him, among other things, what we now know, that John Gordon had died, a man who was in that earlier fracas. And you heard the evidence of the witness Stewart that, having arrived at Tarbet Street with Elliott and having gone into the house and having told them, "John Gordon is dead", some of them were naturally a little upset, and Carraher told them this, that he (Carraher) had been having a cup of tea when he was told Bonnar was in trouble in Rottenrow, that he went out and met Bonnar and that the two of them went to the close in McAslin Street, and found nobody there; and that they went on to the corner of Taylor Street where they met the two fellows and the fight started; and then Carraher said this, according to Stewart's testimony, if you accept it, "I gave one of them a jag and ran away when the fight started." In cross-examination he said, "I gave one of them a wee jag and ran away when the fight started." Carraher, the accused, as Stewart was leaving the house, gave him the chisel which is labelled Nos. 1 and 2 and said, "Chip that away"; and you remember the subsequent way in which that chisel and its handle were dealt with and later recovered. Well, there is Carraher—if you believe Stewart and believe his memory is accurate—giving an account of what had happened in which he had participated as he said, and in which he said to Stewart, "I gave one of them a jag and ran away when the fight started." That is a piece of evidence which you may think tends to corroborate Revie and to suggest where the blow came from.

Now, Elliott had accompanied Stewart into the house at Tarbet Street where Bonnar and Carraher were, and Elliott explains in the course of his evidence how in the kitchen while they were in that house and before Carraher handed over the chisel to Stewart, Elliott says he saw this happening:—the accused put his hand in his hip pocket, took out the chisel, it was in one piece but he

258

THE HONOURABLE LORD RUSSELL

Charge to the Jury.

Lord Russell

pulled it apart, took a dishcloth from the side of the window and wiped the chisel with it, and then later put the chisel into Stewart's hands. That is another second element, and then there is the account given by Bonnar, if you believe it: Bonnar having escaped and run off after the fight, finds his way to a place called Canning Place and there meets Carraher; and you remember at Canning Place Carraher said to Bonnar that he had given Gordon a jag or something. Now, if you accept that evidence—if you think Bonnar is honest, accurate and reliable—if you think Stewart is honest, accurate and reliable—there within a very short time of the occurrence described by Revie and Bonnar at the corner of McAslin Street Carraher had said first to Bonnar, "I gave Gordon a jag or something", or "I gave Gordon a wee jag or something", and later says to Stewart, "I gave one of them a jag and then ran away when the fight started"; and you have Elliott's description of wiping before handing over to Stewart the chisel which is produced, Labels Nos. 1 and 2.

Ladies and gentlemen, what inference do you draw—it is entirely for you—from these words uttered by Carraher in the context in which they occur? Mr. Philip suggested that if you thought Carraher was the man who was in grips or was fighting with John Gordon at that corner that this statement of his about a "jag" might reasonably be taken by you to refer to an injury he has on his finger and does not warrant you drawing an inference that it could refer or did refer to the injury Gordon got on his neck. You will consider that suggestion, ladies and gentlemen. If you think it is intelligible and reasonable you will give effect to it. If you do not think it probable or reasonable then you will not accept it; and if you do not accept it what inference do you draw? What is meant by giving a man a jag, said by a man who, having left to go out on this journey from the house in Rottenrow had remarked to his companion then, "This is the very tool for them"? You will make up your minds upon that matter, ladies and gentlemen. And that is not all: there is finally the evidence of the witness Watt, as you remember, given yesterday, who, having gone back to the house at Rottenrow, says he left Bonnar and the accused before they ever got to the corner—there is a discrepancy in the evidence about that between Bonnar and Watt. It is for you to say how far it really affects the question, but you will bear in mind that on this particular point Bonnar and Watt are in disagreement. However that may be, nearly an hour after Watt parted with those two, as he says, he came back to the house in Rottenrow and there found

Patrick Carraher.

Bonnar and the accused, and you remember what Watt said about that. To be sure I am accurate on that I will just give you a word or two from the notes of evidence: "The first thing whenever I went into that house discussion came up. Q.—What was the discussion? A.—About how they used the weapon." Then after describing what Bonnar said, which I do not read to you, the question is put "Q.—What did Carraher say? A.—He said that he did a bit of a toe dance. Q.—Who did a bit of a toe dance? A.—Carraher, and showing how he came down with the tool. Q.—Just show us what Carraher did?" Then there was a question by the Court: "When he showed you what he did with the tool, what part of his body was he moving? A.—He was moving his right hand backward and forward. Q.—Put your hand into the position you think? A.—That way," and then the witness indicates how Carraher illustrated how he had been tip-toe dancing and so on. "Q.—And what was his arm doing while he was tip-toe dancing? A.—It came down. Q.—Showing how his arm came down? A.—Yes."

Well, all these elements, ladies and gentlemen, are worthy of your consideration and your very serious consideration in making up your minds whether you think that the evidence of Revie and Bonnar as to the meeting, coupled with the corroboration from Campbell and Stewart who were 60 yards or so down the street, coupled with the later evidence that Stewart and Elliott give about the weapon at Tarbet Street, the evidence that Bonnar gives about what Carraher said to him when they met at Canning Place, and the final evidence of Watt demonstrating what he said Carraher showed, is to be relied upon. On that matter you will not leave out of account, of course, that according to the medical testimony the wound in John Gordon's neck has a direction inwards and upwards, and Mr. Philip quite properly suggested to you that if Carraher really was professing to show how he used a weapon in the fight that night and used it by bringing his hand downward from up, that that would never cause a wound in the neck that goes inward and upward. Of course, there are many explanations which might occur to you for that. To begin with, in the demonstrations Watt explained that while Carraher was toe-dancing he was moving his arm backward and forward, and then at the end that he moved it downwards. In a fracas it is quite conceivable, and it is for you to consider whether it could not happen, that the neck of the man may be bent at the time when the blow is struck, and the downward blow on a bent neck might go up. Well, that

Charge to the Jury.

Lord Russell

is for your consideration, ladies and gentlemen, on the assumption that you thought it was proved that Carraher's blow, if he gave the blow, was struck downward, but you will remember the whole description given by Watt as well as a downward movement showed the arm moving from side to side. But it is a matter for your consideration, taken with all the other evidence. If you believe it proved that Carraher acknowledged he gave John Gordon a jag, and that Carraher then handed the weapon, after wiping it with a dishcloth in his own kitchen, to another witness, telling that witness to chip it away, does that corroboration of the story by Bonnar and Revie bring home to your minds satisfactorily beyond reasonable doubt the wound on John Gordon's neck, which was not there immediately before Carraher and Bonnar met them and which was there immediately after Carraher and Bonnar met them—coupled with Carraher's description of jags and so on, and giving away the weapon to chip away—do you think as reasonable men and women that that evidence satisfies you beyond reasonable doubt that the hand holding the weapon that entered John Gordon's neck that night at the corner was the hand of the accused Carraher? Now, that is the first question you have to consider, and you will keep in mind that something was said also about the length of the wound being 4 inches and the measurement of the tool being about 2½ inches if you take the whole of the steel part. You have heard the opinion and evidence given by Dr. Black and Professor Allison. It is for you to judge. You will consider whether there is any reasonable doubt at all that that weapon which is now produced, Labels Nos. 1 and 2, which was handed to the witness Stewart to chip away, is not a weapon which is quite capable of having delivered the blow which caused the wound on John Gordon's neck. You will take that into consideration, but having taken the whole thing into consideration, let me repeat, the first question for you is upon that evidence, the burden of the proof being on the Crown, are you satisfied beyond reasonable doubt that the hand that dealt the fatal blow on John Gordon's neck on 23rd November was the hand of the accused Carraher?

If you are not satisfied about that, then it is your duty to return a verdict of not guilty of murder, which would acquit the accused and the accused would go free. If, however, you are satisfied by the evidence that the hand was the hand, and has been proved to your satisfaction to have been the hand of the accused Carraher, two lines of defence which require consideration have been tabled

Patrick Carraher.

Lord Russell

on the assumption that it is proved that Carraher's hand struck this blow. The first as tabled by Mr. Philip was this: there was evidence of a good deal of drink that night having been taken by the parties involved in this fracas, and that what happened at the corner of McAslin Street and Taylor Street was really a drunken brawl, and there is some evidence that John Gordon may have been the assailant and gone for Carraher or provoked Carraher, and that Carraher, having been provoked, acting with justifiable retaliation, if he killed, cannot be held to be guilty of murder but only of culpable homicide. Now, I have given very anxious and careful consideration as to whether in the evidence you have heard there is in law evidence to suggest for your consideration the existence of provocation directed against Carraher, and causing Carraher to take the action he did. I take the responsibility of directing you in law, and you must take this from me, that there is no evidence on which a reasonable jury could possibly find there had been provocation used on which Carraher's blow ensued. So that I direct you to disregard the first of the defences outlined by Mr. Philip in his able address based on culpable homicide because of provocation; and let me reassure you not to be anxious at accepting and following my direction; you have got to do it. If my direction is wrong there is another Court where it can be reviewed, and where any error I have committed will be put right, but I direct you so far as provocation is concerned, that there is no legal evidence on which provocation could be founded; and therefore that element reducing the character of the crime from murder to culpable homicide is out of the picture.

The remaining question is raised by the second line of defence put forward. It concerns what is called in law the impaired or diminished responsibility of a person who commits an act which, if he were an ordinary normal person, would be murder, but which, if he has diminished or impaired responsibility may, if the jury so think, be reduced to culpable homicide, and on that, as you know, we heard conflicting evidence yesterday. I was invited by the Crown on this topic, on this element of defence, impaired responsibility—I was asked by the Crown to direct you that there is no evidence for your consideration upon which any such impaired responsibility on the accused's part could be established. I have given very anxious and prolonged consideration to that motion on the part of the Crown, and I have with some hesitation come to be of the opinion that I might be usurping your function if I took it on myself to give you that direction and to take this

Charge to the Jury.

Lord Russell

defence out of your hands altogether; and therefore it will be necessary for you to consider such evidence as has been led in so far as it appears to establish the defence of impaired responsibility. Now, first of all, I want to make you quite *au fait* with what the law is on this matter. Diminished responsibility is a condition of mind, of judgment, which is said to make a man not fully accountable for his actions and not fully answerable to the law. Observe this: the accused is perfectly sane and fit to plead. There is no question about his sanity. If the accused were insane or were said to be insane he never would be tried on a charge. There would be an inquiry before a judge, and if found to be insane he would be ordered to be detained during His Majesty's pleasure, and during his detention would be given treatment appropriate to a man with a disease of the mind causing insanity. The accused, as I say, is perfectly sane, but our law does recognize, and it is a comparatively recent introduction into our law, that if a man suffers from infirmity or aberration of mind or impairment of intellect to such an extent as not to be fully accountable for his actions the result is to reduce the quality of the crime in a case like this, which, if you think so, would be otherwise murder—to reduce it to culpable homicide.

Now, I am going to read to you a passage from the Lord Justice-Clerk delivered not many months ago in very similar circumstances in a charge to a jury where the same question was raised, and the Lord Justice-Clerk said this: "I am going to read a sentence or two from the case"—and he mentions the case decided in 1923 by the late Lord Justice-Clerk—"because it seems to me to give as explicit and clear a statement of the sort of thing which you have to look for, as clear a statement as I can find"—and then he reads the late Lord Justice-Clerk's statement to this effect:—"It is very difficult to put it in a phrase but it has been put in this way, that there must be aberration or weakness of mind. There must be some form of mental unsoundness; there must be a state of mind which is bordering on although not amounting to insanity; there must be a mind so affected that responsibility is diminished from full responsibility to partial responsibility. In other words, the prisoner in question must be only partially accountable for his acts, and I think one can see running through the cases that there is implied that there must be some form of mental disease." And then he cites another judge who called the condition partial insanity, and then he goes on, having given that explanation as to what the law is—he goes on to consider the evidence with the jury. Now,

Patrick Carraher.

Lord Russell

ladies and gentlemen, you have heard evidence yesterday from Dr. McNiven and Dr. Blyth to the effect that the accused is in the category of a word they used, psychopathic personality. Well, naturally you and I do not know the meaning of that term, we had to ask them what it meant, and Dr. McNiven's evidence was to this effect. He said, "I am inclined to place the accused in the category of a psychopathic personality. A psychopathic personality is a clinical condition in which are included persons who from childhood or early youth show all the gross abnormality in their social behaviour and emotional reaction, and who do not as a rule show enough insanity to be certifiable as insane." "Broadly speaking," he says again, "it is a condition in which there is an inability on the part of the person affected to adapt himself to the ordinary social conditions, usually less than insanity which is certifiable. It is associated with emotional instability." And then he puts it this way: "If you asked me does the accused know the difference between right and wrong intellectually, does he know if he commits a wrong act he is liable to punishment, I say yes, and then he is responsible; but if responsibility means that he has a proper appreciation of his social responsibility, that he is capable of resisting temptation, capable of exercising control over his actions, then in my opinion he is not as responsible as a normal person." And you remember Dr. Blyth said the same thing more or less. I will not at the moment trouble you with it.

The question of alcoholism was also mentioned as one of the factors, and the doctor said alcoholism would lower any capacity a man may have for self-control. Let me give you a direction first about alcoholism. If by alcoholism the doctor means, as I take it, that a man under the influence of drink has less self-control than a man who is not under the influence of drink, in law drunkenness never excuses or palliates an offence unless it is so extreme as to deprive the man who is drunk of the capacity to form an intention to kill or to do grievous bodily harm. The man must be incapable of forming an intention to kill or to do grievous bodily harm before drunkenness can ever enter the picture in affecting guilt of a crime. So far as the phrase "alcoholism" was concerned I did not understand the doctors yesterday to suggest the accused is suffering from a form of illness due to constant or continuous imbibing of alcohol, because they said, "When we examined him he was showing no symptoms of alcoholism, but from his own statement he seems never to be sober, and at times to be so drunk that he is markedly drunk, and therefore he is a man who has not the same

Charge to the Jury.

Lord Russell

appreciation of moral standards as a normal man. Alcoholism would increase his difficulty in exercising self-control." Very well, ladies and gentlemen, you can dismiss, and I direct you in law that unless you thought it was proved that on the night in question the accused was so drunk as to be incapable of forming the intention to kill or to do grievous bodily harm—you will dismiss any idea of drunkenness, or alcoholism as it is called, from your minds, and you will not forget this, that at nine-twenty, or three-quarters of an hour to an hour before this distressing tragedy happened, the accused left the house making the remark to his friends as he went out to look for Dan Bonnar, "This is the very tool for them." Does that look like a man who is incapable of forming the intention to kill or to do grievous bodily harm?

On the remaining elements which the doctors described as amounting to diminished responsibility they referred to various peculiarities which they said they found in the accused, or at least suspected—that he did not seem to appreciate the consequences of the charge hanging over him, that he had difficulty in resisting temptation, that he could not withstand frustration—and the description, you may remember, was such that it led me to ask whether there were not a great many people in this country who do not act just as good citizens, and whether he would include these in the category of psychopathic personality, and he said, "Yes." Dr. Blyth went so far as to say that people who find themselves in trouble through lack of a social standard, through failure to exercise self-control and through inability to adapt themselves to the social environment in which they live, and who find their way into the courts in trouble—he said these are all or mostly psychopathic personalities. He said it may well be that 2 per cent. of the population, people who are not insane, remember, are psychopathic personalities. Ladies and gentlemen, it is a little disturbing to the lieges, I think, to feel that 2 per cent. of the population are in our midst who, because they have lower than normal self-control, perception of social standards, ability to adapt themselves to their environment, are people who are only partially accountable to the law for their actions; and as the Lord Justice-Clerk said in the course of the passage, part of which I have read to you: "I am going to take the responsibility of telling you," he said to the jury in that case, "in so many words that it will *not* suffice in law for the purpose of this defence of diminished responsibility merely to show that the accused person has a very short temper or is unusually excitable and lacking in self-control. The

Patrick Carraher.

Lord Russell

world would be a very convenient place for criminals and a very dangerous place for other people if that were the law." Now, as I have told you, ladies and gentlemen, I have given very serious and prolonged consideration to the motion made by the Crown to withdraw this defence from your cognisance altogether on the ground that there is no evidence which in law would justify a reasonable jury in holding that there is proof of diminished responsibility in the eye of the law. I said to you I thought I might be usurping your province. I have tried to summarize all the reasons, most of them, I think, given by the two gentlemen who gave evidence for the defence to support their view which the defence here founds upon. They say the accused is a psychopathic personality; they have told us what they understand by psychopathic personality, and the defence says proof of psychopathic personality is enough for a jury to hold that a man has diminished responsibility. Well, it is for you to say, in the light of what I have read to you as the law regulating diminished responsibility, whether really there is evidence to support in your judgment this defence of diminished responsibility, and on the question, when you make up your minds about that one way or the other, remember I read to you the law, which I adopt as accurate, and which gives a formulation of the tests on which diminished responsibility must be decided. Is there aberration or weakness of mind, mental unsoundness, partial insanity, great peculiarity of mind?

These are four of the legal tests, and I ask you in the light of that to consider whether the facts and opinions given by Dr. McNiven and Dr. Blyth really justify you in holding that diminished responsibility is made out. Let me give you a direction about the burden of proof on this point. If the Crown have established here that the accused did this thing, that he wielded the weapon that stabbed John Gordon and caused his death, it is not for the Crown to go further and show that the accused was fully responsible for what he did. It is for the accused to make good his defence of partial irresponsibility, and that means that he must show you that the balance of probability on the evidence is in favour of the view that his accountability and his responsibility are below normal in the sense of the legal requisites that I endeavoured to make plain to you. Therefore, ladies and gentlemen, is there any approach in the evidence which you have heard—and you are the judges here—is there any approach to satisfying, on a balance of probability, the tests formulated upon the evidence which you have heard delivered by these two gentlemen? I do not remind you, because you re-

Charge to the Jury.

Lord Russell

member it for yourselves, that Dr. Scott, a man who has had this man daily under his notice, a man of great experience, gave no countenance to the suggestion that there is diminished responsibility in the accused, and he had seen him every day since the 25th November, and has had an admirable opportunity of forming an opinion. The two gentlemen on whom the defence rely are psychiatrists undoubtedly and you will give careful consideration to what they said, and yet they come forward and profess to give you that evidence as to the mental condition, the mind of the accused, in support of the suggestion made by their counsel that that is enough to justify the defence of diminished responsibility. Now, it is upon the balance of probability on the evidence led that you have got to decide this question, but I am sorry I must leave it to you in this way: it is for you to say. If you find on the balance of the evidence that you are satisfied that diminished responsibility in the sense in which I have read you these legal formulations of it is established, then it is your duty to give effect to it; it does reduce the crime to culpable homicide. On the other hand, if you are satisfied on a balance of probability that diminished responsibility on the part of the accused has not been established, then you reject the defence, and therefore you are left with what? You are left with this, that without provocation by a man who is fully responsible there was an attack in the form of an assault ending fatally against John Gordon. In all that we have been considering for the last twenty-five minutes or so I have been assuming that you are satisfied that it is proved beyond reasonable doubt that it was the accused who did this, and I told you that if you are not satisfied that it was the accused that did it that would end the matter altogether; you would find the charge not proven or the accused not guilty and he would walk off free, but all the rest I have been saying is on the assumption that you come to the conclusion beyond reasonable doubt that his was the hand that did it. Assuming you come to the conclusion that diminished responsibility has not been made out, what is your verdict to be? Let me just tell you what murder is in a word. Murder is constituted by any wilful act causing death, whether intended to kill or whether just displaying wicked recklessness to show in the assailant a regardlessness of consequences; it is also committed by a man where grievous bodily harm is clearly intended or is known to be a likely result of a wilful act, and death follows from that wilful act; that is murder. I do not think anyone in the case has suggested that if provocation is out of it, and if diminished responsibility is out of it, there is any

Patrick Carraher.

alternative to murder, on the assumption that the evidence satisfies you it was the hand of the accused that struck the blow that caused John Gordon's death.

Now, ladies and gentlemen, I do not think that there is anything further that I can usefully say to you. I have done my best to try to ease your labours, but you will realize that in a case of this kind the responsibility is yours. If you come to the conclusion that the defence put forward, which would if established reduce the character of the offence from murder to culpable homicide, is not on a balance of probability established, you must just steel yourselves to the duty you have sworn to perform and find the accused guilty of murder as libelled. On the other hand, if you find that the defence of diminished responsibility is on a balance of probability established, then it would be your duty to give effect to that, and it would be your duty to return a verdict of culpable homicide against the accused. These are the two alternatives for you on the assumption that you are reasonably satisfied that his hand did it. If you are not able to affirm the defence of diminished responsibility you must have courage to do your duty. I cannot help you further; the responsibility is yours.

Now if you will kindly retire and consider your verdict I can take it whenever you have reached it, either unanimously or by a majority.

[The jury was enclosed at 11.35 a.m.
and returned into Court at 11.55 a.m.]

Verdict.

THE CLERK OF COURT—Members of the jury, what is your verdict?

THE FOREMAN—We find the accused guilty of murder as libelled.

THE CLERK OF COURT—Is that verdict unanimous or by a majority?

THE FOREMAN—Unanimous.

THE CLERK OF COURT—Members of the jury, does this correctly record your verdict: "The jury unanimously find the panel guilty of murder as libelled"?

THE FOREMAN—Yes.

Sentence.

Mr. Johnston—I move for sentence.

Sentence.

Lord Russell—Patrick Carraher, in respect of the verdict of the jury the law leaves me no alternative but to pronounce the sentence which I now pronounce. In respect of the verdict of guilty of murder as libelled just received, I decern and adjudge you, Patrick Carraher, panel, to be carried from the Bar to the Prison of Barlinnie, Glasgow, therein to be detained till the twenty-third day of March current, and upon that day, between the hours of eight and ten o'clock forenoon within the walls of the said prison, by the hands of the common executioner, to be hanged by the neck upon a gibbet until you be dead, and your body thereafter to be buried within the walls of the said prison, and ordain your whole movable goods and gear to be escheat and inbrought to His Majesty's use; which is pronounced for Doom.

Patrick Carraher.

APPENDIX

REX v. *CARRAHER*

COURT OF CRIMINAL APPEAL, 20TH MARCH, 1946

BEFORE

THE LORD JUSTICE-GENERAL (The Right Hon. Lord Normand),
LORD CARMONT, LORD JAMIESON, LORD STEVENSON AND
LORD BIRNAM

THE LORD JUSTICE-GENERAL—The appellant was convicted of murdering a man named Gordon in Glasgow on the 23rd November, 1945, and was sentenced to death. He has appealed against that conviction on several grounds which are not closely connected with one another and which I will take up in order.

I shall deal with the objection that the presiding judge misdirected the jury in the following passage:—

> "After all the questions which will have to be considered by you in this case are the broad questions of how the deceased John Gordon met his death, and if you are satisfied by the medical evidence that he met his death on the night of the 23rd November last from hæmorrhage caused by an incised wound in his neck that was put there by a man who assaulted him, wilfully assaulted him or with reckless indifference as to the consequences, then you will come to the conclusion that John Gordon was murdered. I do not think there has been any suggestion to the contrary in the able speech you heard for the defence. Gordon was murdered on the 23rd November last."

The counsel for the appellant stated that the jury might from this passage erroneously infer that the murder was to be taken as admitted if the jury merely found that the deceased met his death on the night in question from hæmorrhage caused by an incised wound in the neck, or that the jury might take it as admitted that the wound resulted from an assault which was wilfully made with reckless indifference as to the consequences. My lords, this submission once more compels me to observe that we

Appendix.

cannot quash a conviction merely because in an isolated passage there may be ground for some criticism. The real question is whether the charge fairly read instructed the jury that they must hold that Gordon was murdered and then had only to inquire whether it was proved that the appellant had struck the fatal blow. If it is capable of being so read, it would be a most serious misdirection. The learned judge had previously instructed the jury that they were the judges of the facts and subsequently he told them that there were two lines of defence, one of which—provocation—was unsupported by evidence and therefore failed as a ground for reducing the crime to culpable homicide. The other line of defence was that of diminished responsibility, and this the learned judge left to the jury with the instruction that it was open to them to find a verdict of culpable homicide instead of murder. It was therefore made expressly clear to the jury that the death of Gordon by a stab, even if they held that the appellant struck the blow, did not mean that Gordon was murdered by the appellant.

The passage quoted in the second ground of complaint was, I think, a slip of the tongue, but then such a slip will only prove fatal to the charge if it stands uncorrected in the Charge itself. In the present case, the correction is afforded by the remainder of the charge which clearly laid before the jury the question whether murder or the lesser crime of culpable homicide had been committed. Therefore, I hold that that ground of appeal fails.

The next ground of appeal is failure to give sufficient and adequate direction on the elements of doubt in the identification of the person who inflicted the fatal wound. The facts are that it is proved that the appellant was present at the locus when Gordon was struck down by a lethal weapon, but there was no eye-witness who could depone that he actually saw the appellant strike the blow; and it was proved also that there were other persons present at the locus, one of whom might possibly have struck the blow, including, for example, the witness Bonnar who according to the evidence had a hatchet in his possession. The Crown case would therefore necessarily have failed if it had depended solely on the evidence of eye-witnesses present at the time of the assault. This, however, was pointed out by the presiding judge in his Charge to the jury. There was in fact other very important evidence tending to incriminate the appellant and this evidence was dealt with at considerable length in the Charge. For example, Revie spoke to seeing the appellant take hold of Gordon and raise his hand, and he said that he saw something in

Patrick Carraher.

the appellant's hand which he also said might have been the chisel which was one of the productions in the case. The witness Watt gave evidence that he was present in the house of the witness Bonnar about 9.20 p.m., some time before Gordon met his death, and that the appellant left that house after hearing that Bonnar was engaged in a fight, taking with him the chisel which was produced, and remarking, "This is the very tool for them"; and also that later and after the fatal blow there was some talk between Watt and Bonnar and the appellant about the blows which had been struck and that the appellant said he did a bit of a toe-dance which he illustrated, at the same time moving his right hand backwards and forwards. Then there were the witnesses, Stewart, Elliott and Bonnar who depone that they heard the appellant say that he gave Gordon a jag or, according to another version, a wee jag. Stewart and Elliott say that they heard that said by the appellant the same evening as that on which Gordon's death took place and at a time when Gordon's death was under discussion, and that after saying this, the appellant took the chisel out of his pocket (that is the same chisel which is produced in the case), that he wiped it with a cloth and gave it to Stewart telling him, "Chip that away", meaning "Take it away". On this evidence the presiding judge directed the jury, that it was for them to consider whether the evidence led to the inference that the appellant had struck the fatal blow. It is to be noticed that he also expressly called the jury's attention to the contention of the appellant's counsel that the evidence did not warrant them in drawing an inference that the jag spoken to referred to the stab in the pursuer's neck. The wound in the neck was in an upward direction and Mr. Philip for the appellant contended that such a blow could not have been struck by the movement spoken to by Watt or, presumably, by Revie. That, of course, was a point which the jury was entitled to consider, but if they arrived at the conclusion that the only reasonable inference was that the appellant had in fact delivered a blow which could have produced the fatal wound, it is impossible to say either that they were wrongly directed or that they arrived at a verdict which was contrary to the evidence. It was, however, said by Mr. Philip that, since the Charge had dealt so fully with the evidence against the appellant, it should also have dealt with the evidence in his favour, that it failed to do so, and that therefore the learned judge had failed to put the defence case fairly and adequately before the jury.

This criticism falls under two heads. First, it was said that

Appendix.

there was conflicting evidence whether Watt had been present at the locus when Gordon was fatally injured, from which it followed that Watt might have been the assailant who inflicted the wound upon Gordon, and it was then said that the presiding judge failed to deal with this point in his Charge. I find, however, that he reminded the jury that there was a discrepancy in the evidence about Watt's movements and he told the jury that it seemed to him not to be an important point but that the jury were the judges of that. This was, in my view, an entirely adequate treatment of the matter. I agree myself that the question whether Watt was present at the locus was not important. There were, admittedly, several persons at the locus and the evidence that the appellant was present was not really the vital and finally significant element in the Crown case against him. His presence had necessarily to be proved, of course, but without the additional evidence of his own statements to which I have referred it could not have justified a conviction. It made little difference whether it was proved that Watt as well as Bonnar and Revie were present. One or other or any of them could conceivably have struck the blow, but it has also to be noted that there is no evidence that Watt had a weapon. The only evidence on the possession of weapons is that the appellant had a chisel and Bonnar had a hatchet, but the wound was an incised wound and not the sort of wound which could be caused by a hatchet.

The other head of criticism is that the charge does not refer to some evidence that Bonnar was heard to speak of having struck someone and of Bonnar having changed a blood-stained shirt after hearing of Gordon's death. With the hatchet I have already dealt. As regards bloodstains, the evidence is that Bonnar had himself received a cut on the head that night. In these circumstances, the learned judge was entitled to treat the evidence about Bonnar as not of sufficient importance to require that he should say more about it than had already been said by counsel. He had warned the jury, as he was entitled to do, that he would not necessarily deal with every point and rehearse the whole of the evidence again but would merely mention matters which appeared to him to be important and he also warned them that it was for them and them alone to decide what was proved. I am of opinion that so far we should not be justified in holding that the Charge, either by what it said or by its silence, misdirected the jury or induced them to disregard the defence case.

The next point arises out of the contention that the presiding judge erred in withdrawing the issue of provocation from the jury's consideration. Mr. Philip submitted to us an argument based on certain cases of high authority which decided that when there is evidence of provocation, the jury should be directed not to convict of murder if they were left in reasonable doubt at the end of the case and on the whole evidence whether the act was provoked or not. This is not the question to be considered. The question is whether the presiding judge was entitled to withdraw the question altogether from the jury's consideration. I have no doubt that it is the law of Scotland, as it has been declared to be the law of England by the Lord Chancellor in *Mancini's* case, 28 C.A.R. at page 65, that "if the evidence before the jury at the end of the case does not contain material on which a reasonable man could find a verdict of manslaughter instead of murder, it is no defect in the summing-up that manslaughter was not dealt with." There is thus no general question of principle to decide here, but only the question whether there was in this case any evidence of provocation. If there was, the Charge is bad; if there was not, the Charge on this head is good. To make the point still more clear— this is not a case in which the learned judge thought that there was some evidence of some provocation, but that it was disproportionate to the appellant's act or that it took place so long before the act that a normal man should have recovered his self-control before the act was committed. The learned judge's direction is that there was no evidence to suggest for the jury's consideration the existence of any provocation against the appellant, nothing which would justify, palliate or explain the delivery of a blow with a lethal weapon against Gordon. In my opinion the Charge is unexceptionable. There was no evidence whatever of any conduct on the part of Gordon which could have provoked the appellant into any loss of self-control. There was some evidence that a witness in the street heard a cry, "Put the hatchet on him, Joe," and it was suggested by Mr. Philip that the appellant might have heard this and might have thought that it was addressed to Gordon and that someone was inciting Gordon to strike him with a hatchet. But all this is the merest speculation. Joe is not Gordon's name. There is no competent evidence that Gordon had a hatchet at any time or that the cry was heard by the appellant or by anyone in his immediate neighbourhood. I therefore reject the contention that the learned judge was not entitled to withdraw this part of the case from the jury.

I come next to the question of diminished responsibility. The

THE HIGH COURT OF JUSTICIARY, EDINBURGH, WHERE CARRAHER'S APPEAL WAS HEARD. IN THIS COURT-ROOM SUCH FAMOUS CASES AS MADELEINE SMITH, DR. PRITCHARD, AND OSCAR SLATER WERE TRIED

Appendix.

ground of appeal here is that the presiding judge erred in his directions to the jury on the issue of diminished responsibility. The facts are that there was evidence that the appellant had that evening taken a considerable amount of drink, and that there was also evidence of opinion by medical men that he was suffering from a psychopathic personality which they said was associated with diminished responsibility. The presiding judge's direction on diminished responsibility is as follows:

> "The accused, as I say, is perfectly sane, but our law does recognize, and it is a comparatively recent introduction into our law, that if a man suffers from infirmity or aberration of mind or impairment of intellect to such an extent as not to be fully accountable for his actions the result is to reduce the quality of the evidence in a case like this, which, if you think so, would be otherwise murder, to reduce it to culpable homicide."

That is an adequate formulation of the law as it has been recognized in previous decisions. The learned judge then goes on to describe by reference to previous decisions the essential elements in diminished responsibility. He quotes from an opinion of the Lord Justice-Clerk in *Braithwaite's* case (1945 J.C. 55). The Lord Justice-Clerk there cites with approval the following passage from the charge of Lord Justice-Clerk Alness in *Savage's* case (1923 J.C. 49 at page 51);

> "It is very difficult to put it in a phrase, but it has been put in this way, that there must be aberration or weakness of mind; that there must be some form of mental unsoundness; that there must be a state of mind which is bordering on, although not amounting to, insanity; that there must be a mind so affected that responsibility is diminished from full responsibility to partial responsibility—in other words, the prisoner in question must be only partially accountable for his actions. And I think one can see running through the cases that there is implied that there must be some form of mental disease."

The presiding judge in a later passage directed the jury to treat as tests of the responsibility possessed by the appellant, these elements which he has taken from previous decisions. Another element was a condition of partial insanity, and yet another the

Patrick Carraher.

existence of a condition of great mental peculiarity of mind. He
dealt with the medical evidence in this case and he says that the
evidence of one of the witnesses was to the effect that he was
inclined to place the accused in the category of a psychopathic
personality; that a psychopathic personality is a clinical condition
in which are included persons who from childhood or early
youth show all the gross abnormality in their social behaviour
and emotional reaction, and who do not as a rule show enough
insanity to be certifiable as insane; that, broadly speaking, it is a
condition in which there is an inability on the part of the person
affected to adapt himself to the ordinary social conditions, usually
less than insanity which is certifiable, and that it is associated with
emotional instability. The Charge also reminds the jury of this
passage in the evidence of the same witness:—

> "If you asked me does the accused know the difference
> between right and wrong intellectually, does he know if he
> commits a wrong act he is liable to punishment, I say yes,
> and then he is responsible, but if diminished responsibility
> means that he has a proper appreciation of his social responsi-
> bility, that he is capable of resisting temptation, capable of
> exercising control over his actions, then in my opinion he
> is not as responsible as a normal person."

The presiding judge, after a direction dealing with the question
of drink, comes back again to the question of diminished responsibility and he says:—

> "On the remaining elements which the doctors described
> as amounting to diminished responsibility they referred to
> various peculiarities which they said they found in the
> accused, or at least suspected, that he did not seem to
> appreciate the consequences of the charge hanging over him,
> that he had difficulty in resisting temptation, that he could not
> withstand frustration, and the description, you may remem-
> ber, was such that it led me to ask whether there were not a
> great many people in this country who do not act just as good
> citizens, and whether he would include these in the category
> of psychopathic personality, and he said 'Yes'."

The learned judge felt, as he says, difficulty about remitting this
evidence for consideration to the jury as a ground for reducing
the charge from one of murder to one of culpable homicide. I

Appendix.

also have great doubt whether it was evidence of anything approaching to mental disease, aberration, or great peculiarity of mind, and whether the judge might not have been warranted in withdrawing the issue from the jury. The Court has a duty to see that trial by judge and jury according to law is not subordinated to medical theories; and in this instance much of the evidence given by the medical witnesses is, to my mind, descriptive rather of a typical criminal than of a person of the quality of one whom the law has hitherto regarded as being possessed of diminished responsibility.

However, the evidence was left to the jury and the jury negatived diminished responsibility. The learned judge also dealt with the effects of alcohol on the appellant's responsibility. He said:—

> "The question of alcoholism was also mentioned as one of the factors, and the doctor said alcoholism would lower any capacity a man may have for self-control. Let me give you a direction first about alcoholism. If by alcoholism the doctor means, as I take it, that a man under the influence of drink has less self-control than a man who is not under the influence of drink, in law drunkenness never excuses or palliates an offence unless it is so extreme as to deprive the man who is drunk of the capacity to form an intention to kill or to do grievous bodily harm. The man must be incapable of forming an intention to kill or to do grievous bodily harm before drunkenness can ever enter the picture as affecting guilt of a crime. So far as the phrase 'alcoholism' was concerned, I did not understand the doctors yesterday to suggest that the accused is suffering from a form of illness due to constant or continuous imbibing of alcohol, because they said, 'When we examined him he was showing no symptoms of alcoholism, but from his own statement he seems never to be sober, and therefore he is a man who has not the same appreciation of moral standards as a normal man. Alcoholism would increase his difficulty in exercising self-control.'"

The presiding judge continues:—

> "I direct you in law that unless you thought it was proved that on the night in question the accused was so drunk as to be incapable of forming the intention to kill or to do grievous bodily harm, you will dismiss any idea of drunkenness, or alcoholism as it is called, from your minds."

277

Patrick Carraher.

That direction is plainly in accordance with the decision in the case of *Kennedy*, 1944 J.C. 171, but the objection was taken that the charge should also have directed the jury to consider the evidence of alcoholism along with the medical evidence of diminished responsibility. The proposition argued to us was that a man who cannot be found to be suffering from any diminished responsibility must nevertheless, if there is opinion evidence that he suffers from what is called psychopathic personality, be entitled to be treated as not having a normal responsibility for his actions, if by taking alcohol he brings about a condition of diminished responsibility. That is plainly inconsistent with the decision in *Kennedy*. I am of opinion that the plea of diminished responsibility, which as was said in *Kirkwood's* case (1939 J.C. 36) is anomalous in our law, should not be extended or given wider scope than has hitherto been accorded to it in the decisions. It may be timely to say also that little weight attaches to medical evidence which is based on a history of the panel's conduct about which no evidence has been led before the jury.

Lastly, we are invited to consider whether we should summon a medical assessor as we are empowered to do by Section 6(e) of the Criminal Appeal (Scotland) Act, 1926. This is a power which has never yet been exercised and it is certainly one which should be used with the greatest reserve. Trial by jury on evidence led before the jury is the dominant principle of our criminal law and we have a duty to be wary against substituting a procedure which might result in so novel a method of trial as taking the opinion of the assessor on such a question as the panel's responsibility. In the present case, however, the question before us turned out to be a purely legal question on which a medical assessor could not possibly have been asked to assist us.

Upon the whole matter, I am of the opinion that this appeal falls to be dismissed.

LORD CARMONT—I agree with the opinion which has just been delivered by your lordship in the chair. I agree with it in its entirety and have nothing to add.

LORD JAMIESON—I concur.

LORD STEVENSON—I also concur.

LORD BIRNAM—I also concur.

Thin

8 May, 1951.